MAG WORLD

MAG WORLD

EMILIA FERRARA

International Publishers
McLean, Virginia

emilia@emiliaferrara.com
www.internationalpublishers.us

ISBN-13: 978-1547277506
ISBN-10: 1547277505

Cover art by Kathryn Zaremba

For Lu

TABLE OF CONTENTS

Chapter 1 / Magazines 1

Chapter 2 / Beauty: History 27

Chapter 3 / Beauty: Business 79

Chapter 4 / Beauty: Science 141

Chapter 5 / Models 231

Chapter 6 / Photographers 269

Chapter 7 / Editors 307

Chapter 8 / Fashion 329

Index 355

CHAPTER 1
MAGAZINES

"And to answer that question, I had to think myself out of the room."—Virginia Woolf

Let's begin in the room. Let's begin with Google. Ask Google, "What is a magazine?" and it can't tell you. Change the words to "the role of magazines," and Google replies.

The first five hits may seem odd at first, but they're instructive.

Hit one is a short history of how magazines turned from regional to national publications. Hit two introduces a study done by the National Center for Biotechnology Information (NCBI) positing whether or not magazines deliver health information to women. Hit three is a post on the blog *Language123*, which at one point exclaims, "[Magazines] are the mouthpiece of the nation." Hit four is a video presented by Black Arts Enterprise exploring a "short take on the defining periodical of the black arts era." And finally, the fifth is an essay for advertisers, a guide on how advertising in a magazine should help a business.

Google isn't always the answer for everything. However, the dictionary often is. According to *Merriam-Webster*'s website, a magazine is:

> 1. A place where goods or supplies are stored, such as a warehouse.
>
> 2. A room in which powder and other explosives are kept in a fort or a ship.

What?

> 3. An accumulation of munitions of war *or* a stock of provisions or goods.

Is this Merriam-Webster?

> 4. A periodical containing miscellaneous pieces (such as articles, stories, poems) and often illustrated; *also* such a periodical published online; *also* a similar section of a newspaper usually appearing on Sunday; *also* a radio or television program presenting usually several short segments on a variety of topics.

Better…

> 5. A supply chamber: as a holder in or on a gun for cartridges to be fed into the gun chamber *or* a lightproof chamber for films or plates

> on a camera or for film on a motion-picture projector.

Strangely, neither Google nor the dictionary explains a magazine very well. How would you explain it, for example, to someone seeing a magazine for the first time? How would you explain it to a child?

There is one more resource to probe: our own experience. I have lived twenty-nine years and have spent half of them obsessed with magazines. I should have something to offer.

How would I put it?

I close my eyes and imagine myself walking up to a magazine rack.

I slow down. I take in the whole wall. My eye jumps to the colors and words, which zip out at me first—yellow, a neon banner, a star, a circle. Then faces appear. One per square. Sometimes none. Some of them smile dimly. Some growl with their eyes. Some are laughing into the wind.

Strange set of faces. Why are they here? What do they want?

"Buy! Buy now! Buy all!"

Why? What do I really need here? How can this help me?

"Eat your weeds." "My life as a punk." "Why rest makes you fitter." "Beauty miracles under $15." "Shiny, sexy hair!" "Free stuff!"

Curious. I guess I could rest more. My hand drifts slowly up.

But I don't need free junk. My hand falls limply back.

After gazing at the wall of colors and words, I begin to step away because I know there is only one reason why I need to buy a magazine: to learn the news.

Magazines are sources of news. They are portals to information we don't already have. Those who work at magazines are hounds sniffing out what makes today different from yesterday, what we can expect out of tomorrow, and a trillion other open questions. They hunt for truth and, when they catch it, they pinch it in their teeth and carefully dangle it onto a page.

Magazines are a monthly heartbeat, each beat per month pushing life into our hands. Magazines are a discovery, like the best books, only a little quicker. Magazines are a safe place, a garden for honesty to grow. They can be pools of compassion for those we must learn more about. They can be fabulous labs where ideas explode into air.

A magazine is a place for a story to unfold in a way it cannot over TV, newspaper, or radio. In a magazine, pictures and words step together and dance through a ballroom of pages. Magazines are a two-dimensional design of words and images that allow an infinitely dimensional imagination to get up and walk around the world differently because our minds have been changed. Magazines send out an alarm as we float through the familiar. They buzz in our face to stop *there*, look *close*, question *now*.

But how do you know which magazine to buy? Is there a type for every person? Does it depend on what place you're in, on where you're going, or on where you came from?

Although magazines are sources of information, it seems buying one—or, more importantly, choosing one—has a lot to do with us. When we buy a magazine, we are making a statement about ourselves to ourselves.

In the documentary *Objectified*, author and *New York Times Magazine* columnist Rob Walker breaks down our choice to buy a car. "When you own the car and you drive the car, and you're making decisions about, 'are you going to put a bumper sticker on it?' there's an idea of an *audience*. I feel pretty strongly that this isn't just true for cars but for almost everything we buy. The real audience is really ourselves, and the person that you're really speaking to when you're speaking about, 'why me?' and, 'is this the right car for me?' – you're making a statement to yourself about yourself."

The audience around which we read a magazine is usually irrelevant at the moment we buy one. When we pick up a magazine, we don't always know every place we will be reading it or who will be around. Maybe I buy it in the airport, but I read it on the beach. Maybe I buy it in a busy supermarket, but I read it at home. There is a public and private context to every environment in which we'll be reading a magazine, but that context is unknown to us at the time we buy it.

So then, what audience is present, as Walker would say, when we choose a magazine? He continues to describe car buying: "In sort of an abstract way, you're thinking about what they might be thinking of you and, like, whether or not they like your Obama sticker or your Christian fish or whatever it might be. But the crucial thing is *the self*. Is your own audience. Your own story of like, 'I'm not that guy' or 'I am that guy' or 'that woman.' Because the truth is: no one cares on the highway."

We've all heard: you are what you read. Unlike with a car, investing in media causes consideration for digestion. Media is food. We tend to be careful of what we allow to become part of us, so we consider, we deliberate, we research, and yet (although the actual, edible food available for women is just as good as the food available for men) is the same also true for media? There aren't apples *for women* and almonds *for men*, but there are magazines with these delineations. Our food, our books, our newspapers, the internet, and thousands of other things we digest

every day are less gender-segregated than magazines. What effect does that segregation have?
In 1929, British author Virginia Woolf reacted passionately to how different expectations were for women and for men. In *A Room of One's Own*, Woolf quotes *Jane Eyre*:

> It is vain to say human beings ought to be satisfied with tranquility . . . They must have action; and they will make it if they cannot find it. Millions [of women] are condemned to a stiller doom than mine, and millions are in silent revolt against their lot. Nobody knows how many rebellions ferment in the masses of life which people earth. Women are supposed to be very calm, generally: but women feel just as men feel; they need exercise for their faculties and a field for their effort as much as their brothers do; they suffer from too rigid a restraint, too absolute a stagnation, precisely as men would suffer; and it is narrow-minded... to say that they ought to confine themselves to making puddings and knitting stockings, to playing on the piano and embroidering bags. It is thoughtless to condemn them, or laugh at them, if they seek to do more or learn more than custom has pronounced necessary for their sex.

For the women of Woolf's time, and indeed Ms. Brontë's, limited expectations meant a narrow narrative. Nearly a hundred years ago, Woolf was highly sensitive to how society confined women, and she knew as well as any that they wanted more than was dictated. In a way, journalism is action. News is never still. And women do have the same curiosity as men to learn the news. So, do magazines "for women" offer the same quality of journalism as magazines for everyone else?

Woolf offers one prediction:

> In a hundred years ... women will have ceased to be the protected sex ... Logically, they will take part in all the activities and exertions that were once denied them. The nursemaid will heave coal. The shop-woman will drive an engine ... Remove that protection, expose them to the same exertions and activities, make them soldiers and sailors and engine-drivers and dock laborers ... Anything may happen when womanhood has ceased to become a protected occupation.

Indeed, women have stepped into a wider range of exertions. Do magazines "for women" reflect this? Do we read about women engine drivers, dock laborers, and soldiers in these publications as often as we read about models, singers, and actresses?

To be sure, Woolf could not make exact predictions of modern society in Britain, let alone of modern society in

America. She could not have anticipated the technological and social revolutions that have come to define our generation. Nevertheless, in the almost two hundred and fifty years of our nation's history, the last half century has seen a vast evolution in our understanding of sex and gender.

Woolf contemplated the result of desegregating the male and female in literature and speculated how that would influence writing styles. There has always been a "male" sentence, she explains, but adds: "Jane Austen [would have] looked at it and laughed at it and devised a perfectly natural, shapely sentence proper for her own use."

Woolf never insists that the male or the female style of writing is in opposition; rather, she believes the creative mind must be both. After reading a more modern female author, she notices that she has "mastered the first great lesson; she wrote as a woman, but as a woman who has forgotten that she is a woman, so that her pages were full of that curious sexual quality which comes only when sex is unconscious of itself."

This quality had been identified before Woolf's time. Samuel Taylor Coleridge said that the great mind is androgynous. "It is when this fusion [of the sexes] takes place that the mind is fully fertilized and uses all its faculties," Woolf summarizes. "The androgynous mind is resonant and porous ... transmits emotion without impediment ... is naturally creative, incandescent and undivided."

So how can Woolf and Coleridge, along with their shared theory that the androgynous mind is stronger than one ruled by gender norms, impact our outlook on the quality of magazines today?

It doesn't matter if a publisher, editor, photographer, or writer is physically male or female; it matters that their mind approaches their work without prejudice, presumption, or bias. The androgynous mind is less a fusion of two flavors and more one that is simply not afraid to break rules. To that effect, a magazine where "sex is unconscious of itself" is just a true record and real account of life. It is full of action, involving both sexes, and less concerned with what women "should be" and more concerned with what women are. Self comes before sex; identity before gender; story before labeling ... and excellence before segregation.

Nearly twenty years after Woolf, in 1950, women were offered a narrow set of expectations in magazines, and perhaps the social climate of the day made that comfortable for them. But ... what about us? In 2017, the female experience has grown—indeed, the full topic of gender differentiation (including LGBTQIA rights) has reached an unprecedented focus. Inappropriate expectations have waned, and women have more legal and social freedom to be, simply, human.

Do "our" magazines reflect that? Have they caught up? And if not, how can we expect our freedom to expand ever more if "the women's magazine" (the one narrative devoted to chronicling our lives) still revolves around "puddings, stockings, bags," makeovers, shopping tips, men, and other airbrushed women?

In light of the political climate of our country today, it might seem silly to find discomfort in the space between a magazine *for a woman* and a magazine *for everyone else.* And yet, given the spread of multiplatform technology, and given that media is food and a choice representing an investment, then that moment when the hand drifts slowly toward the magazine rack is actually critical.

Magazines contain stories. Stories awaken the imagination. The imagination lights a fire under the soul. The soul warms up and acts upon the mind. And then the mind goes on to tell the body what to do, in *this* way or in *that*—all because of a story we once read.

But I don't need to tell you about the magic of storytelling. Whether we are reading *Harry Potter* or the *New York Times*, fiction or nonfiction, they change us.

How do we want to be changed? What change do we find valuable? Who do we trust to help us to change for the better? And should these questions be answered in separate magazines for women and for men?

* * *

Perhaps my curiosity about what magazines are and my passion for what makes them great is best accompanied by some insight from a man who well understood the news.

In 1924, American journalist Walter Lippmann reflected on a passage from Plato's *Republic*: a scene of cave dwellers who only discern reality as shadows dancing on a wall. Americans, Lippmann wrote, inhabited a cave of media misrepresentations—stereotypes, "distortions of distortions … not a mirror of social conditions, but a report of an aspect that had obtruded itself." Journalism became a media "phantasmagoria": "There are no objective standards here. There are conventions."

I see a phantasmagoria of women in media today, most especially in women's and fashion magazines. I see "distortions of distortions"—and I'm not just talking about Photoshop. Sometimes the "news" I am given seems but a "shadow" of another more substantial story. I see stereotypes so crowded that they "obtrude" themselves as well as the subjects behind them. I see products that churn vanity rather than health. Who among us has opened a news magazine with excitement to learn but opened a women's magazine or fashion magazine with anxiety over a club we're supposed to join?

Like Lippmann, my motivations in writing about this

industry are clear. "We shall advance," he wrote, "when we have learned humility; when we have learned to seek the truth, to reveal it and publish it; when we care more for that than for the privilege of arguing about ideas in a fog of uncertainty."

When do we feel surrounded by a fog of uncertainty? When we read women's or fashion titles, what seems to be hazy? What are the conventions that belt these magazines? What are the dimensions of their "cave," and how deeply do those working in the beauty, fashion, and magazine industries dwell in it?

* * *

Right from the cover, magazines seem desperate for your attention. There's a dramatic and demanding tone. The messages are delivered with urgency and consistent hyperbole. There is no "good" or "better"—only "amazing" and "perfect."

Reading a table of contents and seeing what topics are in each issue is like rolling into a car mechanics shop. It's as if we're all banged up, slightly scratched, wheezing versions of ourselves, and *these editors* have a few fine parts to slap on.

They've never met you, but they spend their time and money on the assumption that you do not think you are certain things *enough*. Specifically, they suppose that you do not think you are "sexy," "beautiful," "gorgeous," "ageless," "glowing," "shiny," "glossy," "tousled," "flat," "flirtatious," "romantic," "creative," "dazzling," "racy," "budgeted," "bright," "lush," "tricky," "hot," "fun," "inspired," "loose," or "ready" enough. (All things that women supposedly "hunger" for.) And, in their own words, they are the "experts" on everything.

They assume you want to change the way you dress, what you eat, how you exercise, the music in your ears, the grease in your hair, what kind of friend you are, what kind of daughter you are, and—for all intents and purposes—*who* you are.

Popular topics are on rinse and repeat; it's an inconvenience to find something that is truly new. In a culture where women are more educated and independent than ever, the chronicle of our lives is apparently filled with lipsticks, blow jobs, and diets. Are these really the stories that constitute and commemorate us? The unending "tips" containing sexual standards and how to meet them center us around someone else's perspective, not our own.

The "editorial" control extends far beyond the words. The pictures speak with a force all their own. Magazine staffers take a lot of pictures of real people but then digitally erase what makes them real. A scar on a knee, pigmentation under eyes, creases in armpits, and slightly discolored teeth (for example) are common human attributes that are rarely—if ever—seen in a magazine for women. Stores use mannequins (simplified, fake humans) to sell clothes. Magazines put real people on their covers but then alter them to make them look like mannequins. Even past the cover, every figure on every page is likely digitally changed. I don't have the data, but I'd still wager that not one picture containing a human in a women's or fashion magazine is printed with honesty.

They continue to manipulate in the way they choose "models," perhaps a misnomer altogether. Those girls don't "model" American girls. They do not reflect the height, weight, body mass index (BMI), and other physical attributes of the typical magazine reader. Twenty years ago, the average model weighed 8 percent less than the average woman. Today, the difference is at least 23 percent.

Not only do their looks contrast with the typical reader, but most models also don't communicate the deeper interests of readers. The typical "model" leads quite a different lifestyle from the rest of us who, perhaps, value education and health. Professional models—such as the "Angels" employed by Victoria's Secret—have a limited time in the limelight and "retire" at an average age of 28.5 years old. Only a handful of readers aspire to become models, singers, or actresses; and yet those are the cover girls we receive month after month.

A concerning and overarching thread running through women's and fashion magazines is their preoccupation with quantity over quality. Maybe the number of magazines they sell goes up, but they do not necessarily win more journalism awards. The business of industrial design, says Alice Rawsthorn in the documentary *Objectified*, has always been mass production. "It's been producing standardized objects for production by millions and millions of people."

With the models they reinvent, with the tips they repeat, magazines for women can seem like standardized objects—largely created for the purpose of mass production, to sell, and sell, and sell. In the documentary, Rawsthorn helps us understand the people whose motives are to mass produce.

> One of the earliest examples [of mass production] would be the first emperor of China ... He was waging war to try and colonize more and more parts of what would eventually become China. And one of his problems was that each of his archers made their own arrows. And so if, say, an archer died, a fellow archer couldn't grab the arrows from his quiver and start shooting at the enemy because the arrows literally didn't fit his bow. So the first emperor and his advisors came up with a way of standardizing the design of the arrows so that each arrow would fit any bow.

Apparently, diversity is a problem for mass production—

especially for those trying to colonize as opposed to earn loyalty. Why have we decided that the standard measurements of a model's body are the best way to show off clothes? Why are there only a few ways to Photoshop a picture in a women's or fashion magazine? Have feminine figures in beauty, fashion, and women's magazines become the new standardized arrows, pinning us down and piercing us deep with self-doubt and shame?

When it comes to photography, editors of news magazines understand that every detail of a picture is relevant. Immense research goes into context, environment, and technological possibilities ... but the most important asset is the photographer. Experience, skill, and a love of taking photographs are vital. Would *National Geographic* Photoshop a wrinkle or increase someone's chest? No, because they are not trying to persuade, perform, or establish an ideal. Some photographs tell stories with artistic value, some with photojournalistic value, and some with both. Regardless, photographs should give layers of meaning to the material, not take layers of meaning away through digitally edited fantasies.

Successful editors (photographic and editorial) feel satisfaction when a story has pulled back a curtain to illuminate that which is not often seen. These editors never reach for the limelight. It's not about them. Pseudo-celebrity is irrelevant, as is promoting a self-centered Instagram account, appearing on talk shows, and making "lists" for others to "follow." Editors of women's magazines often seem excited by superiority, flattery, and inane girl-to-girl competition. The satisfaction of "beating" the other girl holds true from the lowest intern snagging a clothing sample to the most senior editor squashing the seating placement of another during fashion week. It's rarely about earning the best scoop. It's often about feeding the biggest ego.

News magazines are exclusively interested in truth. They invest in thorough reporting and fact-checking, and their journalistic skepticism is healthy. News isn't always comfortable. When women stretch boundaries, we ask ourselves: is that really a good idea? Do I really believe in this? Women's magazines, and those who report for them, should be skeptical and demand more information before hailing a salute.

Lippmann saw frivolous publications as a waste, but not exactly a threat. "All the gallant little sheets expressing particular programs are at bottom vanity," he said, "and in the end, futility, so long as the reporting of daily news is left in untrained and biased hands." Today, news magazines and women's or fashion magazines do demonstrate notable disparities, but so what? Who cares? Just don't buy them.

Even if these missteps make us want to dismiss them altogether, it's not that easy. Today's "gallant little sheets" exert real power and influence—and not just in print. The audience of women's and fashion magazines is hard to beat. The total collection in America claim at least fifty million readers.

Is this not fertile ground to plant the seeds of change, of encouragement, of a truly healthy life? Women, today, have the opportunity to make choices never before open to them.

Elizabeth Gilbert (author of the novel *Eat, Pray, Love*) described the journey of choice for the modern woman in a *Big Think* interview back in 2012:

> It's a really interesting point in history … I think this era of women has become sort of hamsters in a great, unprecedented social experiment, which is: what happens if you give women a little bit of power? What happens if you give them autonomy? What happens if you give them control over their reproduction? What happens if you give them earnings? What happens if you give them options? You know, that social experiment has never been played out before. And so we're all sort of hamsters in the maze, it's this big sociological test that's going on.

Later, she adds, "This is why this is the age of memoir. This is why this is the age of Oprah … we need to get up and look into each other's mazes and we try to see how the other women are doing it … we need to see how others are solving these questions. We are all looking into

each other's lives to try to get clues for our own scavenger hunt."
This is exactly the kind of exercise to which magazines for women can contribute. A magazine's capacity for research, for telling the truth, for shedding light on positive examples, can all serve the process of climbing up and out of the maze. Are we really burning to match the right eye shadow to our iris? Are we awake at night trying to come up with nine new outfits for fall? Is this a satisfying way of being fed? When you stand in front of a rack of women's and fashion magazines, you have the right to ask for more.

* * *

The ballet *Sleeping Beauty* is about a princess, Aurora, and her royal court. Her father, the king, is adored by the entire kingdom. As an only child, Aurora is the jewel of the family. She is beautiful, poised, and yet full of her own brilliant spirit.

Aurora's father throws her a ball. It is luxurious and grand—everything a girl could want. Aurora puts her party dress on and goes downstairs, but when she comes through the door she finds a surprise waiting for her. Three surprises. Her father presents her with three princes and announces that, tonight, she is to dance with each of them because they are her suitors. They have come to marry her.

Aurora arrived just wanting to celebrate. While getting ready, she was oblivious to the fact that she would be expected to pick a husband that night. The music in this moment, composed by Peter Ilyich Tchaikovsky, acknowledges her unease and genuine fear.

For this young princess, love is a dream. She has never fallen in love before, but the world famous theme from this ballet—"I know you, I met you once upon a dream"—suggests falling in love for Aurora is an intimate, private, delicate affair—as delicate as a dream. At your father's command, in front of the entire court, with your family standing by, and all the guests studying your every move, how could this be an opportunity for true love?

But Aurora goes with it. Never one to crack under pressure, she is a dutiful servant of the crown. She dances a *pas d'action* with harp accompaniment. Her performance is both excruciating and excellent. She is a slow, methodical dance partner to each suitor. She treats each prince as if they are the only being in the room. She turns as if on a pedestal, letting the men circle around her. They admire her from every angle, but she stays cool, distant, mechanical—and captivating. She literally winds each prince around her finger and, although we cannot be sure, it is perhaps the same finger which just moments later she pricks on a spindle, sending her into a century-long sleep.

Tchaikovsky's music in Aurora's *pas d'action* is soft at first. The harp draws you into her beauty. Then the music is regal with a sense of commanding attention that could only belong to a princess. Then it becomes tense, very tense, and we sense a true struggle. It is as if we have traveled from the party inside Aurora herself. She feels sad; she doesn't want falling in love to be like this. She is tired; dancing again and again with each prince is exhausting. She is determined to do her duty in the moment perfectly, but to save her heart for another night. And the passion of Tchaikovsky's score comes when you realize that—for this young girl—the experience nearly breaks her. Aurora is a young mind, and the pageantry is heavy. Aurora has promise and potential, but the expectation and the dictation are paralyzing. Aurora has a strong inner spirit (the only thing in the world she needs to listen to), and yet the thoughts of those in the court only get louder and louder inside her mind.

Nevertheless, she goes on. Aurora finishes the dance. And yet for us, we know it was all just work. Hard work.

We all operate under pressure. We all cope with others expectations—whether from family or society. So do we also have to open a magazine only to manage pressure there too? Are we going to pay $3.55 to be thus exhausted?

This scene in Tchaikovsky's ballet reminds me very much of what all women—young girls, in particular—go through in encountering content (print or online) from the beauty, fashion, or magazine industries. When a teenager is met with a curious and overly abundant sense of pageantry, stuff is thrown at her—bags, lipsticks, baubles—and she is in a swamp of gloss and glamour. She reads and listens to what they want her to do, and suddenly there is an army of expectations. List upon list upon list. How to date, how to breathe, how to sneeze. Month after month, rule after rule—as narrow as they are harsh. She is trained to believe that she is the only one who feels this way—that there are other readers, other editors, writers, editorial assistants, celebrities, fashion interns, and so on who all live in Mag World, who are all doing these things, who all function happily within these rules, who only want more and more and more.

But it's not true.

There is no distant kingdom where some "court" of women are elegant 24-7, always moisturized, always dressed, and ready to take on anything. Women working in the beauty, fashion, or magazine industries do not live in Mag World, they live in our world, and to realize they are just like anyone else is to give them the compliment they wouldn't even give themselves.

Do publishers want to push women and girls to the point where they don't want to pick up an issue but feel like they have to? Unlike Aurora, many women lack the strength to finish the job. And for those like Aurora who steal that strength, they actually forgo the fairytale ending and end up asleep for an eternity, missing out on experiences, ceasing to grow, and eventually losing themselves.

I fail to meet expectations, especially when they are unhealthy. I am insufficient, especially in qualities that clasp my freedom. Virginia Woolf taught me that being on the outside of a system is sometimes better than being in it. She was on the lawn of a prestigious university knowing that men in the administration would not give her access to the library because she was a woman. She reflected, "I pondered what effect poverty has on the mind; and what effect wealth has on the mind; and I thought of the queer old gentlemen I had seen that morning with tufts of fur upon their shoulders; and I remembered how if one whistled one of them ran; and I thought of the organ booming in the chapel and of the shut doors of the library; and I thought of how unpleasant it is to be locked out; and I thought of how it is worse perhaps to be locked in."

In Woolf's day, female authors were rarely published and, it would seem, even less often allowed into the library. She was locked out of the system entirely. Today, we marvel at how a genius like Woolf could be kept out of anything. How could it be possible?

Perhaps the doors to the library have been opened for us, but what about the doors to accepting the human self in media? What about the doors to a bathroom containing no self-loathing? What about the doors to a kitchen stocked with delicious food and fear free? What about the doors to a magazine workplace safe from the prick of the coworker's stiletto? What about the doors to beauty without a makeup drawer? What about the doors to a women's magazine that tells stories from the soul?

We can open those doors. We are already in a new age of media and a new age for women. These magazines can claim the dawn, rediscover their readers, and serve them well.

When you know what good a magazine is, and when you see what women can do today, change is more than possible. It's inevitable.

CHAPTER 2
BEAUTY: HISTORY

For as long as priests have been praying and farmers have been feeding, women have been plumping, glossing, slicking, and sculpting. A look, a style, a standard has forever been obtainable through little rituals—expensive or inexpensive, reasonable or wild.

In some societies, women used makeup under pressure; in others, women adorned themselves as an expression of freedom. In our American history we have both. These trends of beautification as conformity, as well as beautification as liberation, have ebbed and flowed through time as indiscriminately as various streams in one ocean.

Richard Corson, who died just before he had the chance to see the turn of our new century, is perhaps most well known for his sociological study of the world's beauty industries. A former theater professor and backstage aficionado, Corson is the author of *Fashions in Makeup: From Ancient to Modern Times*, which covers much of the ground for this chapter. "Sociological changes are usually interlaced with economic, technological and psychological ones," Corson explains. We beautify "for what it can do for us and to others." Primitive people did at times use makeup to frighten enemies, but it has most commonly been used to attract friends and lovers.

In the beginning, makeup was sunblock—or, you could say, life block. Face painting among the earliest known tribes reveals that the first makeup also coated the skin as protection from the sun, as well as camouflage from afar. Often, face paint was a mark of hierarchy. Native chieftains used it to express their success in hunting. We know of at least one Persian king who always took his makeup to war, carrying them into the battlefield in elaborate cosmetics cases.

When face painting wasn't about strength, it was about performance. Women were always playing a part and using beauty products to do so. "Women of fashion have always used makeup surreptitiously with the intent of deceiving," writes Corson, "gradually seducing their less aggressive compatriots into following their lead until the deception becomes so widespread and so much a matter of common knowledge that acceptance of the artifice is forced upon a reluctant public." At first, this behavior leads to tolerance, says Corson, "then to permissiveness and sometimes to wild abandon."

Corson marks these with a "forthright use of makeup," saying that they indicate "a general permissiveness in so-called moral behavior and, in fact, may well be designated as permissive makeup. During these periods of extremism, makeup gradually departs from a representation of nature to ornamentation of the human face purely for purposes of decoration."

Decoration and performance are the themes that have lived

on to our day, more so than battlefield valor or hunting prizes. And yet, one performs differently for different audiences. Hindu women stained their teeth red. Japanese women stained their teeth black. And Elizabethan women shaved their teeth. And today, we never would.

Overall, Corson stipulates that the psychological experience among users has been positive. "As our self-confidence increases, so does our willingness, even eagerness to [beautify] resulting in an apparent reversal of the natural law, with demand following supply as technology improves both the quantity and quality of the product."

He also offers a theory for this low tide and high tide. "When the flamboyance has reached a peak beyond which it cannot reasonably seem to go and beyond which no one really wants it to go," he writes, "it subsides, at least for a time, in favor of greater naturalness. This naturalness is always greeted with sighs of relief, which are then forgotten as a new peak of permissiveness eventually approaches."

Corson sees this pattern of extravagance and modesty as perpetual; it is never meant to stop. "Anyone who tries to interfere with this natural rhythm of change, and many have, would do better by far to cultivate patience, secure in the knowledge that whatever women are doing to their faces today, tomorrow it will be something else."

One group Corson blames for trying to interfere with

this natural rhythm is the moralists. "Ensnared in their own theology, they are not always concerned with psychological needs or sociological changes they have threatened hellfire and eternal damnation to those who dared defile God's handiwork with artificial color."

I have no lightning bolts in my back pocket, but I can't promise to agree with Corson entirely. From my vantage point, I do not see expansive psychological positivity, and I cannot promise interminable revolution. I'll save my opinion until the history has been shared, but I will say that although I am in contrast with Corson's conclusions I support his study, presentation, and style.

Let's hope you hold no lightning bolts either. In chilly England in 1583, Philip Stubbes became one of the most furious of moralists, bemoaning endlessly over British women using "certain oyles, liquors, unguents and waters," to flaunt God's will by "[coloring] their faces with such sibbersauces." To nobody's surprise, it never made him very popular. He warned that they "seethe not that their souls are thereby deformed, and they brought deeper into the displeasure and indignation of the Almighty, at whose voice the earth doth tremble and at whose presence the heavens shall liquefy and melt away."

Four centuries later, American women would be spending half a billion dollars per year on these sibbersauces, with little hope for an end in sight.

* * *

Many look to Mesopotamia as the first real start of civilization, and the same is true for beautification. The Sumerians lived in the southeastern section of Mesopotamia (modern-day Iran), close to the Persian Gulf. They lived peacefully and were keen on perfume, which they mainly made from soaking plants in water and oil. Some of their cosmetics were kept in seashells, which have been found inside tombs along with various color pigments.

Women put kohl around their eyes less as a fashion statement and more to protect against bacteria, the sun, and conditions like pink eye. Eye makeup was mixed by specialists and made from kohl and charred frankincense resin, for its antibiotic properties. Lip coloring was not used as often as eye makeup because it usually consisted of henna, which took weeks to wash off and only needed to be applied occasionally. Still, lipstick may have its roots in Mesopotamia, as women created a vivid paste made from crushed jewels and gemstones.

Mesopotamia was a relatively supportive culture for women. They were welcomed into the marketplace on a daily basis and usually bought and sold for themselves or on behalf of their fathers, brothers, and husbands. They managed legal matters when men were absent, and were allowed to own property, receive loans, and settle certain business matters. Upper-class women, such as female priests or royals, were able to read and write. There were even many powerful goddesses the whole population worshiped.

Despite their relatively generous civil liberties, many inequalities still existed for women in Mesopotamia. Enheduanna, known as the first female poet in history, was a priestess who, after her father's death, lost her job and was left with barely any rights. "It was in [the goddess's] service that I first entered the holy temple, I, Enheduanna, the highest priestess. I carried the ritual basket, I chanted your praise. Now I have been cast out to the place of lepers. Day comes and the brightness is hidden around me. Shadows cover the light, drape it in sandstorms. My beautiful mouth knows only confusion. Even my sex is dust."

Enheduanna would have been one of the Mesopotamians who dabbled in cosmetics until their use was widespread. However, the Egyptians probably had the longest-lived beauty industry, which grew fast and became complex in only a short period of time. Archeologists have found Egyptian palettes for grinding eye paint from around 10,000 BCE. "All evidence indicates," writes Corson, "that throughout their history, the Egyptians … had, in some form, most of the cosmetic aids which have ever been devised."

The majority of men and women in Egypt used makeup every day. Makeup was just as important in this life as it was in the next. Countless tombs have been uncovered with ample cosmetics ready for use in the afterlife. "Some of the cosmetic jars found in the tomb of Tutankhamun," explains Corson, "still contained a three thousand-year-old skin cream composed of approximately nine parts of animal fat to one part of perfumed resin." Egyptians used oils to soften the skin, and then paints and dyes to color it. Perfume was an absolute necessity. They rouged their cheeks, rouged their lips, and used henna on their nails, hands, and soles of the feet.

The cosmetics production process was meticulous. "Both cosmetics and perfumes were compounded by professional cosmetics makers or, in earlier times, by the priests," explains Corson, "who kept their formulas secret and sold their products only to those who could afford them." Some paint lightened the skin (usually yellow ochre) and some darkened it, but the creation began with "the pigment, mined in large chunks and ground by the cosmetic makers into a powder, [then] supplied in tubes, wooden boxes, and metal pots."

Kohl was used as widely as perfume, and cosmeticians were very particular. This precise formula reveals an ancient Egyptian eyeliner mixture composed of "a black, grey or colored powder made variously of powdered antimony (stadium), black manganese oxide, burnt almonds, lead, black oxide of copper, carbon, brown ochre, iron oxide, malachite and chrysocolla, [and] a green-blue copper ore."

Still, much like our beauty industry today, the more you spent in ancient Egypt the wilder your choices. Many stained their nails, hands, and feet, but wealthy women highlighted the veins on their breasts as well as their temples with ethereal blue paint. Most shaved off their eyebrows and painted on new ones. And the perfumes that were most luxurious contained ingredients like "frankincense, myrrh, spikenard, thyme, marjoram, origanum, balanos and oils of almond, olive and sesame."

Beauty advice was not scarce, and the Egyptians loved to write recommendations. According to Corson, a woman who needed help fixing her complexion, for example, was instructed to "wash her face with a concoction of bullocks bile, whipped ostrich eggs, oil, dough, refined natron, and hautet resin combined with fresh milk." One wrinkle-fighting secret: "add to milk a mixture of incense, wax, fresh olive oil, and cypress crushed and ground, and apply [to the] face for six days." Although painting protected the skin, after-sun care was needed. One general beauty restorative contained "writing fluid, hippopotamus fat, and gazelle's dung"; another was composed of "phallus, vulva and black lizard."

Indeed, a dark-haired culture feared oncoming grays. For aging hair, one needed "the blood of a black cow, tortoise shell, and the neck of a gabgu-bird cooked in oil." Other hair coloring treatments required "the horn of a fawn, warmed in oil; the bile of many crabs; dried tadpoles from the canal, crushed in oil; and the womb of a cat, warmed in oil with the egg of the gabgu-bird."

Creativity and invention were never lacking in Egypt, and beautification only spread in the Middle East. Assyrians were not as keen on wigs as the Egyptians, but their interest in hair irons, dyes, and curling tongs matched if not surpassed their painted friends. Other Middle Easterners, such as Babylonians, kept their skin soft with pumice stone and, due to their elaborate hair up-do, anointed their head with oil to keep out any insects or rodents.

One tomb excavation near Ur found a mani-pedi set. Among the five-thousand-year-old artifacts were "a cosmetics pot of blue-green malachite and a tiny, shell-shaped gold cosmetics case with a miniature cosmetics spoon, tweezers for removing superfluous hair from the eyebrows, and a metal rod for pushing down cuticle." Lip rouges, "believed to have been used by [Queen Puabi] more than four thousand years ago," were also uncovered.

The Medes loved richer perfumes, and Scythian men's colognes contained "cinnamon, saffron, spikenard, crocus, lotus, thyme, marjoram, and other herbs and spices." Men of Persia often carried cosmetics to war and took particularly great pride in their beards. Facial hair and beards were often curled and oiled and sometimes extended with fake hair..

Women focused on their eyes and believed a certain spiritual power came from applying the right eye makeup. "Excavations of graves at Susa and [El Obeid] have brought forth small conical vases containing remnants of a green eye paint. It was believed … certain colors were thought to have magical powers.".

The Hebrew Jezebel enraptured men and made history with her painted face. According to the Old Testament, when Jehu came "[Jezebel] painted her face, and [adorned] her head, and looked out a window," no doubt to casually show off her features.

Despite the regular use of makeup, people often suffered painful consequences because the ingredients were simply not healthy. Assyrian women, according to Corson, "painted their faces with white lead ... Babylonians—young men, as well as women—painted their faces with white lead and vermilion and lined their eyes with stibium."

Excavations in the Mohenjo-Daro, located in the modern-day Sindh province of Pakistan, revealed numerous "4,500 to 5,000 year-old cosmetics pots of clay, stone, ivory, faience and alabaster, in a variety of shapes, most of them only two or three inches high with very small openings." One small bottle was a perfume sprinkler with tiny holes in the bottom. Their perfume was a little different, "smelling like damp earth, fish, lotus flowers, or goat's urine" and colored "dark red, greenish yellow, black or brown."

People in this region loved using materials that made the most of their own land and natural resources. Ingredients at the time included things like "collyrium and antimony (for the eyes), vermilion, realgar, yellow orpiment, and lamp soot." Many of their creams and ointments were also "perfumed with sandalwood, black zedoary, tagara and an essence made from bhaddamuttaka," a kind of local grass. In other regions, ingredients included "galena and probably lamp black mixed with fat" for eye makeup and "terre verte was used instead of malachite" for green eye paint.

Elaborate and well-designed public baths were critical to the beauty industry in the Indus Valley. They particularly loved to be scrubbed and believed in the physical and spiritual benefits of exfoliation. "In ancient India … rasps and scrapers of various types were used for cleansing and stimulating [the body and the skin]." They scraped their bodies using a perfumed powder and "a wooden hand-shaped instrument [such as] crocodile teeth, the jawbone of an ox, a twisted cloth, or by other means." If accessories were lacking, they rubbed themselves against trees or columns to stimulate circulation. After exfoliation, moisturizing was important. Body treatments depended somewhat on the season. Oil, saffron, musk, and aloeswood smoke were considered suitable in the winter and a body-paste of camphor, sandalwood, aloeswood, and saffron in the spring.

One of the most distinctive aspects of cosmetics in ancient India was their artistic value. Women were rarely painting their faces in response to societal pressure or ideals. Rather, they treated their skin as a sort of canvas. It was not unusual for women to paint their face with shapes, symbols, and designs depending on the week or the day. "Women painted their faces with suns, moons, flowers, stars, and birds as well as geometric designs," says Corson. Makeup had less to do with correcting deficiencies or hiding imperfections, but more to do with celebrating and expressing the beauty that already surrounded them. Perhaps these women did not sport a natural face, but they certainly felt they were aligning themselves more with nature after using makeup.

Cosmeticians in the Indus Valley were so good at using the land and natural resources to their advantage that they also became valuable trade partners to other beauty industry centers to the west. Indeed, their beauty economy was as vast as it was organized. "Street vendors, especially in the seaports, sold all sorts of perfumes and cosmetics … and many exotic scents and costly ointments were imported from Arabia and Somaliland." And yet, perhaps no ancient civilization brought such a diversity of ingredients and practices together into one place than Ancient Greece.

The earliest Homerian Greeks never wore makeup. Living around the seventh or eighth century BCE, their era was influenced by the namesake poet, Homer, and their ideals were toward human naturalism and personal style. Later on, however, with the expansion of the empire and growing wealth among all classes, Greek women began adapting elaborate cosmetics. By the fourth century BCE, the use of makeup was well established in Greece. Jean-Jacques Barthélemy described "one of the prettiest women of Athens" as being painted.

Greeks were fond of blondes. Fine, soft Mediterranean hair could be lightened in a variety of ways—with more than a little effort, of course. Social critic and author of comedic plays, Menander, captures a scene in downtown Athens of women soaking up their blonde. "The sun's rays," he wrote, "are the best means for lightening the hair … After washing their hair with a special ointment made here in Athens, they sit bareheaded in the sun by the hour, waiting for their hair to turn a beautiful golden blonde. And it does."

Greece was also perhaps the first place where cosmetics were clearly defined among classes. It is also the first time that we know of when makeup began an association with performance. "Lower class working women did not, so far as is known, wear makeup," writes Corson. Except, of course, for actresses. "A traveling entertainer is described as having a brownish red cream rouge spread generously over her cheeks and lips," and this was not uncommon.

A great deal of natural resources contributed to healthy, easily produced cosmetics, and olive oil was a foundational ingredient to almost everything. Olive oil made for cosmetics was handled in a particular way and only used when unripe. "When the olives could not be conveniently picked from the tree, they were beaten down with canes. They were then crushed in stone mills and the pulp placed in a wicker basket and weighted with stones. The oil thus forced out of the olives ran through the wicker of the basket and was caught in another vessel. Later, a wooden-frame press was used instead of the wicker baskets."

Similar methods worked for extracting oil from sesames, almonds, and palms.

However, not all Greek ingredients were healthy. Pale faces were sometimes painted with lead. The rouge was sometimes made of vermilion, although more often "of vegetable substances, such as mulberry, seaweed, and paederos," a root similar to alkanet. "Later, cinnabar (red sulfide of mercury) was used as well as white lead. Orpiment, a compound of arsenic, was used as a depilatory."

The first known reactions to unhealthy cosmetic choices were captured in both the literary and scientific spheres of ancient Greece. In a seventeenth-century translation of the Greek physician Galen (who, incidentally, was the inventor of cold crème), women were warned about cosmetics that had a nice immediate effect but a nasty aftermath. "The excellence of this Mercurie sublimate is such that the women who often paint themselves with it, though they be very young, they presently turn old with withered and wrinkled faces like an Ape, and before age comes upon them, they tremble (poor wretches) as if they were sicke of the staggers, reeling and full of quick-silver." He even offers a scientific defense. "The Soliman and the quick-silver differ only in this, that the Soliman is the more corrosive and biting; insomuch that being applied to the face, it is true, that it eateth out the spots and staines of the face, but so, that with all, it drieth up and consumeth the flesh that is underneath, so that of force the poore skin shrinketh."

In Xenophon's *The Science of Good Husbandry*, Ischomacus is fully frustrated with his fifteen-year-old wife, and his commentary is vibrant. "When I found her one day painted with rouge, I pointed out to her that she was being as dishonest in attempting to deceive me about her looks as I should be were I to deceive her about my property. I told her that although her artifice might deceive others, it could not mislead one who saw her regularly. I was sure to catch her in the morning before her cosmetics had been applied, or [when her] tears would betray her, or [her] perspiration, or the bath."

The wealthier Greek women grew, the more fiercely they depended on makeup. Petronius describes watching a lady take her false eyebrows out of a box. "Taking care her eyebrows be not apart, not mingled neither, but as hers are, stolen together. Met by stealth, yet leaning too, o'er the eyes their darkest hue." Men loved it when a woman's brow met above the nose.

Philosophical connotations of cosmetics were also seriously considered in Greece. According to Plutarch, cosmetics were banned from Sparta as a "flatterer of the senses" and "forbade the city to all who used the art of painting the body, for evil arts corrupted men's manners.". It is possible that Lycurgus only objected to what was seen by day, and not to the "face-packs of meal which were applied at night and removed with milk in the morning."

Morning, noon, day, and night, women in Greece pored through cosmetics, and it was much the same in Rome. Roman debate covered the sociological, psychosocial, and moral consequences of makeup—and it seems everyone took part in the discussion. Comedic Roman playwright Plautus invented two girls from Carthage, one arguing for the regular use of makeup and one against it. Their two-thousand-year-old debate is as humorous as it is delightful. One proclaimed it was necessary for the art of beauty; the other chimed that good food needs no seasoning. The rebuttal: "a woman without makeup is like a fish without salt"—or something to season it to help keep its fresh flavor.

Ovid saw a need for makeup and recounted a light layer of vermilion that would "supply the color denied by nature." Horace liked diversity and suggested women use three kinds of paint: "red lead, carmine, and an extract of crocodile dung." Yet others insisted it was all rubbish. Tibullius asked, "What's the use of lighting up your cheeks with a sparkling paint?" Propertius proclaimed that the "best face" was the natural face. Martial complained of his mistress Polla a great deal: "Leave off thy paint, perfume, and childish dress; And Nature's aging honesty confess; Twofold we see those faults which art would mend; Plain, downright ugliness would less offend." Pope Clement I, of course, lashed out at everyone—especially the women.

Much like his fellow Greek politician from Sparta,

Augustus followed Lycurgus in regulating the use of makeup. He particularly banned patrician ladies from using cerise (white paint), but the restrictions did not hold long. White paint was popular, and "light complexions were considered essential for fashionable women, in Rome." Apparently, "the more sympathy a woman wanted in a situation, the whiter [her] makeup." Rough was also popular, and ingredients ranged from the regular to the extravagant. Ovid wrote that he had seen, as a substitute for rouge, "[p]oppies soaked in cold water and rubbed on the cheeks."

Ovid's work reveals he has the most tricks of the trade. Among his lengthy suggestions is a pimple-fighting recipe:

> "Of these take six pounds each and grind it all in the mill. Add to that white lead and the scum of red niter and Illyrian iris. All this must be kneaded by strong, young arms. And when all are duly mashed, an ounce should be the proper weight. If you add to this the mud with which the Halcyon cements its nest, you will have a certain cure for spots and pimples. An ounce applied in equal parts is the dose I recommend. To make the mixture more adhesive and easier to apply, add honey from the honeycombs of Attica."

Ovid also had a specific cure for blackheads, involving a mixture of incense and niter. "Take of each four ounces, adding an ounce of gum from bark and a small cube of oily myrrh—nine scruples of myrrh and five of fennel. Add to this a handful of dried rose-leaves, sal-ammoniac, and frankincense. Pour barley water over it and let the weight of the incense and the sal- ammoniac equal the weight of the roses. A few applications of the mixture will give you a beautiful complexion." Wrinkles were a major concern, which they treated with an astringent called tentipellum, mainly preventative.

Some of Ovid's descriptions reveal modern motivations. "When you are well rested and your body is refreshed from a night of sleep, let me teach you how to make your skin a dazzling white. Take the barley from which our ships bring back Libyan fields and strip it of its straw and husks. Take of this two pound and of vetches an equal quantity and with ten eggs mix them well. Dry this mixture in the open air, then let it be ground by a mill-stone worked by the patient ass." Next, they must pulverize one sixth of a pound of hartshorn into a fine powder and pass it through a sieve. Then they added a dozen skinned narcissus bulbs, pounding the mixture in a marble mortar. Then two ounces of gum and Tuscan wheat and nine times as much honey. Finally, "any woman who uses this cosmetic paste," Ovid proclaims, "will have a face more shining than her mirror."

It is no wonder that some cosmetics were regulated, given how exhaustive and elaborate these routines became. In *The Lady's Toilet*, Lucian describes what the scene of a

Roman lady's bathroom looked like.

> "She must, these days, use powders, pomades, paints ... each chambermaid, each slave carries one of the essential objects of the toilet. One holds a silver basin, another a chamber pot, a third a water pot; still others the mirror and as many boxes as one could find in a pharmacy: and all these boxes contain only things she would not want anyone to see. In one are teeth and drugs for the gums; in other, eyelashes and eyebrows and the means of restoring faded beauty. But it is especially on the coiffure that they use the most art and spend the most time. Several women who fancy changing their black hair to blonde or even golden, rub the hair with a pomade which they then dry in strong sunlight. Others, whose black hair still pleases them, spend their family fortune on ointments scented with all the perfumes of Arabia. The heat irons [are used] to make curls which nature has denied them. The hair must fall over the forehead nearly to the eyebrows ... The curls behind hang very low on the shoulders."

Pompeia Paulina, wife of Seneca, allegedly required a hundred slaves to put her together. Her routines began at night: "a nightly face-mask, made of moistened and perfumed meal, which dried into a hard mask, was washed off in the morning with asses milk." She also bathed in milk, in hopes of preserving her complexion. She then covered her skin, however, with chalk and white lead. "She used fucus, a red or purplish paint, to rouge her cheeks and lips, antimony to darken her lids, lashes, and brows and blue paint for her veins." Her nails, according to Corson, were covered with a lacquer of "dragon's blood mixed with sheep fat." In addition, Pompeia had "depilatories for stray hairs, meal paste and lemon juice to bleach her freckles, pumice stone to whiten her teeth, barley flower and butter for pimples, and Hessian soap, as it was later called, to bleach her hair." As many reported, the effect of this routine was hardly subtle.

The Roman woman experienced all kinds of social pressure and expectations. Her painted or plastered face literally became known as the "domestic face." It was worn at home and was intended to please her husband. Not unlike Ischomacus, Juvenal felt it was the only wife he ever saw. "She duly, once a month, renews her face; Meantime, it lies in dawn, and hid in grease; Those are the husband's nights, she craves her due; He takes fat kisses, and is stuck in glue. But to the loved adulterer when she steers, fresh from the bath in brightness she appears; For him, the rich Arabia sweets her gum; And precious oils from distant Indies come. How haggardly soe'er she looks at home, Th'eclipse then vanishes; and all her face is opened, and restored to ev'ry grace; The crust removed, her cheeks as smooth as silk, are polished with a wash of asses milk; And should she to the farthest north be sent, a train of these attend her banishment. But hadst thou seen her plastered up before, 'Twas so unlike a face, it seemed a sore."

Indeed, there was no one as critical as Ovid. In *The Art of Love*, he takes the subject a step further.

> "You know how to whiten your skin with wax and to supply with carmine the rosy blush of Nature. You have the art to fill the space between your eyebrows, if that is necessary, and white makeup to conceal the telltale marks of the advancing years. You do not hesitate to increase the brightness of your eyes with powdered ash or with saffron gathered on the banks of the Cydnus… But on no account let your lover come upon you surrounded by the accouterments of your cosmetic art. Your artifice should go unsuspected. Who could help but feel disgust at the thick paint on your face melting and running down onto your breasts? How can one describe the obnoxious smell of the oesypum, even though it comes from Athens, of that oil extracted from the fleece of sheep … Do not use the marrow taken from deer or clean your teeth in front of others. I realize that all of this can heighten your charms, but it is nonetheless unpleasant to watch. If we arrive before you've finished your toilet, have the servants tell us you are still asleep. You will seem all the lovelier when

> you do appear. Why do I need to know what gives your skin its whiteness? Shut your door, and let me not see the work till it's complete. There are many things we men had best know nothing of. Most of these artificial aids we'd find distressing if you'd let us see them … Rare is the face without fault."

Martial speaks to a woman who remains nameless and, perhaps, surpasses Ovid's criticism by infusing his own with a blend of poetry and contempt. "You are but a composition of lies," he writes. "Whilst you were in Rome, your hair was growing on the banks of the Rhine; at night, when you lay aside your silken robes, you lay aside your teeth as well; and two thirds of your person are locked up in boxes for the night. The eyebrows with which you can make such insinuating motions are the work of your slaves. Thus, no man can say, I love you—for you are not what he loves, and no one loves what you are."

We know little of how Roman women answered back, but it is easy to imagine the impact was grave. As Martial said, "Lycoris, who is blacker than the color of the ripe mulberry, [only considers] herself beautiful when she paints her face with white lead." Martial describes another woman, Fabula, saying she "feared the rain" because of the chalk on her face. Others, like Sabella, were neurotic and "took pains to avoid the sun." Were they proud of their performance? Torn down by it? Did they feel their husbands loved them more than their fake hair, or loved them for their fake hair?

These questions of tenderness and connectedness would only become more opaque in the early Christian period. The first few centuries after the birth of Christ were marked by an elevated debate over the morality of makeup. Most of our information about this time comes from the writings of churchmen who objected to it. Ironically, their choice in writing about the very thing they were trying to purge is precisely what allowed it to live on so that we might look back on it and learn.

There is a long list of men who wrote and argued for a greater value to be placed on natural beauty. Not surprisingly, their logic was often motivated by saving the soul. Clement of Alexandria, for example, argued that when women who wore wigs were blessed, "the blessing remained on the wig and did not penetrate the wearer beneath." Clement was insistent on the effects of cosmetics on spiritual health. "They are not once, but thrice worthy to perish, which dawbe their browes, and weare their cheekes with their painted stuffe." Apparently, he felt a special circle in hell existed for cosmetics users.

Akin to the Greeks and the Romans, St. Ambrose separates the woman from her cosmetics by naming it her borrowed face. "And thou who displeaseth thy maker, who seeth his work to be defaced. O woman, thou defacest the picture if thou daubest thy countenance with materiall whitenesse or a borrowed red … Do not take away God's picturing and assume the picture of a harlot." St. Ambrose may not be seeming to protect the woman, but he certainly believes that God is in that woman, and seeks to protect the face of Him in her. Later on, toward the end of the fourth century, he says, "Painting is deceitful ... lasts but a while, and is wiped off with either rain or sweat." He interestingly anthropomorphizes makeup. "It deceives and beguiles," he asserts, and "cannot please him who thou desirest to please, who perceiveth this pleasing beauty to be none of thine, but borrowed."

"The women which are exercized in frizzling their haire, in anointing their cheekes, in painting their eyes, and dying their haire, and following other wantonness with unlawful artes, doe seeme to me to draw on unhappy lovers: but if any man shall open the vaile of the Temple, I meane their dressing, colouring, dying, and those things, that are plastered on them, thinking to find true beauty, I wot well he will grow into a loathing and detestation." It would seem the warnings of men to fellow men about uncovering the veil of beautification echoes through the centuries.

While the lecturing and preaching may have dimmed the general popularity of cosmetics for the first few centuries after Christ, they were certainly still used, and the world of beautification became a bit darker in the Middle Ages. When medieval-era women wanted to be whiter, they simply removed any red. "Almost without exception," writes Corson, "upper-class European women in the Middle Ages wanted to be pale, and frequently they achieved this by [being] bled." Letting a woman bleed was a very common practice, and it achieved an overall white visage all across the face, hands, and chest.

For an even complexion, one medieval potion involved "asparagus roots, wild anise, and the bulbs of white lilies in the milk of asses and red goats. This was aged in warm horse manure before being filtered through felt. The lady rubbed her face with pieces of soft bread dipped into the filtered liquid, and she did this 'for as long as it takes to say the credo thrice.'"

Thin may not have been in, but for the eyebrows it was true. Eyebrows were usually natural, until about the fourteenth century. Corson tells us, "A thirteenth century English poet describes a lady's brows as 'white between and not too near,' and a French one admires brows which are 'brownish, narrow and delicate.'" Before eyebrows had an audience, they were just eyebrows. "The admiration for narrow brows evidently increased, for in the fourteenth and fifteenth centuries fashionable women plucked their eyebrows into a thin line. In England, it appears, even lower-class women plucked their brows—like the carpenter's wife in *The Canterbury Tales*: 'Full small y-pulled were here browes two, and they were bent and blake as any solo.'"

Women around Europe had different practices. A thirteenth-century French verse lists just a few of the cosmetics that would have been offered by a traveling merchant: "I have all the various things a woman needs who would be fair; Razors, forceps, mirrors too, combs and irons for her hair; Picks and brushes for her teeth, baneaux or a fancy pin; Cotton to apply her rouge, white enamel for her skin."

We know that the more remote medieval Anglo-Saxon tribes were keen on paint, especially war paint. It was Caesar who first accounted these fierce warriors and recalled them being painted blue, often with woad. Indeed, the modern name "Britain" takes its root in the Celtic word "brith," meaning "paint." The Anglo-Saxons also had an affinity for blue hair. "Since the hair of both men and women is consistently painted blue in illuminations of the period, we assume that [it] was colored with dye or powder."

One magazine's entry from March 10, 1860, recounts this trend. The comedic magazine *Punch* comments: "About the fact of blewe haire … it was worn thus being thoroughly established, we may fancy that young ladies of the Anglo-Saxon period spent a good deal of their leisure in colouring their hair, more especially perhaps when they were asked to spare a lock of it. 'My mother bids me dye my hair to a cerulean blue,' doubtless was a ditty much in vogue about this period, and matchmaking Mammas no doubt insisted on their bidding being put into effect, if they thought blue hair increased the girl's capillary attractions."

Regardless of the factual utterings of "matchmaking Mammas," the author notes that there were indeed exceptions to those who liked the trend, such as the poet of this couplet. "Youre nose is redde, your haire is blew; Youre nailes are blacke, styl I loave yew! Andd if youre pa wyl stande the shine; Sweete maybe, E'll bee youre Vallentine!"

We even have this group of early Anglo-Saxons to thank for a popular haircut. Medieval natives in Scotland were whimsical indeed, incorporating magic into their culture. One tribe known as the Picts are featured in Terry Pratchett's *Discworld* novels, where he references a race of tiny wood-fairies who spoke a kind of ancient Scottish-Gaelic language and tattooed themselves with blue war paint. In *Carpe Jugulum*, they are called "the Pictsies," and today a short haircut resembling a fairy is called a "pixie."

One ancient Celtic hair restorative described by Ivor Griffith helps men—but, he warns, wear gloves. "With mice fill an earthen pipkin, close the mouth with clay and let it be buried beneath the hearth-stone, but so as the fire's too great heat reach it not. So be it for one year, at the end of which take out whatever may be there. For baldness, it is great. But it is urgent that whoever shall handle it have a glove on his hand, lest at his fingers ends the hair come sprouting forth."

When hair growth formulas didn't work, extensions were used. "At the end of the thirteenth century," explains Corson, "false hair was often used by women to provide the projecting rolls of braids over the ears. These false pieces, called atours, early in the fourteenth century were shaped like horns, which upset the clergy even more than the use of paint. The horns, filled out with flax or hemp, are mentioned in *Le Roman de la Rose* … [and] another satirist says: 'They have horns with which to kill the men; They pile up other peoples hair upon their heads …

The bishop is aware of all the horns and hair, and in his sermon duly notes that he will give his solemn blessing to those who'll mock this sort of dressing, by shouting loudly, 'push, you goats!'" Even then, mockery didn't shame a determined woman.

In addition to this mockery and shaming, there was praise for the natural face. "Although many women throughout the Middle Ages did paint their faces and dye their hair," writes Corson, "natural beauty [was] admired by most men and certainly by the poets. 'Nor was she painted or disguised,' says [one poet], 'for she had no need.'" Gautier de Coincy, an abbot and poet from the thirteenth century, describes a modest and prudent maiden who does not "associate with those who go together pair by pair, who paint themselves to counterfeit youth and incessantly comb their hair."

Henry VII of England, in considering marrying the Queen of Naples, first "instructed his ambassadors to note, among other things, 'whether she be painted or not' and 'the clearness of her skin.' She did not appear to be painted, reported the ambassadors, and her skin, what they could see of it, was clear," writes Corson.

Thanks to Charles Darwin, we can see how these traditions developed in Asia and Africa. He observed that "not one great country can be named ... in which the [natives] do not tattoo themselves." Although the practice of tattooing throughout tribal peoples had social as well as religious significance, beautification remained the predominant purpose. "The natives undergo considerable physical pain in the process," writes Corson, "which involves repeated puncturing of the skin and introducing of the blue paint into the wounds." For the Mayans, the art of tattooing developed to high sophistication, with "very elaborate patterns, even animals and mythical figures." Other painful routines involved having the front teeth "filed to points, holes drilled in them, and precious stones inserted."

In Australia, makeup among the Aborigines included both painting and tattooing. Columbus was surprised when he found that native men in the New World used cosmetics, painting themselves "white and red or other colors, sometimes the whole body or only the face, the eyes, or the nose." According to Corson, "the skin was lubricated with deer's or bear's fat before the vegetable and mineral colors were applied." Columbus also observed that the paints were protective as well as decorative.

Henna remained a familiar ingredient. Near Kurdufan, Sudan, "[the] Fallatah women stained their fingers and toes by wrapping them with henna leaves, shadowed their eyelids with sulfide of antimony, dyed their hair with indigo, and stained their teeth yellow, purple and blue."

For the Bantu women in Southern Africa, natural resources were key to beautification. Where red clay was plentiful, it was mixed with oil and rubbed on both skin and hair, primarily as a protection from the elements. Depending on the tribe, cosmetics included ingredients such as soot, leaves, dung, butter, antelope blood, and blue mica schist.

"Tattooing and deliberate scarring of the skin in patterns were and still are commonplace."

In Asia, makeup was no less common. "Fashionable Japanese ladies, like the Chinese, used white face paint, rouge, and nail coloring," writes Corson. "Sometimes they also gilded the lower lip." Women across Asia blackened their teeth, shaved their eyebrows, and created new brows with paint. "[The Japanese]," writes Corson, "had fifteen choices for the style of the hair in front and twelve for the back."

Trade from the Orient was key to cosmeticians in the East and West. Although the Arabians introduced alternative cosmetics to Spain near the beginning of the eighth century, the Crusaders were responsible for bringing Oriental perfumes into Europe. Spices and oils from the East were high luxury, especially in Italy and France, where new scents began to be developed. Catherine de' Medici, for example, liked to combine her perfumes with poisons.

It is easy to imagine a woman like Catherine de Medici taking a bath in her Asian spices and herbs just before a dinner party because recorded scenes from the renaissance are just that elaborate. Our own modern consciousness of the history of beauty seems to be linked to this time, where Venus was born and hell was written.

The Italian Renaissance brought one of the earliest books devoted to beauty expectations. In 1548, the author Agnolo

Firenzuola was quite a handful. Both monk and lawyer, Firenzuola wrote a text with some contradictions of its own—perhaps, first and foremost, that expectations for looks are implicated, but the means for achieving them are restricted. In other words, there is a beauty lottery, but it's genetic and very few will win.

He begins with the cheeks. "The cheeks should be fair; and such fairness is in things which, beside whiteness, have a certain glow, as snow." Then, the breasts. "And whereas the cheeks to be beautiful must be of this fairness, the bosom must be white." Next, the hair. "The hair ... should be fine and fair, in the similitude now of gold, now of honey, and now of the bright and shining rays of the sun; waving thick, abundant." Very important, as well, was the forehead. Measurement was required. "The forehead must be spacious, that is, wide and high and fair, and serene ... The height ... must be equal to half the width, [and] should shine after the manner of a mirror, not by wetness or by painting, or by foul washes, like that of Bonivetta." The cheeks of course, should not be "so white as the forehead, with a patch of sunset vermillion." The nose, "should be of proper size, more narrow than wide, slightly turned up at the tip, and colored but not red." The mouth should be "small with medium lips, vermillion in color and not to show more than five or six teeth—uppers only, when parted." Not even the tongue was an exception, as he thought it should "neither [be] pointed nor square [and] to be scarlet." There is no question that he favored a long, slender neck, but he also wanted a slight double chin.

Everything had to look as natural as possible. Firenzuola "complained of the cosmetics" that were used, as he put it, "to paint and whiten the whole face," and compared them to "lime and plaster [which] cover the face of a wall." He publically shamed those "foolish maids [who] believe that men, whom they seek to please, do not discern the foulness, which I would have them to know wears them out and makes them grow old before their time, and destroys their teeth, while they seem to be wearing a mask all the year through." He names names. "Look now at Mona Bettola Gagliana—what do you think of her? The more she paints and the more she dresses up, the older she seems; nay, she is like a gold ducat that hath lain in aqua-fortis."

Men were opinionated and vocal, but also shared scientific concerns. "Physicians in general," during the Renaissance, "warned women against using poisons on their skin—not only white lead, but mercury sublimate, which was frequently used to remove imperfections in the skin and make it smooth," writes Corson. Laguna spoke of the dangers of mercury, as they were "infamous inconveniences which … might be somewhat more tolerable if they did sticke and stay only in them who use it, and did not descend to their offspring. For this infamy is like to original sinne and goes from generation to generation." That passing down of corruption of makeup from mother to child was, of course, just as fervent a warning as lead and mercury, although not scientifically sound.

Firenzuola offered alternatives to poisonous chemicals. "Use barley water or the water of Lupines, or the juyce of Lymons, and infinite other things, which Dioscorides prescribes as cleanly and delicate to clear the face, and not goe continually with rank smells of ointments and plasters about them."

Laguna casts out a warning. "Wherefore let all gentlewomen and honorable matrons, that make price of their honesty and beauty, leave these base arts to the common strumpets, of whom they are best fitted to be used, that by filthiness they may be known and noted."

Andres Laguna was a sixteenth-century pharmacologist and botanist originally from Spain who became doctor to the pontiff. He weighed in, with similar views to Firenzuola, toward naturalness and restraint. "There are many who have so betard their faces with these mixtures and slubbersauces," writes Laguna, "that they have made their faces of a thousand colors." "Slubbersauces" was a slang term comprised of "slubber," for slime, and sauce. "Some [women] as yellow as the marigold, others as dark as greene, others blunket color, others as of a deep red died in the wooll … Thus the use of this ceruse, besides the rotting of the teeth and the unsavorire breath which it causeth, being ministered in paintings, doth turn faire creatures into infernal Furies."

A passionate man indeed, Girolamo Savonarola joined the cause. In 1497, young supporters of this determined Dominican took to the streets of Florence and made a heap in the piazza. They collected mirrors, hairbrushes, cosmetics, and even works of art and burned them. It came to be called the Bonfire of The Vanities.

Savonarola even moved to have cosmetics banned, and for a time they were. But he made the small mistake of not including the Medici women, who went on with their beautification techniques while the other nobles walked about barefaced. Of course, this did not last long; the other women were outraged, and the makeup was back on the streets in a month.

Still, the beauty industry in Renaissance Italy raged on. And they had a style for everything. Catherine de' Medici worked for the fairy-look quite hard. In trying to achieve beauty that looked as natural as possible, her physician instructed her to "go into the royal gardens at dawn and gather dew-drenched peach blossoms, which should then be crushed with oil of almonds by the light of the moon." Perhaps all this royal blossom-dew scampering from dawn until midnight simply gave Catherine the natural glow of exercise.

"The eyebrows of fashionable women," writes Corson, "were still being plucked into a thin line, but eye makeup was not commonly used. By the end of the sixteenth century the brows had returned to their natural fullness [and] beauty spots were occasionally worn."

Cosmetics, paints, and styling didn't stop at the skin, but went on to the hair. "Blonde hair was in fashion," Corson tells us, "and women spent hours in the sun bleaching their own." Giambattista della Porta, a philosopher and scientist from Naples, suggested one lightening recipe. "Add enough of honey to soften the lees of white wine and keep the hair wet with this all night. Then bruise the roots of celandine and greater olivers-madder, mix them with oil of cummin seed, box shavings, and saffron; and keep this on the head for four and twenty hours, when it should be washed off with a lye of cabbage-stalks and ashes of rye straw."

Della Porta even wrote a toothpaste recipe, "for white and pearly teeth." Take "three handfuls each of flowers and leaves of sage, nettle, rosemary, mallow olive, plantain, and rind of walnut roots; two handfuls each of rockrose, horehound, bramble tops; a pound of flower and a half a pound of seed of myrtle; two handfuls of rosebuds; two drachms each of sandalwood, coriander, and citron pips; three drachms of cinnamon; ten drachms of cypress nuts; five green pine cones; two drachms each of mastic and Armenian clay, reduce all of them to a powder, infuse them in 'sharp black wine,' and macerate them for three days, during which time she might presumably take a well deserved rest." To apply toothpaste, women "[filled] the mouth with it and [rubbed] the teeth with a finger wrapped in fine linen."

The beauty industry took off in the Renaissance and grew into a strong economy. Different groups were able to isolate their business only to cosmetics. Even parts of the Church made a way of life by contributing to the beauty economy. In 1508, Dominican monks in the convent of Santa Maria Novella in Florence established what Corson calls "one of the most celebrated perfumeries in Europe." It was patronized by the Medicis and the popes, who gave generous donations. Over the centuries, each new director of the perfumery added recipes and ingredients, as trade increased and the exotic became the accessible. "Pope Innocent XI contributed a recipe to cure burns, thereafter called Balsamo Innocenziano." In a catalogue hundreds of years old, we can see the delicacies available, like "quina elixir, long life elixir, rhubarb elixir, melissa water, and Regina water (the invention of a Medici queen). Their Orris powder was used to perfume linen, brush the teeth, and dust on to the skin after bathing," writes Corson.

Collective knowledge and understanding of this developing economy was largely in the hands of men, but leave it to the noble women of Renaissance Italy to take control. "Venetian ladies even formed a society (and elected officers) for learning and testing new discoveries in the cosmetic arts," writes Corson. It was a popular group with regular meetings and distinct initiatives. "Isabella Cortese was president at one time, and Catherine de Medici was an honorary member."

These were women of great consequence in their communities. And yet, perhaps no woman would rise to the same influence in Europe as Queen Elizabeth I. Her era of beauty was a sight to behold. Cosmetics in Elizabethan England grew to infuse the beauty and fashion industries together, such as gloves that became popular because they were sewn with potpourri: "perfume gloves."

However, Queen Elizabeth's goals contrasted with those of the "peacocks" of Renaissance Italy. In a country newly without a pope, the Queen was the supreme ruler—for God and man. And as the Virgin Queen, she looked directly to the Virgin Mary for spiritual leadership and, perhaps also, visual inspiration. As Elizabeth got whiter, many followed.

Egg whites "give a fashionable glaze to the skin," but they were—by far—the most timid approach. While women bled for white skin in the Middle Ages, Elizabethan women "[swallowed] gravel, ashes, coals, dust, [and] tallow candles," writes Michel de Montaigne, just to outdo each other. And it was all in vain, for they would be sick, "labour and toil themselves to spoil their stomach, only to get a pale-bleak color," he says.

For the few who wanted to forgo paint or swallowing wax, they were advised to "wash in your own urine," and perhaps mix it with a little rose water and wine. They could even "make a Decoction of the Rinds of Lemon" on their faces. Diane de Poitiers, famous simply for her complexion, is said to have "used no cosmetic other than rain water.".

Hugh Plat's recipe for the white face begins: "take the jaw bones of a Hog or Sow well burnt, beaten and searched throrow a fine Searce, and after, ground upon a porphyry or serpentine stone, is an excellent focus, being laid on with the kyle of white poppy. To take away spots and freckles from the face or hands. The sappe that issueth out of a birch tree in great abundance, being opened, in March or Aprill, with a receiver of glasses set under the boring thereof to receive the same, doth perform the same most excellently & maketh the skin very clear. This sap will dissolve pearl; a secret not known unto many."

To be sure, this period in Europe was not lacking in creative approaches to beautification. Patching still generated the weirdest reactions from men. "In 1616, court ladies in Berlin were observed to be heavily patched," writes Corson. "And somewhat later [Johann Michael Moscherosch] reported seeing 'a group of women looking as if their faces had been scratched, pecked, and cut, for on those parts to which they wished to attract special attention, they had stuck small black plasters which looked like gnats and fleas of every imaginable shape and size, as well as other singular lures to finger and eye.'" Patching was complicated and, indeed, an upper-class goal; if it went wrong, the face was scarred for life.

And yet it would seem, the devil was still in the details. A meticulous face-wash recipe from the period was made popular by Ben Jonson. "Madam, you take your hen, plume it, and skin it, cleanse it o' the inwards; Then chop it, bones and all; add to four ounces of carravicins, pipits, dope of Cyprus; Make the decoction, strain it. Then distil it, and keep it in your gally-pot well glider's: Three drops preserves from wrinkles, warts, spots, moles, blemish, or sun burnings, and keeps the skin 'in decimo sexton,' ever bright and smooth, as any looking-glass; And indeed is call'd the virgins milk for the face." "Virgins' milk" would have been an advertising catchphrase sensation at the time.

Despite the "virgin skin," there were many "flaming heads." Hair dyes were rampant. In 1602, Hugh Plat instructed: "How to colour the head or beard into a chestnut colour in halfe an hour: take one part of lead calcination with sulphur, and one part of quicklime, temper them somewhat thin with water, lay it upon the hair, chafing it well in, and let it dry one quarter of an hour thereabouts; then wash the same off with fair water divers times, and lastly with some and water, and it will ver naturals hair colour. The longer it lyeth upon the hair, the browner it growth. This coloureth not the flesh at all, and yet it lasteth very long in the hair."

Plat also had a recipe for teeth for women who wanted to "keep the teeth both white and sound." Its relation to Della Porta's is, as such, unknown. "Of honey take a quart, as much vinegar, & half so much white wine; boyl them together, and wash your teeth therewith now and then." At the end of the recipe, he adds, "if your teeth be very scaly, let some expert barber first take off the scales with his instrument, and then you may keep them clone by rubbing with the aforementioned rules."

Elizabethan women loved beauty marks, although they required quite a bit of skill to create. The end of the sixteenth century, writes Corson, saw the beginning of "a new era in patching, thus providing the clergy with one more sin to preach against." It became a custom to wear "little black beauty spots to set off the whiteness of the skin," explains Corson, and "is believed to have begun with the use of black velvet or taffeta court plasters on the temples," which originally was done to relieve a toothache but then became a trend unto itself.

This beauty industry grew in size and even made its way into the art of the time, particularly plays. In *A Midsummer Night's Dream*, Shakespeare writes of Hermia who calls Helena a "painted maypole," and Hamlet accuses Ophelia of overdoing it: "God hath given you one face," he says to her, "and you make yourself another."

Indeed, the Elizabethan cosmetic economy boomed. Manufacturing became, in *The Countrey Farme*, quite a feat. Published in 1600, Richard Surflet's translation spoke to the "country wife," suggesting that she "achieve some skill" in making "fumes and such things as are apt for the decking and painting of the body," not that she would make great use of them herself, but that she may "make some profit and benefit by the sale thereof, unto great lords and ladies and other persons that may attend to be curious and paint up themselves," says Corson. Of what we know of the Elizabethans, a country wife would have had much to roll her sleeves up for.

A good marriage was often the highest if not the only goal of a woman of this era—another major reason why makeup was not only popular but crucial. Beautification figured heavily in how men picked mates. The unknown author of "How To Choose a Wife" explains, "Good sir, if you will shew the best of your skill to picke a virtuous creature, then picke such a wife, as you love a life, of comely grace and feature; The noblest part, let it be her heart, without deceit or cunning; With a humble wit, and all things fit, with a tongue that's never running; The hair of her head, it must not be red, but fair and brown as a berry; Her fore-head high, with a christall eye, her lips as red as a cherry."

The poet Robert Herrick also describes the ideal beauty: "Black and rowling is her eye, double chinn'd and forehead high; Lips she has, all Rubie red, cheeks like creame enclarited; And a nose that is the grace and Proscenium of her face." It seems Herrick expected a little makeup, but not a lot. Sir John Suckling, whose name will be forever remembered for his favorite body part, wrote of a lady he admired: "Her lips were red, and one was thin compared with that next to her chin, some bee had stung it newly."

Some persisted with damnation. John Singer, the author of *Quips Upon Questions*, does it with wit. "Where's the Devill? He's got a boxe of women's paint; Where pride is, thers the Devill too." In 1616, Thomas Tuke echoed earlier Christians when he argued for the natural face. "What a pride it is that thou canst not bee content to appeare in thine owne likeness and to seems that to others which thou art in thy selfe? The bird appeares in her owne feathers, the Peacocke shewes himselfe in his owne colours, the sheepe is seene in her owne fleece and likeness, white or black; the tree hath her own rind, appears in her owne blossomes and fruites; and shall it be horrible to a woman to seeme to be, as she is indeed, displeasing to her to appeare in her owne likenesse, her owne haire, her owne complexion? She was borne in her owne, nature would shew itself in her proper colours; she was not borne painted in this world ... neither shall she ride painted in the next world, and I thinke she would be loth die painted, why then should she live painted, why should she love it? A painted face is a superfluous face. It were well if the world were well rid of all such superfluous creatures."

Most men of this period seemed tolerant of artificial aids, but only if they were not a distraction. "Despite the voluble complaints [among] clergymen" of this period, writes Corson, "men in general accepted the painted faces with resignation—as a foolish conceit, perhaps, but hardly a mortal sin." From a similar perspective, George Chapman, who wrote in the early part of the seventeenth century, used more vivid language. He compares the women of his day, always made up, to the temples of Egypt. "With alabaster pillars were those temples upheld and beautiful, and so are women; Most curiously glazed, and so are women; Cunningly painted too, and so are women."

If it was a distraction, men pointed out the differences between the two faces. In *Wit Restored*, Sir John Mennis writes of "A Painted Madam": "men say y'are fair; and fair ye are, 'tis true, but (hark!) we praise the painter now, not you." He wrote similarly about "A Painted Curtezan": "whosoever saith thou sellest all, doth jest, Thou buy'st thy beauty, that sells all the rest." We learn from John Saris that voyagers to Japan in 1613 found local women, "Their haire very blacke and very longe, tyed up in a knot upon the crowne in a comely manner; their heads no where shaven as the mens were. They were well-faced, handed, and footed; clear skind and white, but wanting colour, which they amend by arte."

Saris also tells us that the Moors around the Mediterranean and Morocco were very fond of perfumes and oils. In 1610, Muslim women were observed "with their chinnes distayned into knots and flowres of blue, made by pricking of the skinne with Needles, and rubbing it over with Inke and the Juyce of an herb, which will never weare out againe."

Similar practices were shared by Turkish women who, in 1630, were gathering in seraglios—or homes for wives and concubines. According to Samuel Purchas, the virgin chosen by the Sultan "hath all the art that possibly may be shewen upon her by the Cadun, in attiring, painting, and perfuming her."

Nevertheless, the Italians were best at combining beauty with cunning. "In seventeenth-century Italy, it was possible to find among ladies' cosmetics a colourless preparation of liquid arsenic called Aqua Tofana (after Giulia Tofana, who concocted it), or sometimes Aquetta di Napoli or Manna of St. Nicholas di Bari," writes Corson. This was a strange liquid. Sold in special vials and packaged with a picture of St. Nicholas, this arsenic water gave women glowing results, but had another effect on men. "In lieu of printed information about its use, private instructions were given to the lady at the time of the purchase." When more than six hundred husbands and lovers were found dead in southern Italy, it was discovered that they had died of arsenic poisoning—not entirely by accident. Signora Tofana and her daughter were arrested for running an elaborate scheme, and the Signora herself was eventually "executed as the most prolific poisoner of the century." That cosmetic surely attracted the kiss of death.

* * *

Throughout history, the beauty industry may have looked different north, south, east, and west—but it was always open for business. There are vast commonalities between historic practices and pressures and ours today.

First, the industry has always been (in slightly varying degrees) big, organized, and immersed in society. Its integration into everyday life has been such a constant quality that Gautier de Coincy's description of the girls who "incessantly comb their hair" doesn't seem like an eight-hundred-year-old image to me. I can name five right now.

Another constant quality of the beauty industry then and now is its experimentation with new technology. We can be grateful for certain advances, infusions of technology, and improvements for health. Perhaps we can feel lucky, for example, that when we walk into our bathrooms at night we don't have to go through the twelve steps that della Porta lays out in brushing teeth. My thanks to Colgate.

Along with experimentation, the results of developing technologies have not always been so positive—and so too, today. New beauty practices are not always introduced for the sake of health. In fact, the industry then and now has been much more about the power of transformation.

Cosmetics never were, and still aren't, health aids. A woman's beauty was just a means to an end. Makeup was used to achieve something: scare an enemy, win a lover, climb up society, or land a job. If there is one uncharted isle the beauty industry has never settled on it is that of supreme individuality. The global beauty industry has never focused on being yourself: rather it produces a means to an end; transformation for the sake of performance.

What have women been trying to transform into? Muses. Although he would not easily admit it, I think Ovid is asking the woman he addresses to transform into a muse when he says her face needs to be "more shining than [a mirror].” Pressure fell onto women to be the muses, the inspirations, the saviors, the sirens.

And what is a muse? It is nothing but a character. A muse is an ideal. A muse is perfect. Muses are not human; humans are not muses. I am particularly drawn to Greece, Rome, and Egypt when I think of all their goddesses and heroines. Their cultures seem to have focused on women performing as muses, and I wonder if it isn’t coincidence that these are the cultures that created history’s greatest legends.

With the creation of heroes, both in story and in art, comes a collective, cultural lust for fantasy. Dreams are difficult to ignore. Dreams have prompted both men and women to transform into figures from tales, into the stuff of legends. In this way, we know Greek women did not just want golden hair; in fact they wanted golden hair like Helen. Are we not just as guilty when we fawn over actresses walking a red carpet? We don’t even call them Hollywood people; we call them Hollywood stars because they are the culturally established, socially accepted modern muses of our time. We marvel when they do anything “just like us!”—as if they were ever anything other than human.

Characters, heroines, sirens, muses, and dolls. They’ve all played a role in the beauty industry. Perhaps when Firenzuola gives his laundry list of the perfect woman he is doing exactly that, designing a doll.

Not to be discounted, there has always been a male presence in the beauty industry. Indeed, men and women have been working equally hard to churn this wheel. The industry is present because of their dual, shared activity. Snapshots of the male role that stick out to me are the painful ones. "Two thirds of your person are locked up at night," says Martial. "Rare" is the face without fault, says Ovid. "No man can say, I love you," he continues, "for you are not what he loves, and no one loves what you are."

And yet, playing the muse has been the only exclusively female role in the beauty industry. All other roles men and women have shared. Perhaps men would have liked their role to be thought of as the observers, or in the audience. But the truth is, except for the women who have stood on stage giving the performance, both men and women have been in the audience, backstage, and playing director.

These characteristics and others have remained constant. The beauty industry has always been large, organized, and well immersed in society. It has always been affected by new technology. It has always served as a means to an end. It has always helped the female performance of playing the muse. And it has already involved men. However, some aspects of the beauty industry today are not shared with history, are totally modern marks, are completely unique to modern society—being unequivocally negative.

Never in the history of the human race, that I can gather, have women starved, bled, and burned themselves in the name of beauty as widely and as eagerly as they do now. Eating disorders, plastic surgery, and tanning, for example, are joined by a fourth characteristic that distinguishes our beauty industry from that of history: our advertising business. The fifth and final modern distinction to our industry is the holistic introduction of children into it. Have girls so young ever been allowed to buy into the industry the way they do now?

When we starve and diminish the shape of our body, or when we break our noses to build a new one, are we not "[taking] away God's picturing"? Women in the Middle Ages and the Renaissance, in a way, wanted to be more like paintings, and so they painted their faces to mimic the image. Did that set the precedent for what we do now? Do we want to be more like photographs? Are we so caught up in advertising that we starve to mimic the image of the day, a Photoshopped model? Those paintings, of course, smoothed over hairs and lines that actually existed, as Photoshop does. When we mimic them, are we erasing the human? The beauty industry has continued to grow, but never has it been so large as it is today. Ideals of beauty were at one moment about romance and love, but are they now about mass production? Indeed, is that not why hundreds and hundreds of models have the same dimensions?

I discuss these phenomena in several different sections of this book, but perhaps most directly in the next chapter. For now, I think these modern distinctions need only be introduced, because they really do put our activities in a new light. We do things that even the women swallowing wax would not do. We do things that, I hope, generations after us will never do.

When I researched and wrote this chapter, I realized just how little I knew. And yet, I think it is also true that the average American woman reading this would now know more about the ingredients, production process, and warnings of the cosmetics used by women one thousand years ago than she knows about the ingredients in the products in her own bathroom right now. How do they make this stuff? What exactly is in it? Can I be sure of what it's doing for me? We see, we use—but how much do we know?

I am also keen to call on Virginia Woolf. What would she make of all this? Are we still like George Chapman's temples? Is not the painted sex the protected sex, because we feel there are things we need to cover, shield, and hide from the world? Or is the most important person we're hiding these things from ourselves, because even we can't accept us?

Of one thing, I am sure: the painted face is the "superfluous face." Men only have to have one. Why do I have to have two? Are we all living with our own modern version of "the domestic face"? If we took a break from it all for some time to reflect, our routines and our rituals might seem as foreign as painting a star on one's cheek or a tree on one's head. Why should I put tan paint under my eyes, because otherwise I look tired? Am I not allowed to be tired? I mean, at least I'm exerting myself, at least I'm trying, at least I work. I'm not made of porcelain. And if I am a little bit tired from doing my best, then shouldn't it be allowed to show?

Cosmetics in overuse can seal the transformation of woman to muse. It's time for the curtain to close on that role. Isn't the human race done conquering other people, parading into war, stealing lovers, playing Puck, and inventing ourselves again and again into something that we're not? Isn't it time we simply measure how much money we spend on beauty products per month and then put that toward the house we always wanted, the exercise classes we said we can't afford, or donate it to charity? If men have evolved from thinking war is the best option, when will women evolve from thinking that performing the muse is their most important role?

I am not impressed by muses. Some see women who are so beautiful, supermodels in ads looking like creatures from the sea. And I say, "Same devil. New dress." We have been bleeding ourselves, burning ourselves, and cutting ourselves long enough. It's time to heal.

To those youngest of all, I would say: You don't need to be a doll. You don't need to dress up. You don't need to try, or to buy, or to apply. You just need to be, and be well. For this measure, truth is beauty and beauty is truth.

Let's turn a new page of history. Let's make a new beauty industry. When I think back on it, we don't know of

Amelia Earhart for how she powdered her nose. We know her for how she flew through the sky. There are only so many hours in the day. So what are we going to do with them? Figure out how to inject mother-of-pearl into our eyeballs? In the end, it's a simple choice: we're either taking the world's beauty for ourselves, or giving our own beauty to the world. And I think it a truth universally acknowledged that giving is better than taking.

CHAPTER 3
BEAUTY: BUSINESS

If society decides there is a "look" more desirable than another, and if people are willing to go to lengths for tips, tricks, and products to get it, then an industry is born. Objectifying beauty is one of the first steps toward making it a business.

The ten-thousand-year-old industry that once was is still up and running today. Now we are the customers and cosmeticians. Now we are the salesmen and CEOs. Our beauty industry isn't actually ours. We inherited it. We knew what we inherited was valuable and lucrative, so we run it harder and faster than anyone has before.

Some ingredients and habits from history are similar to ours. However, the eating disorders, cosmetic surgery, tanning, advertising, and involvement of children in the industry now make our beauty business unique. Not only is our technology extremely advanced, but also the psychological landscape has darkened. Unhealthy and wrong practices in ancient times were also—at least, partly—done out of ignorance. We have developed these five new problems consciously, actively risking our health.

This chapter is not about the financial value proposition

underlying modern cosmetics. Rather, this is the story of the behavioral economics, the human choices, and the cultural value proposition behind our beauty industry. We know this "beauty" world is monetarily lucrative, but by examining the bigger picture we can ask: What are the complex incentives that support these five modern developments? How do consumer choices, large and small, enable this psychological environment? And finally, what ideologies laid the foundation for these issues?

Perhaps the first question that needs to be addressed: how is this relevant to Mag World? If women's and fashion magazines change, why does the beauty industry have to change as well? Aren't they in different offices, run by different bosses, and producing different products? True, but they also basically have the same schedule, attend the same meetings, work off the same budget and have offices on the same street—trading and hiring executives all the time.

Journalist and critic Walter Lippmann was familiar with such webs. In *Liberty and the News* (1920), he noted that newspapers did deals with everyone. He found crossovers where he didn't even know there were connections. Senators, doctors, even street laborers had a button to push in a paper's office—and he was frustrated by it. He didn't believe their interests should take priority over the integrity of journalism.

One could argue the "mistakes" editors and publishers

sometimes make are done with a forced hand. Can an editor really call up a beauty advertiser after seeing the first glimpse of an ad they're meant to run and say, "I don't know about this … Isn't your model a little bit underweight?"

In July 2013, Katy Perry was a guest on Jay Leno's *Tonight Show*. She sipped and swooned and talked about what she had been up to lately. "I went on a cleanse," she told Leno. She changed her routines and started taking vitamins and supplements. She switched from coffee to green tea. She stopped drinking alcohol. "I was, like, really in the zone."

Why was Perry (potentially) working with dietitians, cosmeticians, and personal trainers? It wasn't because she was going to be in a wedding, or because she was taking a trip to the beach, or because she was giving the commencement address at her alma mater. It wasn't even just because—just for herself, for the sake of a healthy future. Perry was going to appear on the cover of Vogue. And that simple invitation triggered a whole host of new beauty activity.

"I just wanted to be glowing for that cover," she said as she turned to appeal to the audience. Indeed, Perry was only another name on a long list—Oprah Winfrey, Elizabeth Hurley, even the seven-year-old Bea Weiss—of people who have dieted to appear in Vogue.

Perry's choices may seem obvious, common, and certainly

not new. However, they are an indication of the actions one person can take to show just how connected the beauty industry is to magazines and fashion. Perhaps Perry didn't technically diet or go hungry; she just made healthier choices. Even then, why is a magazine the reason to change at all? If she had been sitting down with a senior writer at the Wall Street Journal (who probably would have also taken her picture for a story), would she have changed from coffee to tea for the three months prior to that interview? The distinction may be slight, but it does matter.

Beyond the fashion, magazine, and entertainment industries, the beauty industry's impact also reaches fields more connected to the very young, particularly toys. In the summer of 2013, Mattel reported low earnings, falling short of projections by about $0.10 per share, but their iconic Barbie was sinking more severely than that. Her sales had fallen 12 percent that quarter, the fourth quarter down in a row.

In January 2014, Mattel continued to show sales falling: down 6.3 percent; the brand's revenue dropped $25 billion short of projected earnings. Global revenue from Barbie also fell 13 percent, during a time that included the busy holiday shopping season. In February 2014, Mattel stock continued to drop, declining to a fifty-two-week low at $36.50 per share. As 24/7 Wall St. put it, "for all intents and purposes, the huge toy company [was] stuck in neutral."

A previous story in the Globe and Mail from 2013 featured two young girls out shopping with their mother. The girls had been avid Barbie buyers, but now they chose American Girl. "Less hourglass, less makeup, the hair's more realistic, someone they can relate to more," the mother told the reporter. "Real girls!" one of her daughters chimed in. "Barbie dolls are nice," the mother answered back, "but they've become very repetitive." Not for nothing, American Girl doll sales surged a reported 14 percent in the fourth quarter of 2013.

Although classic Barbie had a lifespan of fifty-seven years, the last ten years also included valuable social studies—all of which furthered the argument that dolls representing an unhealthy body image for girls is also an unhealthy toy. Finally, in January 2016, Mattel announced that Barbie would only be available in three new body types and a variety of skin and hairstyles—a meaningful makeover, in more ways than one. One month later, Mattel stock rocketed back up 12 percent.

This theme of large industries redesigning something that is natural (like a human body) is a concern shared by many industrial designers—in particular, Dieter Rams, the former Design Director of Braun Kronberg, Germany. In the documentary Objectified, Rams explores the notion that it can be problematic when objects are designed in such an oversimplified way that they are not really designed but distorted. He thinks there is a carelessness behind anything that is so inorganically designed it results in a slanted or misleading product. He says:

> In my experience, users react very positively when things are clear and understandable … That's what particularly bothers me today, the arbitrariness and thoughtlessness with which many things are produced and brought to market. Not only in the sector of consumer goods, but also in advertising … We are doing a lot to design our world now. We even design the nature.

I can't help but wonder should Rams pick up a classic beauty magazine or stand in Times Square surrounded by banners or sit in a hair salon for an hour, whether he might also think: has the visual narrative in media become subject to the same pattern of over-design leaving nothing, not even nature, untouched? Should the beauty industry, either in product development or in advertising efforts, take on the task of "redesigning nature"? Or are there fundamentally healthier goals?

I think back on my middle school makeup drawer. Products and contraptions overflowed everywhere—most of which I barely used (not unlike my messy toy bin when I was little). "We have too many unnecessary things everywhere," Rams says in the documentary. How well were these things in my bathroom designed if I really didn't need them? "Good design should be innovative," he says, "good design should make a product useful." Was there one object that I could have used in middle school to make myself beautiful? My bathroom shelves were not the only ones fully stocked. Americans are offered billions of products every day.

* * *

What if personal beauty were not a goal? What if the same aesthetic standards couldn't be applied to everyone?

At the moment, a few private companies intend for the vast American public to buy products that remove socially defined flaws, iron out kinks, and correct mistakes. They "fix," they "mold," they want you to have the best head of hair, the best skin, the best nail beds money can buy. Still, their "best" is rarely the healthiest. They present a standard of their own and they sincerely want to help you reach it. However, this is not the first time a booming American industry made the severe mistake of assuming there was only one "best" or one "perfect" for everyone. Almost thirty years ago, another massive American industry believed this, and when they changed the results were sweet. Literally.

In 2004, Malcolm Gladwell gave a TED talk about one of his personal heroes: the scientist of great acclaim, the obsessive, the brilliant, the beloved Howard Moskowitz. He transformed the American food industry and, as Gladwell explained, "has done as much to make Americans happy as, perhaps, anyone over the last twenty years." He did this by reinventing spaghetti sauce.

Moskowitz was a psychophysicist. He supremely enjoyed measuring things. After getting his doctorate from Harvard, he set up a little consulting shop in White Plains, New York, and one day Pepsi knocked on his door. The artificial sweetener aspartame had just been introduced to the market, and they were aiming to make the first Diet Pepsi.

They wanted Moskowitz to test mixtures in a range between 8 and 12 percent in order to know the tastiest amount. He created experimental batches, each at different increments, and gave the samples to thousands of people. After plotting the points on a curve, he expected to take the most popular concentration as the answer, but it didn't work. When Moskowitz looked at the data, it was not a nice bell curve. "In fact, the data doesn't make any sense," said Gladwell, "it's a mess. It's all over the place."

The conundrum bothered Moskowitz for years until he found himself at a diner in White Plains with the answer. He realized that when they analyzed the Diet Pepsi data, they were asking the wrong question. They were looking for the one and only perfect Pepsi, and they should have been looking for any and all perfect Pepsis. "Trust me," Gladwell said, laughing, "this was an enormous revelation."

Moskowitz took his new discovery and went on the road. He visited conference after conference, lecture after lecture, but no one could quite understand him, until pickle company Vlasic came along. They asked him to design the perfect pickle, and he said, "There is no perfect pickle, there are only perfect pickles … you don't just need to improve your regular, you need to create Zesty."

Finally, Campbell approached with their Prego sauce, whose sales were trailing behind Ragu. Campbell asked Moskowitz what they could be doing better. To their surprise, Moskowitz did not suggest higher quality tomatoes, better packaging, or fresher basil. He made forty-five varieties of spaghetti sauce and varied them in every conceivable way.

"Then he took this whole raft of forty-five spaghetti sauces and he went on the road [again]," Gladwell continued. "He brought in people by the truckload, into big halls, and he sat them down for two hours and he gave them, over the course of that two hours, ten small bowls of pasta with a different spaghetti sauce on each one." This time, when Moskowitz analyzed the data, he didn't look for the most popular sauce. Rather, he tried to group all the different data points into clusters.

This time the data did show a natural pattern. Americans had three main tastes for tomato sauce: people who like their spaghetti sauce plain, extra spicy, or extra chunky. And of those three, the last was totally unheard of in the market. So when Moskowitz brought his findings back to Prego, they looked at the evidence and they reinvented their products. In those few years, during the early 1990s, Prego came out with a line of extra chunky that "immediately and completely took over the spaghetti sauce business," explained Gladwell. "Over the next ten years, they made $600 million off their line of extra chunky."

Gladwell claimed that Moskowitz was responsible for more than just bringing great tomato sauce to the table. "Howard [made us] realize the importance of what he likes to call horizontal segmentation."

Before Moskowitz, the food industry thought very differently. As Gladwell explained, they were convinced by the story of Grey Poupon. There used to be only yellow mustard in plastic bottles, but then Grey Poupon came out with Dijon. It had individual mustard seeds, a little white wine, and was packaged in a glass jar to make it look French. The commercial showed two millionaires eating Grey Poupon in their Rolls Royces. And, as Gladwell said, "everyone's take home lesson from that was the way to make people happy is to give them something that is more expensive, something to aspire to, to make them turn their back on what they think they like now and make them reach out for something higher up the mustard hierarchy … A better mustard. A more expensive mustard. A mustard of more sophistication, and culture and meaning."

This strategy was not only aspirational, it depended upon people being unhappy with what they had, wanting to change, wanting to transform, wanting to escape reality. Moskowitz's contribution proved that popular desire does not exist on a hierarchy. "There is no good mustard, or bad mustard, there is no perfect mustard, or imperfect mustard," summarized Gladwell. "There are only different kinds of mustards that suit different kinds of people." This revealed the natural importance of individuality of taste, and it fundamentally democratized the way we think about identity and aspiration.

Moskowitz confronted the notion of the platonic dish. "For the longest time in the food industry … there was a sense that there was one way, a perfect way, to make a dish," explained Gladwell, "and that same idea fueled the commercial food industry as well." They had a platonic notion of what tomato sauce was. "In other words, people in the cooking world were looking for cooking universals. They were looking for one way to treat all of us."

For the last two centuries, science was obsessed with universals. "Psychologists, medical scientists, economists were all interested in finding out the rules that govern the way all of us behave," Gladwell said. However, our generation is responsible for an accidental scientific revolution: understanding and embracing variability. "Now, in medical science," he said, "we don't just want to know how, necessarily, cancer works; we want to know how your cancer is different from my cancer. Genetics has opened the door to the study of human variability." The development of genetic science has not only helped us understand who we are and where we come from, but it has enhanced our cultural belief that our differences make us special.

Moskowitz looked at his clients and decided that same thing needed to happen in food. "When we pursue universal principals in food," reflected Gladwell, "we aren't just making an error, we are actually doing ourselves a massive disservice … In embracing the diversity of human beings, we will find a sure way to human happiness."

So how can a psychophysicist, a ten-year-old TED Talk, and a jar of tomato sauce make the beauty industry healthier?

* * *

I have not developed an extra-chunky tomato-sauce hair conditioner—at least, not yet. Rather, I seek a less direct connection to Moskowitz. I want to examine the platonic dish and horizontal segmentation a little more closely.

Moskowitz witnessed the initial notion that there was one great tomato sauce, one platonic dish, and one perfect Pepsi. In almost exactly the same way, we are now witnessing the same ideology, beliefs, and attitudes in the beauty industry: there is one great skin, one great hair, one great nose, etc. We have acknowledged, adopted, and supported the belief that there is "perfect" beauty—and if we use this product or that, we will get there. We are wrong.

Only when we fully appreciate the power of diversity will we be able to understand beauty. Only when our diversity is seen, present, paid for, and published, will we be supporting it, believing in it, and standing up for it. We have yet to recognize that we can either be some common version of "perfect," or we can be beautiful. They are not one and the same. The only thing better than beauty is many beauties.

This is the ideological mistake (and market research failure) that inhibits most companies. Anyone who seeks one socially defined "perfect" will not see it in this lifetime. It only seems to exist in Photoshop, oil paintings, and in highly crafted performances with a herd of people behind the curtain (such as the typical beauty magazine photo shoot, or beauty ad). Their "perfect" may seem like it exists through one lens, but it does not exist in real life. Indeed, it is healthier to find comfort in real life than in some artificial, contrived fantasy.

Using the concepts of horizontal segmentation, behavioral economics, and clustering in developing products, selling products, hiring models, and nearly every aspect of the beauty business is crucial for its economic and social survival. The introduction of horizontal segmentation also includes the negation of the quest for materialistic and superficial universals.

Gladwell said that "people in the cooking world were looking for cooking universals. They were looking for one way to treat all of us." Today, the largest beauty companies think monetary success comes by finding the one way to treat all of us. They want all of us to wish our freckles were gone. They want all of us to wish our curly hair was straight. They want all of us to wish. They depend on our desire to perform or transform because, again, their hierarchy is vertical.

Moskowitz may have thought the mustard world was aspirational, but clearly he never spent a Friday night in a crowded bathroom with a bunch of girls getting ready to go out. The beauty industry bases its economics and its future on exactly the same principles. They bet that they will be around tomorrow because they bet that you won't want to be the same person tomorrow as you are today. They have decided, and they promote with billions of dollars, the idea that the Dijon version of you is better, that the more expensive version of you is better, that you will "turn [your] back on what [you] think [you] like now" and they will "make [you] reach out for something higher up the hierarchy. A better [you]. A more expensive [you]. A [you] of more sophistication." The number one product the beauty industry sells is an appetite for upgrade, escape, and the deeply emotional conviction that you are never enough.

Lippmann found many untruths in the standards and universals of his day. In Liberty and The News, he wrote:

> The battle [for social popularity, cultural dominance, and public opinion] is fought with banners on which are inscribed absolute and universal ideals. They are not absolute and universal, in fact. No man has ever thought out an absolute or a universal ideal in politics, for the simple reason that nobody knows enough, or can know enough, to do it. But we all use absolutes, because an ideal which seems to exist apart from time, space, and circumstance has a prestige that no candid avowal of special purpose ever had. Looked at from one point of view, universals are part of the fighting apparatus in men.

I agree: finding universals has been a constant challenge for mankind. Today, in the beauty industry, there are "banners on which are inscribed"—both with images and with words—"absolute" but not necessarily "universal" ideals. These standards from the beauty industry are circulated and promoted by women's magazines, fashion ads, and the internet. They are recirculated down catwalks and in catalogues.

Lippmann openly acknowledged that, in the news business and in politics, there can be no absolute ideal that isn't universal. In our beauty industry, there cannot be one socially defined "perfect" expected of women.

In regards to weight, skinny is not perfect. In regards to hair, straight is not perfect. In regards to skin, clear is not perfect—and so on.

When I am looking at a Photoshopped woman, a picture distorted either greatly or with subtlety, I feel I am looking at "an ideal which seems to exist apart from time, space, and circumstance," not real life. I would prefer "a candid avowal of special purpose," because all I ever see when I look at these images are the opinions of a few people.

For Lippmann's generation, standards bled into their news and politics and played an intimate role in their lives. For women of this generation, "perfect" is also part of a daily inner choice: who am I going to believe (and invest) in? Them or me?

"Looked at genetically, these idealizations are probably born in that spiritual reverie where all men live most of the time," said Lippmann. "In reverie, there is neither time, space, nor particular reference, and hope is omnipotent." Lippmann thought idealizations come out of daydreams, reverie, and omnipotent hopefulness—a mental state suspended in fantasy and disconnected from any realistic reference point. This is, indeed, the exact point of view required to enter and exist in Mag World.

I understand those who, as Lippmann put it, "live most of the time there." I am a writer, and I have lived my entire life with an overactive imagination. I am so captivated by the past and its mysteries or the future and its possibilities that I am hardly able to keep my eye on the present. I learned, both as an artist and as a student, how familiar dreams are to the American story. So if I'm asking to negate standards in the beauty industry involved with dreaming, idealizations, and aspirations, am I not also asking us to let go and to forget one of the most classic cornerstones of American identity: dreams?

Not necessarily. It depends on the dream. We get most of our ideas about beauty from beauty industry "make believe." As Lippmann said, "a world of reverie." And after living in this Mag World, we have come to confuse wanting "to improve" with wanting "to perfect." So, if your dream is to become stronger, more educated, more kind, a better community server, a hula dancer, a lawyer, an astronaut, or simply healthier, then yes—your aspirational life is like the American dream. However, if you're waking up in the morning swearing to yourself that your day would be just a little bit better if you were just five pounds skinnier, your nose straighter, your breasts bigger, or your hair lighter, then I would say you are not living a dream but a nightmare.

In considering the difference between a standard, an ideal, and a universal, I may be in contrast with both Lippmann and Moskowitz. A standard is like a rule in a sorority—an understanding between a small group of people usually upheld by social pressure. An idealization is a disconnected fantasy facing east toward the sunniest possibility (but not the most probable). However, a universal is like gravity; it is a constant in nature beyond ourselves and out of our control.

Do I believe our beauty industry now operates with social pressure and standards? Absolutely. Do I believe the business harbors idealizations? Sometimes. As a sweet drink can give us a quick and enjoyable high, certain beauty fads can lift or spark the industry now and again, but they are nothing on which to sustain a multibillion-dollar business. Do I think we conduct business with a reverence toward universals? No—or perhaps not enough; we are just beginning to. To survive, the beauty industry must unite and collectively store faith in at least one universal: women are human, humans are natural creatures, and natural creatures require health—both physical and mental.

A successful beauty product only preserves or restores the natural, unique features that define our own individual, personal, and human identity. Perhaps our first step is to untangle our misconstrued understanding of the word "perfect." It has only meant "exactly one" in recent centuries. The word is derived from the original Latin "per" (completely) and "facere" (to make or do). For thousands of years, it meant to do wholeheartedly, to make complete, or to bring to full development. Embracing who we are and striving to be as true to ourselves as we can be is the only "universal" or "perfect" beauty.

* * *

How has the beauty industry tried to treat us all the same? What examples can we learn from? In February 2013, Sally Holmes wrote a five-part series for The Cut on her efforts to get ready for the Oscars. I would have titled it: "How A Twenty-Something Takes the Long, Long Journey From Our World to Mag World." In each installment (exercise, liposuction, skin care, gown fitting, and makeup) she gives a glimpse into the collision of girl-next-door with this hyper corner of the industry.

"With so many awards shows clumped together … stars spend most of January and February having to look really freaking good," Holmes writes. Her first step is a juice cleanse. Holmes is neither over- nor underweight, but she says, "doing something really drastic, really fast, seemed like the way to kick start a new routine." Her reactions to the vile concoctions she forces down are both charming and startling: "Apparently, I don't like the taste of earth." She had to sip "almond milk, dates, [and] vanilla bean" while watching her boyfriend inhale ravioli. Her reflections are open and honest. "Many people raved about the 'glow' juicing gives you, and the renewed energy. In reality, you're out of it and tired," she says. "I could barely concentrate long enough to sit in front of my computer to work."

Next, she seeks out a fitness regime that mimics what stars go through. As she describes, there are only coy advisers in the beauty industry. "I talked to Hollywood PR people and workout gurus who were hesitant about the language of the whole thing. No one says this is what you have to do to lose weight, because no one wants to [openly] promote the idea that being skinny is the goal."

She signs up for workout classes with intimidating names. "Even the older women in the class looked like Lululemon mannequins." She is unapologetically frank on how much red-carpet preparation is work. After endless ab crunches, she writes, "there's always a moment halfway through the class where I think I can't believe humans pay money to have this done to them."

She gains some new opinions of Hollywood. "For most celebrities who work out regularly—many twice a day—exercising isn't just a priority, it's part of their job, but it's hard to imagine being able to maintain that on a weekly basis for, uh, forever? Even thinking about that has me wondering how these women have the energy to be a celebrity in the first place."

Holmes's diary, her journey through the extremes of the beauty industry, is powerful. Guru trainers, dietitians, dermatologists, liposuction artists, and of course stylists, all blow the whistle from dawn until dusk. The five-part series is funny, staggering, and worth reading thrice.

I can only imagine how many hours she must have spent playing games on her phone out of sheer boredom, and how grateful she must have been when it was all over. And yet, I don't have to imagine because this has become the norm for so many women and girls, especially wannabe "celebrities," who go through routines. There are varying degrees between a night at the Oscars and dinner at the newest restaurant in town, but most women and girls go through some ritual preparation before "going out." How many teenagers on their way to prom would kill for Holmes's Oscar treatment?

How many of us can say that the time we spend in preparation to simply greet the world is full of nourishing, healthy activities? We use products, contraptions, machines, and more stuff generated by this industry. And when we bought them, we also guaranteed we would be at least twenty or thirty minutes late because it is impossible to use them and still take the same amount of time as a guy who is, comparatively, doing nothing. Given the thoughtlessness, low quality, unhealthy ingredients, and unreliability of the majority of beauty products out there, buying into this industry means signing away real time and hard-earned money in return for the belief that the way we actually look just isn't good enough.

Who deserves to live like this?

Like the food industry's relationship with the "platonic dish," this is an example of the beauty industry wanting to treat us all the same. We have accepted it, and we have made it a part of our lives. This is a reflection of who we think is looking at us. What is the character of our "audience" if we can't leave the house without thirty minutes of alterations?

Author and New York Times Magazine columnist Rob Walker reflected in the documentary Objectified on our mental relationship with "audience" when we're on the road.

> [When] you're making decisions about [what car you're going to buy], 'are you going to put a bumper sticker on it?' there's an idea of an audience. I feel pretty strongly that this isn't just true for cars but for almost everything we buy. The real audience is really ourselves and the person that you're really speaking to when you're speaking about, 'why me?' and, 'is this the right car for me?'—you're making a statement to yourself about yourself … The hurricane is coming. You have 20 minutes. Get your stuff and go … You're going to pick the most meaningful objects to you because those are the true objects that truly reflect the true story of who you are and what your personal narrative is. A story that you're telling to yourself and no one else because you're the only audience that matters.

Is it perhaps true, as Walker describes, that the audience you imagine waiting outside before you walk out the door really doesn't care whether a wisp of your hair is frizzy or if a zit on your chin is red? Are all the other people just going about their daily business really an audience? And if everyone is constantly the audience, are we constantly on stage?

Perhaps this stress relates to how poor our language is when we discuss these issues. In December 2012, Lauren Bans reported for The Cut on the use of the word curvy. "All a woman has to do to be called 'curvy' these days is possess a human body," she writes. Over a period of six months, Bans counts eleven actresses who were either called curvy or called themselves curvy. These eleven women, however, looked drastically different and varied in dress size, ranging from size 2 (Lindsay Lohan) to size 18+ (Gabourey Sidibe).

Bans was perplexed by the use of the word even outside Hollywood. New York magazine photographed an executive assistant in New York City for her street style, citing her "just-rolled-out-of-bed look." The lean and athletic-framed girl commented on her style choices to the photographer, saying that she rarely showed much skin because she was too "curvy." Bans also found a Marie Claire columnist who "treats curvy and plus-size as interchangeable terms." In her own profile on the dating app OKCupid, Bans herself was knocked for using the word to describe her body type. Someone named "Anonymous" wrote, "P.S. Don't say ur 'curvy' cuz guys will think ur fat ;)".

Bans's criticism has less to do with the inconsistency when the term is used, and more on the attitude that goes along with it. "Whenever magazines do feature more regular-size models and actresses, it always comes with a note of self-congratulation," she writes, as if curvy is a kind of cultural accolade. She cites a Health magazine article featuring Christina Hendricks, which was "obsessively preoccupied with her 'shattering expectations' body and taking notes of her 'health regrets' and 'health rule-breaking.' (She's so naughty, that curvy one!)"

Bans also looks at Glamour magazine's June 2010 Crystal Renn cover, which was quickly run over by consecutive months of non-average-weight cover girls. The magazine rooted for her and then quickly went back to "using traditionally straight-bodied size 2 models." In September 2010, Michael Kors was quoted in Teen Vogue praising actress Nikki Reed because he loved dressing a woman with a full figure. "I'm so excited to be dressing you," he said, "because if there's one thing I love, it's a girl who has a real body—I love curves." However, three months later, Bans points out, he insisted on his use of stick-thin runway girls to the Montreal Gazette saying, "Models, by nature, are not supposed to look like you and me. They are exemplary."

Using the word curvy, Bans concludes, is "unwarranted self-congratulation. If curvy can mean anything we want it to—on a scale of size 2 to size 22—then our reductive thinking on the subject of bodies and beauty standards hasn't actually changed. The ubiquity of 'curvy' is just a gloss of body acceptance, not actual body acceptance."

A "curvy" label also represents our hesitation to test discomfort with things outside the norm. In 2013, an organization called Pro Infirmis created new mannequins for a store window. Instead of tall, slender men and women, these models had totally different dimensions. Not only did the mannequins represent people outside the height and weight ranges of typical models, the mannequins represented figures outside the ranges of average people: disabled people.

"Behind you is a male mannequin just as it is actually used," explains the sculptor involved in the project. "We will now take all the measurements [of the disabled person] that are different," he said, gesturing to his body, so that they could create a mannequin just like him. The mannequins built and molded after disabled men and women would be displayed in shop windows in downtown Zurich in honor of International Day of Persons with Disabilities.

"The people passing by will be irritated," suspects one disabled person about to have their measurements taken for a mannequin.

"Seeing it there for real is quite a shock," says another, after she looks at the finished sculpture of her body.

Nevertheless, the individuals were left with pride and

smiles after the mannequins were finally displayed in the shop window. “It’s special to see yourself like this, when you usually can’t look at yourself in the mirror,” added another.

Perhaps some would argue that mannequins in windows are the territory of the fashion industry. And yet, fashion is an expression of change. It is not innate in fashion to work in a mindset of standardization. This is an example of the beauty industry twisting the arm of another industry into believing in “one perfect” or the “platonic dish.”

Maybe a shop window is a quintessential location to look for clues about our pervasive dependence on standardizing our looks. The US Army, however, is a more unusual place to look.

In 2013, the Christian Science Monitor published a story by Julie Watson about the little known use of liposuction in the military. The news was also covered by Kathleen Hou for The Cut. Both stories reported on the fitness test the military regularly uses, which measures body fat with a neck-to-waist ratio instead of the more popular body mass index measurement.

“The archaic sounding ‘tape test,’” writes Hou, “takes neck-to-waist ratio measurements that are used to pass or flunk soldiers. Men who fail are required to join the, ‘pork chop platoon’ or ‘doughnut brigade,’ which, contrary to those delicious-sounding names, is actually an intense exercise and nutrition program." Julie Watson noted the unspoken tolerance throughout the military. "[One plastic surgeon] said liposuction works for those with the wrong genetics. 'I've actually had commanders recommend it to their troops,' [the surgeon] said. 'They'll deny that if you ask them. But they know some people are in really good shape and unfortunately are just built wrong.'"

It seems incongruous to honor and salute brave men and women serving our country, while allowing them to degrade themselves by asking them to join something called "the doughnut brigade." What is wrong with their measurements not meeting a visually and aesthetically pleasing standard—which, by the way, has absolutely nothing to do with their capabilities and talents for fighting?

Do the high-ranking military leaders, who directly or indirectly support the use of liposuction and the controversial test itself, aim to make American soldiers with a highly pleasing neck-to-waist ratio so attractive that they will shock a dust-covered cave-dwelling member of the Taliban and stun him to death merely at the sight of GI Ken? Do they expect our enemies will falter in intimidation at their first glance of our perfectly measured good looks?

One successful advertiser argues that standardization and believing in "perfect" can really only go so far. In

2014, Donny Deutsch joined Mika Brzezinski and Joe Scarborough on MSNBC's Morning Joe to discuss Super Bowl commercials. The advertising executive (who is also a father and author) discussed the direction of ads in America by identifying successful and unsuccessful strategies.

They rolled clips of old Super Bowl favorites, classic commercials, and the spots which generated the most buzz from the previous year. Finally, Deutsch was asked: what is it about a Super Bowl ad that makes it so successful? He began his answer by pointing to the 2014 Darth Vader Volkswagen commercial, with the father and son story line. Deutsch explained that even after all the technological advancements in the industry, the best advertisements portray an encapsulated human story. He said that when a human story is crisp and clear, and also relevant to the brand, it makes a lasting connection.

Deutsch's assessment of Super Bowl commercials not only makes sense, it is a modern-day analysis that applies beyond TV. Beauty advertisements with a phony airbrushed model, or a woman inflated with plastic surgery, will not establish a lasting connection. When looking at beauty ads in magazines, billboards, online and beyond, we should be looking at images of women who are human, relatable, and honestly photographed.

Why is an honest photograph such a big deal? Why are the majority of current marketing strategies in the beauty industry not sustainable? Why must our beauty not be standardized? Why must the industry's attitudes and practices turn a new page? Why is an under-eye bag, armpit fat, or wisp of frizzy hair so important to keep in a picture? Aren't there more visible physical features that define us, such as our eye color, our hair color, or our smile? And for that matter, aren't those the more recognizable, larger, more often noticed features that people like about us? Aren't they the things we should be protecting (if not enhancing)? What's the big deal with changing hair color anyway? If someone wants to go and change their hair color for any reason whatsoever, shouldn't that be okay? Why is wanting to change your own beauty such a big deal—even if behind your choice was a billion dollars' worth of marketing?

Because you're too worth it. You are too valuable to throw away even an inch of you. You are too valuable to cover up even an inch of you. You are too valuable to starve, or deprive, or deny for one second. You are too important. You are too worth it. You are too beautiful to be veiled. And those eye bags? They're not just eye bags. They're the hours you spent up late last night with your kid as he did his homework. And that frizzy hair? It got wet with the sweat you burned in the gym. And those dark spots? Those are the sunspots you earned while on the beach with your partner, falling in love. Those lines are the years you have lived. That hair is from your grandmother who, like you, also loved to play piano. Those hips, like Sophia Loren, are bowls of pasta you can't help but enjoy. Every inch of you is yours. Whether you believe it was given to you by God, your parents, yourself, or whoever, your body matters because it was the first and it will be the last thing that belongs to you … and to no one else. Chip away one detail and, no, you're not going to stop being who you are; but at the end of the day, you're the only one who can decide or control how much chipping away results in losing yourself. Be careful, be accountable, but most importantly: be deeply grateful.

"Suppression is felt," wrote Lippmann, "not simply by the scattered individuals who are actually suppressed. It reaches back into the steadiest minds, creating tension everywhere; and the tension of fear produces sterility. Men cease to say what they think; and when they cease to say it, they soon cease to think it."

We will not cease to say, we will not cease to think, because we cannot cease to be ourselves.

* * *

Shailene Woodley is perhaps best known for her performance with George Clooney in *The Descendants* or for her dazzling strength in *Divergent*. Woodley is from Simi Valley, California, and was born in 1991, so she is part of the generation that grew up with Mag World. However, unlike a hundred girls her age in Hollywood, Woodley finds that the most important thing she can be is herself.

"I saw somebody—what I thought was me—in a magazine once," Woodley told Emma Stone in Interview, "and I had big red lips that definitely did not belong on my face. I had boobs about three times the size they are in real life. My stomach was completely flat. My skin was also flawless. But the reality is that I do not have those lips and my skin is not flawless and I do have a little bit of a stomach. It was not a proper representation of who I am."

"I realized," Woodley continues, "that, [while] growing up and looking at magazines, I was comparing myself to images like that—and most of it isn't real. So (a) I don't really wear makeup that much anyway, so part of it is just a selfish, lazy thing, and (b) I want to be me. I do think it's fun sometimes to dress up for the Oscars or for certain events—I get to be like a five-year-old again, wearing my Cinderella dress. But for some events where it's a more casual vibe, I just want to be me."

When Woodley identifies the origins of Mag World as being the stuff of fairy tales, like Cinderella, she connects with Lippmann's description of "a world of reverie." She appreciates the difference between a more made up face and a more natural one. Her choices aren't on either extreme, but she recognizes the variance between identity and anonymity.

In speaking about her recent film The Spectacular Now, Woodley told Interview magazine that one reason she identified with her character was because she didn't wear any makeup. She looked at the scenes later on and, for a moment, she wished she had not been so barefaced. "But once I let go of my insecurities, I could see how it added a lot to the film. The fact that we weren't wearing makeup made it seem much more real and relatable because we're playing awkward high school students, not beauty queens."

Woodley takes an unusual approach to personalizing makeup. Instead of just finding the hues that work for her, which most women might try to leave as natural-looking as possible, Woodley went back to basics. For an interview with The Hollywood Reporter, Woodley introduced her makeup artist, Gloria Noto. Noto is an artist with Jed Root, edits The WORK Magazine, and spent much of her time growing up with extended family in Sicily, Italy. Woodley was drawn to her because "she uses very light makeup." So light, in fact, she barely has to leave the kitchen for supplies.

"It's a perfect lip stain," Noto told Pret-a-Reporter, as she started slicing up a juicy magenta beet. "It's got, like, the right amount of red and the right amount of purple in it. And it stays on for a long time. And there's no chemicals in it," she added with a smile.

It may seem like child's play, slicing up vegetables and imagining how they might look on your face, until Woodley tells the story of her frantic preparation for the

Golden Globes. "We were trying to figure out what color lipstick to use," interrupts Noto, "and she was like, 'We're going to use this beet!' And [she] put it on."

Indeed, Woodley did attend the Golden Globes in 2013, with her hair swept up neatly behind her neck, in a glittering Marchesa gown, and fresh-from-the-chopping-board beet juice on her lips. "We don't ever do anything too crazy … because it's about her, it's about her face, it's about what's there. So it's all about bringing her natural beauty into play."

Shailene Woodley is not alone in urging a return to basics. Lady Gaga has formed her career on empowerment and individuality, so it's no surprise that the beauty industry could learn from her stubborn positivity.

In the fall of 2012, the entertainment media began noticing Gaga's fluctuating weight. She told a radio show that she had been enjoying visiting her father's Italian restaurant in Manhattan. "I love eating pizza and pasta, I'm a New York Italian girl," she told the radio hosts. "I gain five pounds every time I go in there."

However, the story took a turn when Gaga herself took to social media that September. In a yellow bra and underwear, with little makeup, not posing for the camera, Gaga posted a vulnerable picture of herself captioned, "Bulimia and anorexia since I was 15." According to Melanie Haiken of *Forbes*, the choice was "more cultural-challenging than sashaying around town in wigs, costumes and towering platforms."

Gaga then organized a new section of her website, turning a typical fan page into a "dramatic public forum" on her struggles, the fears of eating disorders, as well as cutting and other body-hating behavior. "The photos popping up are startling in their honesty. Reed-thin anorexics, those who are overweight, kids with dwarfism, disfiguring scars and artificial limbs. All baring their souls along with their bodies," wrote Haiken.

Although many stars have "come out," as Jezebel put it, about their self-image and health issues, Gaga's efforts reflect a strong use of platform, a refreshing sensitivity, and a true connection with her fans—for which even the greatest artists of all time would give an arm and a leg.

By starting her message on social media and then creating a forum on her website, "these discussions aren't just transpiring in the ephemeral world of Twitter and Facebook," writes Haiken, "but in a site where they will continue and be preserved into the future for those who want to come back again and again." Indeed, within a beauty industry like ours, the naked body online and the naked face in public (whether you're Lady Gaga or Stefani Germanotta) seem to be more uncomfortable than anything else.

The comparison may not seem obvious at first, but perhaps

Lady Gaga's use of makeup and her interaction with the beauty industry are not unlike Woodley's. They are both very aware of being "on" and "off" in performances. They both regard makeup as a tool, a separate entity from themselves. And, although not explicitly stated on either part, both seem to have arrived at a place of social understanding and inner self-acceptance: they both agree the non-made-up face is truly as acceptable as the painted one.

While Gaga's private pain, public choices, and the release of her single "Born This Way" have revealed her efforts to rise above and live outside beauty industry standards, another celebrity has managed a leadership style all her own.

Jennifer Lawrence may have never made private pain public the way that Lady Gaga has, but her straightforward, no-nonsense ease in talking about the difficulties of her environment make her one of the few admirable celebrities who does not desire Mag World.

Gaga's genius paired with her bravery has inspired many others. And yet, it is Lawrence's girl-next-door public persona that makes her choices and her messages truly compelling. With her down-to-earth, funny, and seemingly well-adjusted outlook on life, she makes healthy choices and healthy thinking seem obtainable by anyone. Indeed, she makes leaving Mag World seem as easy as tripping on your dress at the Oscars.

Lawrence has had tough expectations laid on her by the industry. First, critics doubted whether she would be a successful Katniss (a lead character in The Hunger Games). While her acting capabilities and professionalism were not called into question, rather, it was her weight. "A few years ago Ms. Lawrence might have looked hungry enough to play Katniss, but now, at 21, her seductive, womanly figure makes a bad fit for a dystopian fantasy about a people starved into submission," wrote Manohla Dargis for the New York Times.

In this instance, accuracy seems less important than audience. The Hunger Games trilogy was so popular with young adults that the person filling Katniss's cinematic shoes needed to be as a healthy as possible—not as starving as possible. Otherwise the film industry would be indirectly endorsing unhealthy images and unhealthy dieting of a girl who was healthy and well fed in the first place. (Talk about dystopian fantasies and unnecessary hunger.)

Lawrence describes seeing distortion on top of distortion in her environment. "In Hollywood, I'm obese. I'm considered a fat actress. I'm Val Kilmer in that one picture on the beach. . . I'm never going to starve myself for a part," she continues. "I don't want little girls to be like, 'Oh, I want to look like Katniss, so I'm going to skip dinner,'" she explains to Elle magazine. "That's something I was really conscious of during training, when you're trying to get your body to look exactly right. I was trying to get my body to look fit and strong, not thin and underfed."

Indeed, true to her character, Katniss really isn't as starving as other girls her age because she's strong enough and smart enough to hunt fairly well. Lawrence, in congruence, isn't starving like some other girls her age because she is strong enough and smart enough not to enter Mag World.

"The world has a certain idea. We see this airbrushed, perfect model, and then if you don't look like that … You have to look past it. You look how you look," she said in conversation with Yahoo! CEO Marissa Mayer. "Be comfortable. What are you going to do? Be hungry every single day just to make other people happy? That's just dumb."

"[Certain shows] are just showing these generations of young people to judge people … they put values in all the things that are wrong," she said. "And it's ok to just point at people and call them ugly or call them fat. They call it fun. And 'welcome to the real world'… that shouldn't be the real world. It's going to keep being the real world if we keep it that way. It's not until we stop treating each other like that … with these unrealistic expectations for women. It's disappointing that the media keeps it alive."

"Why is humiliating people funny?" she asked Barbara Walters in an ABC Special. "I get it, I do it too. We all do it … But I think when it comes to the media, the media needs to take responsibility for the effect that it has on our younger generation, on these girls that are watching these television shows and picking up how to talk and how to be cool … So then all of a sudden being funny is making fun of the girl that's wearing an ugly dress."

"And the word fat!" she continued. "I just think it should be illegal to call somebody fat on TV. I mean, if we're regulating cigarettes and sex and cuss words because of the effect it has on our younger generation, why aren't we regulating things like calling people fat?"

"We have the ability to control this image that young girls are going to be seeing," she said to BBC Newsnight. "Girls see enough of this body that we can't imitate, they will never be able to obtain … it's kind of an amazing opportunity to rid ourselves of that in this industry. It's better to look strong and healthy. Kate Moss running at you with a bow and arrow wouldn't really be scary."

The multibillion-dollar beauty industry today could gain so much more by placing the real prize on these well-spoken women. These companies should show their admiration for voices like Jennifer Aniston, Adele, Serena Williams, Mindy Kaling, Amy Schumer, Lena Dunham, Kate Winslet, America Ferrera, Alicia Keys, Emma Watson, Meryl Streep—and the list goes on. So how could a capitalistic for-profit industry start over with the example of these women in mind?

First, forget the muse. Let her fade into the mist of the Aegean Sea. Splash your face with some saltwater and bring back the woman. She is more important. Indeed, Woodley's connection to nature and the earth, Gaga's mastery of performance, and Lawrence's candidness all have at least one thing in common: they help us understand a term coined by Stella Bugbee—"the undone woman."

Bugbee says Woody Allen has managed to create female characters and to cast actresses in ways that have broken the mold for Hollywood—and, I would say, which have broken the mold for Mag World. "The Woody Allen women are memorable for their quirks of dialogue, but also for their fashion sense," writes Bugbee for The Cut:

> If I had a dollar for every time I've heard someone who works in fashion cite Annie Hall as a "style icon," I could fund Woody Allen's next production. But an under-appreciated joy of many female leads in Allen's (non-period) films is their "'real woman" beauty. By Hollywood standards, his characters are delightfully un-dolled-up, with easy hair that doesn't point to hours under a dryer and is sexier for lack of trying. You never have those irritating moments in one of his movies when you are watching, thinking, They are post-coital, why is she wearing a full face of makeup? There are very few fake lashes, hair extensions, or gratuitous hints of artifice. And

> even though that seems sort of "duh" for an indie filmmaker who's trying to capture "real" life, it's a welcome relief.

Bugbee continues:

> The unstyled, snapshot haircuts on the poster for Hannah and Her Sisters hint at the mess that will ensue as the movie's love triangle unfolds, but it also looks like the hair that busy modern women have. The halo of Léa Seydoux's Botticelli-blonde locks in the last scene of Midnight in Paris is all you need to signify her free spirit and willingness to just let life unfold.

Bugbee uses hair as a small example of a larger choice to be holistically "undone." Allen's female leads may not be all crunchy granola, but they're not stuck in Mag World either.

This director has actually cleared the path for other industries, like the beauty industry, placing women before the public in a healthy, successful, and attractive way. I agree with Bugbee: "Credit should be given to the director and his team for leaving them looking like they might actually look on a Saturday in the park: gorgeous in a real way; gorgeous when they cry; gorgeous when they hate you; gorgeous when they are cheating, moving on, or making you laugh. Just gorgeous because they look like themselves."

This wise editor's observations and the work from Allen together are more than enough to set the tone for new goals for companies in considering representatives, models, and slogans, etc. The real question is, How "undone" are they willing to go?

* * *

Bugbee and Allen are not the only individuals whose observations and choices are setting a positive example. Some recent changes, in the industry as a whole as well as amongst particular companies, represent the percolations of this new philosophy.

In 2012, the Food and Drug Administration created a new set of guidelines for sunscreen. Research found that UVA rays and UVB rays were equally damaging, and yet products all over the market were poorly labeled, not clearly distinguishing which type they covered, if any at all. "A product's SPF indicates only its ability to defend against sunburn-causing ultraviolet-B rays—and not against ultraviolet-A, which penetrate deeper into the skin and cause premature aging. (Both types contribute to skin cancer)," reports Emily Holmes for the Wall Street Journal.

Now, packaging includes a "broad spectrum" phrase to confirm that it is as protective as possible. Conversely, a warning label also appears on any product with an SPF lower than 14: it will not protect against skin cancer. No company can use the term "waterproof," only "water-resistant." And packaging must also indicate when products need to be reapplied, for example after forty or eighty minutes. In addition to the new terms allowed, companies must also print a "Drug Facts" section listing active ingredients, uses, and warnings.

The FDA hopes that more testing and better labeling will protect consumers from skin cancer, which has become an increasing threat. According to the Mayo Clinic, cases of melanoma multiplied eight times from 1970 to 2009 among women between the ages of 18 and 39. Tanning, and especially tanning beds, have been to blame. Now they are considering a proposal to ban any products labeled with an SPF higher than 50, as research has found anything above that is only slightly better, and yet people tend to reapply it less often.

This is terrific leadership on the part of the FDA. They are really participating in steering the industry toward a healthier future. It is important to see companies turning toward these regulations and making positive change, not only in abiding by new rules but also in raising their priorities on health and safety.

Another milestone has less to do with regulation than deregulation—or the regrowth of freedom. In January 2014, American Apparel opened their Lower East Side storefront window with a new look for a new year. The mannequins were different from every other mannequin in Manhattan, as well as every mannequin to ever appear in that window. They were furrier. Three mannequins sported full-length unsculpted pubic hair. The dolls were dressed with sheer undies and a sheer bra, so that the bush and the painted-on nipples were in clear view.

"People clogged the sidewalk on Lower Manhattan's East Houston Street to get a glimpse at a surprising sight from an unsurprising source," wrote Laura Stampler for Time magazine. "The mood [was] light," and "people [were] laughing," reported Jen Chung for Gothamist. "American Apparel is a company that celebrates natural beauty," American Apparel's Ryan Holiday told Gothamist, "and the Lower East Side Valentine's Day window continues that celebration. We created it to invite passerby to explore the idea of what is 'sexy' and consider their comfort with the natural female form. This is the same idea behind our advertisements which avoid many of the Photoshopped and airbrushed standards of the fashion industry. So far we have received positive feedback from those that have commented and we're looking forward to hearing more points of view."

American Apparel has made some questionable modeling choices (namely, in their provocative displays of girls who look inappropriately young), but they demonstrate leadership in simply allowing their mannequins to be different. They are revoking the need for standardization.

It was, as Holiday expressed, an opportunity for people to rethink what is sexy. Indeed, the entire effort to prompt people to explore what is sexy means that they will arrive at a true answer for what is sexy for them. These mannequins actually encourage the viewer to be more concerned with their own individuality than with the task to conform. Industry leaders should never decide for a consumer what beauty is; rather, they should be given the opportunity to contemplate their own health and decide on their own terms.

At the end of the day, pubes are messy. That's why they were rarely painted in murals or chiseled into marble. These mannequins are more about diversity than about conformity; they encourage you to imagine how you could look, as opposed to how you are supposed to look; and, given that the function and form of every mannequin ever in the last century has been the opposite, it is quite a mini revolution. Should every mannequin have pubes? Not necessarily, but every company should decide how their marketing displays an appreciation for individuality.

A mini revolution began stirring in the European modeling industry too. First, an ad was banned in the UK in 2011 in which a seventeen-year-old Dakota Fanning posed for Marc Jacobs holding a perfume bottle suggestively. The government stepped in immediately, and the British Advertising Standards Authority (ASA) pulled all the ads for Jacobs's new perfume.

Following that, another ad was banned for being overly Photoshopped. An image of Rachel Weisz for L'Oréal Paris was removed because it had been so manipulated that it was misleading. According to Women's Wear Daily, "The ASA said that the ad was misleading in relation to the claims that the [skin care] product made skin look smoother and the complexion look more even, as the committee believed Weisz's image had 'been altered in a way that substantially changed her complexion to make it appear smoother and more even.'" Also, the ASA told L'Oréal "not to continue to use postproduction techniques that could misrepresent a product's claims."

Unhealthy and misleading images are currently being regulated in Israel; legislation passed in 2012 banning the use of underweight models in local ads and publications and in fashion shows.

"Models must prove that their Body Mass Index (BMI) is higher than the World Health Organization's indication of malnourishment (a BMI of 18.5) by producing an up-to-date medical report—no older than three months—at all shoots to be used in the Israeli market," Charlotte Cowles reported for The Cut. "Meanwhile, all Israeli publications and advertisements must have a clearly written notice when they alter images to make women and men appear thinner," she said. Although the US has relied on the industry to regulate itself (mainly through the CFDA), this was the first instance of a country passing a law to regulate these issues.

The first economic study of anorexia, done by the London School of Economics in 2012, shows that cultural environment plays a huge role in the decision of a woman or girl to starve herself. "SHOCKER," wrote Cowles for The Cut. "Government intervention to adjust individual biases in self-image would be justified to curb the spread of a potential epidemic of food disorders," concluded Dr. Joan Costa-i-Font, an economist at LSE.

"The distorted self-perception of women with food disorders and the importance of the peer effects may prompt governments to take action to influence role models and compensate for social pressure on women driving the trade-off between ideal weight and health," the authors observe. It is exciting to finally receive such helpful research, and the beauty industry can only thrive from learning from these leaders how to be healthier.

* * *

These stories speak of recent changes throughout the industry, but there are specific companies already making waves; particularly, The Honest Company, Miyu, MAKE, and Dove have all set different and positive examples. Although their goals, products, origins, and centers of market differ, each is a leader with something specific to teach.

The Honest Company was founded by someone who had

to juggle life in and out of Mag World. Someone who called Hollywood home and to whom performing the muse was not unfamiliar: Jessica Alba. Alba may be the only actress who has founded a company in this industry, and one of the few from Hollywood who is involved in one.

"Once upon a time … a dad named Christopher and a mom named Jessica found themselves utterly frustrated trying to find the perfect products for their babies and homes," says their website. "We both wanted an ideal: not only effective, but unquestionably safe, eco-friendly, beautiful, convenient, and affordable—everyone should have it. We believed every baby deserved the best we can create for them. We are dreamers," they say. "But, more importantly, we are doers."

The Honest Company originally focused on infants and toddlers, with face and body lotion, shampoo and conditioner, sunscreen, body oil, hand sanitizer, laundry detergent, dishwasher gel, and more. Their Sweet Orange Vanilla shampoo, for example, received 4.5/5 stars from 99 people on Amazon. Then, in the spring of 2015, Alba debuted Honest Beauty, a full makeup and skincare line made with the same natural philosophy.

A rundown of the company's financials from Business Insider traces their growth from 2011, with initial funding of $27 million, provided by General Catalyst Partners, Lightspeed Venture Partners, and Institutional Venture

Partners. By November 2013, the company added $25 million in new funding. Soon they may be seeing brick-and-mortar stores. In October 2015, the company hosted an "Honest Beauty" pop-up shop with a massive press attendance, and shortly after they were valued at $1 billion.

Although The Honest Company has been called many things—"a baby company," "a lifestyle company," and "a beauty company"—it seems to be a mix of all. It is not surprising, given their strong dedication coupled with their ease and approachability, that they have been able to raise capital and sustain it. The Honest Company works on a subscription-based system. Customers need a membership and create an account to buy products online. Their most popular items are sold in "baskets," or packaged subscriptions that deliver monthly at a discounted rate. And they give back, so that with every product purchased, they "[donate] product, money, time, and effort to addressing critical health & social issues affecting children and families."

Their commitment to health is remarkable. They use "safe" ingredients in everything, based on plants, with the least possible "presence of petroleum in [the] products and packaging." All ingredients are "natural, organic, sustainably harvested, renewable, pure [and] raw materials," according to their website. Transparency (and honesty) is key to everything, so ingredients are listed and explained for each product online. Overall, the entire company holds themselves to high "health and sustainability standards," and their priority is to "reduce the ubiquitous presence of toxic chemicals in our natural environment (air, soil, oceans, etc.), man-made environments (homes, schools, offices), and our personal environments (industrial pollution inside our own bodies)." They track all the materials used, they monitor their environmental footprint and "cradle to grave impact" in production, they make reusable packaging, use higher post-consumer recycled or FSC-certified materials, their shipping material is recyclable, all the electricity used in their headquarters and warehousing is from 100 percent renewable sources, their warehouses use natural daylight, energy efficient lighting, electric forklifts—and the list goes on. Their attention to health, safety, and wellness is so obsessive and absolute that, had the CIA itself tried to make baby lotion, they could not have done it better.

Their website is light and airy, which is difficult for a two-dimensional platform meant for speed and efficiency. They say their dream brand is a combination of "savvy style, sustainability, and extraordinary service & convenience all wrapped in a passion for social goodness, tied with a bow of integrity and sprinkled with a little cheeky fun ... We are obsessed with product design that's functional, effective and durable—and also beautiful, fresh and fun." Indeed, their branding has been a welcoming, well-organized fun-mom home run from start to finish.

"People thought I was nuts," Alba told Jimmy Fallon

on Late Night in 2014. People had strong reactions to her leaving Mag World and rolling up her sleeves to become an entrepreneur. "'Can you just do a perfume or something?'" she recounted with an eye roll.

It is important to see a Hollywood icon like Alba not only giving back but also encouraging others to do so. Another new company, more exclusively geared to the beauty industry, is producing makeup that gives back. Indeed, their appreciation of philanthropy is noteworthy.

Nikos Mouyiaris founded the We See Beauty Foundation, launched in the summer of 2013, which serves as a nonprofit supporting women's cooperatives. It helps get women-led, worker-owned cooperative businesses up off the ground, according to Christina Han for The Cut. To do this, Mouyiaris created a makeup company whose sales would directly benefit the foundation, donating one third of its profits toward community based businesses. The makeup is made by MANA Products, also a Mouyiaris company, from which François Nars's was founded.

The concept sounds complex at first, but it is based on a business model Mouyiaris remembered from his great-uncle back in Cyprus. As he told Vanity Fair, "the villagers collected money and started an agricultural cooperative and a cooperative bank. That was in 1920. These institutions still exist today, and they are still thriving." Their first project was devoted to incubating a Brooklyn-based cooperative to make cleaning and personal-care products.

"I wanted to create a way to bring more equitability and security to women and community members who have an entrepreneurial will, and allow them the opportunity to become stakeholders in a business that will also better the community it is in," Mouyiaris continued in Vanity Fair. "Our collective goal is to empower local economies, elevate women, strengthen communities, and see a more beautiful world where there may be equitability, hope, and opportunities for all."

The structure and vision is truly extraordinary. After all, how many nonprofits are out there promoting cooperative development? "This all seems like a no-brainer: Women wear makeup, so why not buy makeup that helps other women in our very own nation?" writes Han. Indeed, Mouyiaris makes introducing philanthropy into the beauty industry seem more possible than not, and although his focus on cooperatives is special, he is opening the doors for other philanthropic choices his peers could be making across the industry.

Certainly Mouyiaris is turning new pages, and Alba has broken the mold by conceiving and directing a company instead of spritzing on perfume. And yet, Connie Tai is breaking the mold in a completely different way.

Tai is a chemist who has a degree in marketing from FIT and who, after working for Bliss in New York City, also went on to get an MBA. Tai always wanted to change the beauty industry, and she is doing that now with a self-made line of tea-inspired products. That is, there is the tea that you drink and there is the tea you put on your face. The tea starts from within because Tai believes that beauty starts from within. Where Mouyiaris's key innovation lies in creative economic choices, Tai's main innovations lie in her scientific intuition.

Tai's company is called Miyu, inspired by the Chinese phrase "mei yuan," or "the origins of beauty." While living the fast-paced NYC lifestyle, she noticed, as explained on her website, "it was taking a toll on her previously problem-free skin," She had discovered the impact that lifestyle has on complexion. In fact, Tai found 80 percent of skin aging is caused by factors such as UV exposure, pollution, stress, poor diet, and lack of sleep. "Lucky for us," the website notes, "these factors are well within our ability to control."

Of course, the first special quality of Miyu is its leader. That is, Tai is an actual scientist, who also understands her market, and who also resembles her customer. Her position has a unique intimacy. The second quality making this company special is Miyu's topical and beverage based line.

"Miyu pairs teas and skin care," and the products are categorized by lifestyle needs rather than skin type, writes Cheryl Wischhover for The Cut. The two lines, Hydrate

Mi and De-Stress Mi, both have a tea and a beauty essence, "an amped-up facial mist that has the same level of active ingredients as a more traditional serum, and is loaded with hyaluronic acid for maximum hydration," Wischhover explains. "You use the beauty essence in the morning and evening, and drink the corresponding tea whenever you want."

Miyu bases its philosophy in Chinese medicine. As the website explains, "Borrowing wisdom from the philosophies of ancient Chinese medicine, Miyu combines those teachings with the advancements of today's skincare technology," Each product contains some measure of three key ingredients: green tea, pearl, and white peony. In fact, women in Ancient China were keen on pearl powder, which they used often because it was easily made from oyster shells. The shells contain amino acids and "calmed" the skin against inflammation or irritation. Green tea worked against any signs of aging. Peony extract contained high amounts of tannins that brightened complexions. In other words, after two thousand years of guinea pigs, Tai and her team were well onto something.

Miyu products are free from parabens, sulfates, phthalates, synthetic dyes, and synthetic fragrances. Their philosophy is just as fresh. "While we love our coveted creams and lotions," Tai told blogger Ashley De Filippis, "we believe that beauty extends beyond the topical and should encompass all your lifestyle choices including diet, exercise, sleep and emotional state-of-mind … After all, your complexion is a direct reflection of your internal health!”

Perhaps great leaders are defined by their creativity, or perhaps by their size. For Dove, both are the case. This company has thrown its full weight behind a mission that defined a generation.

Dove soap hasn’t changed much. Products have diversified and grown slightly. What they sell is good, but the way they sell it is awesome. Indeed, their choice to start a marketing revolution made them the only company in the industry whose products are being bought perhaps more for the message than for the material. “It’s not just soap; it’s a soapbox,” wrote Elizabeth Olson for the New York Times.

Dove is a section of Unilever, an Anglo-Dutch company headquartered in London and founded in 1929. Unilever was a merger between the Dutch company Margarine Unie and the British company Lever Brothers. The first product was margarine; the second was an overnight soap sensation. Brothers William and James Lever teamed up with friend and chemist William Hough Watson in 1885. Watson had invented a chemical process that made a new kind of soap, lightly lathering and easy to wash off (based off glycerin and vegetable oils, such as palm oil, as opposed to tallow). The product was an overnight success; production reached four hundred and fifty tons per week in 1888 after only three years, and Lever soap became a household name.

Today, the company is divided into four sections: food, beverage, home care, and personal care. There are more than four hundred in-house diversified brands, with fourteen enjoying net sales of more than a billion euros. Among them are Axe, Hellmann's, Sunsilk, and, of course, Dove—with their unforgettable bar of soap.

Unilever was worth $4.97 billion back in 2003, which doesn't sound bad—but they had problems. Growth had been relatively steady, but in 2004 Unilever said they not only would not meet their target of 5 to 6 percent sales growth that year, but they were in debt 12.6 billion euros. Change was in store and, that September, Unilever announced chairman Niall FitzGerald would retire one year early and would be replaced by Patrick Cescau, then the head of the food division.

One of the first changes he made was meeting with Edelman, their advertisers at the time. Right away in 2004, "they conceived a campaign that focused not on the product, but on a way to make women feel beautiful regardless of their age and size," explained Melinda Brodbeck and Erin Evans, in a marketing study from Penn State University.

Dove outlined the new task on their website: "The Dove

Campaign for Real Beauty is a global effort that is intended to serve as a starting point for societal change and act as a catalyst for widening the definition and discussion of beauty. The campaign supports the Dove mission: to make women feel more beautiful every day by challenging today's stereotypical view of beauty and inspiring women to take great care of themselves."

The company had done its homework and discovered exactly what women wanted. The company-commissioned study, The Real Truth About Beauty, documented some revealing emotional truths.

"StrategyOne, an applied research firm, managed the study in conjunction with Dr. Nancy Etcoff and Massachusetts General Hospital, Harvard University, and with consultation of Dr. Susie Orbach of the London School of Economics," Brodbeck and Evans explain. "Between February 27, 2004 and March 26, 2004, the global study collected data from 3,200 women, aged 18 to 64. Interviews were conducted across ten countries: the U.S., Canada, Great Britain, Italy, France, Portugal, Netherlands, Brazil, Argentina and Japan."

The conclusions were surprising. "Dove knows that the relationship women have with beauty is complex … It can be powerful and inspiring, but elusive and frustrating as well. We sponsored this study in order to probe more deeply into this intricate relationship. Dove wanted to understand how women define beauty; how satisfied they are with their beauty; how they feel about female beauty's portrayal in society; and how beauty affects their well-being." As the authors note, this was the first comprehensive scientific exploration of its kind.

Without literally putting an ear to the ground, Dove would never have known which way to turn. Larry Koffler, senior vice president of consumer brands at Edelman, said that the follow-on advertising and marketing campaigns could not have been conceived "without having a foundation in the global research study, which showed that the image of beauty was unattainable," according to Brodbeck and Evans.

"Our mission is to make more women feel beautiful every day by broadening the definition of beauty," Philippe Harousseau, Dove's marketing director told NBC News in 2005. Just a glance at their billboard, seeing women of all sizes and all colors, harkens back to Howard Moskowitz's theory of horizontal segmentation. As Malcolm Gladwell summarized, "In embracing the diversity of human beings, we will find a sure way to human happiness."

The women from the original campaign included a manicurist, kindergarten teacher, two students, and an administrative assistant. "Most girls don't have that type of body [of a model] and they know they won't get to that," a twenty-two-year-old woman told NBC as she passed by the billboard. "But seeing this they say, 'I can do that.'"

"We are telling them we want them to take care of themselves, take care of their beauty," a managing partner at the ad agency told NBC. "That's very different from sending them the message to look like something they're not."

This approach worked for Dove. It is precisely what made their message organic, and what continues to make it so today. After the first study was underway, they conducted two more in 2005 and 2006. The new strategy, research, and campaign helped Dove soar into new heights. Where Unilever's earnings per share were less than $0.50 in 2000 and wobbled to just under a dollar in 2004, they jumped to $2.50 in 2008, increasing more than 150 percent in barely four years. And they only continue to grow. Honesty, empowerment, and natural beauty of all kinds seem to be the right direction for a company that has transformed itself from a sitter to a player. Dove continues to soar onward: they have spent more than $17 million on the Self-Esteem Project, an education initiative to raise girls' self-confidence. This unprecedented level of care and concern reveals an utterly fresh and pure ideology that puts the girl first.

* * *

Does a beauty industry have to be a vain industry? Is it automatically ugly to think of beauty as a business? What is beauty if not a business? What other name would I give the industry we have?

If it is possible for a beautiful girl to also not be a vain girl, then it is possible for a beauty industry to also not be a vain industry. In the same way a beautiful girl does not put her looks first, does not think of her looks first, does not concern herself with her looks first, and thinks more of her heart, her mind, and her health, then it is also possible for an industry to drain away less time and money on looks and more on the science of why health and how health has all sorts of positive inward and outward results. It is up to all consumers, girls and women, to charge them with that mission.

Performers get themselves back at the end of a performance. They take everything off, wash their faces, and—because they are professionals—they have the privilege of going home. People who live in Mag World put themselves on an imaginary stage, before an imaginary audience, which they almost never leave, and which almost never returns them to themselves. This, in some cases, is the sadness of plastic surgery, the sadness of platinum blonde after platinum blonde after platinum blonde, the loss of individuality and the loss of diversity.

Virginia Woolf knew that women had to be separated from all this. She knew that women were surrounded by a multitude of "stuff" and that they had to recognize it was all irrelevant.

In A Room Of One's Own, she wrote:

> All these infinitely obscure lives [of average, everyday women] remain to be recorded ... All that you will have to explore, I said to [the future female author], holding your torch firm in your hand. Above all, you must illumine your own soul with its profundities and its shallows, and its vanities and its generosities, and say what your beauty means to you or your plainness and what is your relation to the ever changing and turning world of gloves and shoes and stuffs swaying up and down among the faint scents that come through chemists' bottles down arcades of dress material over a floor of pseudo marble.

Woolf wants women to pay attention to their well-being and illumine their own souls with self-care. Woolf saw the industry of her day as an ever-changing, ever-turning world where women are surrounded by stocked shelves. She charged future female authors to draw back the curtain and lift the "veil," allowing women to stand alone without anonymity and standardization.

Woolf wanted women to focus more on their own lives than on all this "stuff." Where could they go? What could they accomplish? She even questioned the economics of their choices. Why were women always coming up short on money? "At the thought of all those women," she wrote, "working year after year and finding it hard to get two thousand pounds together, and as much as they could do to get thirty thousand pounds, we burst out in scorn against the reprehensible poverty of our sex. What had our mothers been doing then that they had no wealth to leave us? Powdering their noses? Looking in at shop windows? Flaunting in the sun at Monte Carlo?"

Almost one hundred years ago, Woolf asked: what do we invest in? Is the frivolity of shop windows and nose powder the same as the frivolity of hair spray, lip-gloss, and Botox today? Why were those women always broke, falling behind and absent on otherwise male adventures? Why had they no wealth to leave behind? Perhaps they were investing in the beauty industry, and not in themselves. Until the beauty industry starts focusing on the individual and on health, it will always be about the muse instead. Investing in the self means understanding science. Investing in the self is the only activity that yields beauty. And a valuable investment like that is a valuable way to build a business.

CHAPTER 4
BEAUTY: SCIENCE

In southern Italy, off the coast of Naples, there is an island called Capri. Best known today for shopping, parties, and celebrity-spotting, historically it was known for magic. There are many legends about Caprese magic, and one of them involves a spot where the cliffs meet the sea. A grotto—a cave—once called La Gradola and now known as La Grotta Azzura (the Blue Grotto) is hidden at the base of the northwest coast. At first, the cave does not seem noteworthy. From the outside, you see a small opening rising about a meter above the water. But with a tiny boat, when the tide is low, you can safely enter this archway and … step inside a sapphire. Immediately your eyes are distorted by the darkness that surrounds, but when they adjust, an ethereal, untraceable blue glows and glitters and dances all around. The water below seems to be breathing with its own light, and the jagged walls of the cave soften with a spectacular shimmer.

The Blue Grotto has been a destination for kings, emperors, and explorers. Treasures and statues are scattered across the floor. Stories of enchantment, witches, and monsters are memorized by the local people. However, the beauty of the Blue Grotto is no mystery at all. It is science. Special algae grows on the walls, fading the appearance of jagged edges. Its shape, sixty meters long and twenty-five meters wide, gives it visually advantageous proportions. And the light enters the cave in such a mathematically perfect way that the entire space fills with blue without so much as a corner in shadow.

You can't see the science that creates the Blue Grotto's beauty, even from a boat. At first, it seems the small outside archway must be the source of the cave's light, but it is only the beginning. Below the entrance, beneath a bar of rock, there is a second hole several feet underwater. This hole is nearly ten times the size in surface area of the entrance opening. The light from this hole, at just the right time of the day, triggers the beauty of this famous place.

Our own beauty is a by-product of life cycling through our bodies. Some say the body is a temple. I say the body is like a grotto, reverberating and echoing its own dazzling light—and whatever else we allow to enter it. Everything that enters is captured, and how it progresses through the body determines what leaves it—or, the appearance on the outside.

We've heard a million times that our most beautiful self is our best self—but so many different people define what is "best." Health, on the other hand, is what allows us to reach our full potential. Health is our body at peace, a peace supported by a secure and sustaining routine. But health is also action—and the more we are active the more we are free.

Health is controlled by three things: what surrounds you (your environment), what you introduce into your body (food, exercise), and what you apply to the outside of your body (skin care, cosmetics). In most cases, these three choices are in our control.

This chapter is about learning. I am not a scientist. I used to stare out the window in chemistry class (even though I wanted to be a good student) so when I knew I had to write a chapter of which chemistry was a component, I not only wanted to run in the opposite direction, I knew I needed help. The findings and the science I share here are not my own. Even the few scientists, authors, journalists, and so on who I reference only represent pools of other individuals who have also been working to collect this knowledge. I commend and honor those who have studied the science of the body and how to care for it, and I hope only to share their work with the purest ease and simplicity.

There is no question that the products mentioned in this chapter are healthy. However, I am not promoting one over another. I am showing how some companies have entered into, and have been successful in, understanding the science of beauty. To write this chapter, I had to enter into a particular quest: What are the basic ingredients and practices we can look for and take advantage of, and which should we avoid? How could understanding the science of beauty be made easier? Is there anything government could do to help? And of course, how does this product or these choices represent an investment in personal health?

Just as the Blue Grotto depends upon algae and location, environment is the first factor that determines a scientifically healthy (and beautiful) body.

* * *

"Lifestyle" choices often sound vague, but everyday we make key decisions that directly affect our quality of life. The way we sleep, our ability to manage stress, our friends and family, our drug use, our technological exposure, and our spiritual choices all blend with other threads to make up our "lifestyle." And, perhaps surprisingly, each of these choices plays a role in physical appearance.

Recent studies of lifestyle's connection to appearance have shattered more than a few old wives' tales. For example, it was once thought that UV exposure was the only environmental threat to premature skin aging, but now we know there are more complex factors at work. An article published in the *Dermatology Times* in 2014 by Dr. Ilya Petrou explains that "[p]otential contributors to [intrinsic and extrinsic skin aging] can include smog, pollution, cigarette smoke as well as other pollutants [which are solely] in the air." Nanoparticles (such as those generated from internal combustion engines, cigarettes, or other industrial processes) affect the skin.

"Polycyclic aromatic hydrocarbons (PAH) bind to the nanoparticles in the air from pollution [and] are converted to quinones," Petrou continues. "These quinones are the redox cycle chemicals that in turn produce reactive oxygen species (ROS)" which cause the same type of skin aging as UV light. Quinones, from air pollution, also prematurely age skin through discoloration and spotting.

Therefore, although step one seems impossibly simply, the skill is in the execution: people with urban lifestyles should wash their faces regularly and consume antioxidants. Dr. Zoe Draelos—interviewed for the article by Petrou—says, "It has been shown that there is more facial dyspigmentation in individuals who dwell in high PAH environments (i.e. cities) compared to those who live in rural areas."

Controlling one's environment, however, has less to do with the traditional geographic definition of environment and perhaps more to do with everyday bodily functions—like sleep. Most of us learn the hard way that sleep not only allows us to do our best but feel our best. And, as studies over the past fifteen years have confirmed, the chemistry of sleep helps us to look our best, too. We need seven to nine hours of sleep every day to churn out human growth hormone, the chemical responsible for the production of collagen—which contributes to skin elasticity, plumpness, and youthful appearance. Another chemical benefit of a full night's sleep: a reduction of the stress hormone cortisol, which is linked to acne.

Dr. Mehmet Oz offers suggestions to enhance sleep. One option is an open window or—for the city girl—several houseplants so your room has plenty of oxygen. Try to sleep in one position: on your back with your head raised slightly above your shoulders, and in total darkness (because light suppresses the production of melatonin in the brain, the chemical that allows you to fall asleep naturally). Melatonin also allows the body to form its own regular sleep cycle, so Dr. Oz recommends developing a schedule in which you go to bed on the early side—and wake up naturally, without an alarm clock. Relaxing with a glass of red wine (which offers cardiovascular benefits as well) may be helpful, but not necessary.

A good night of sleep starts with a good "slowdown" routine. As Dr. Rubin Naiman explains in *O, the Oprah Magazine*, "It's an opportunity to literally practice the fundamental art of letting go, of surrendering." Some start by giving someone a big hug. Others include an opportunity to "take stock" like organizing, journaling, sunset provisions, the Ignatian Examen, or other activities that tie up loose ends at the close of the day. The slowdown logically includes presleep hygiene—flossing, washing your face, etc. You can continue the slowdown once in bed, with meditation, prayer, or reading. A different sort of presleep routine (which may not seem like "slowdown") would include a passionate massage or sex—which release relaxation chemicals in the body.

Oz also has advice on tossing and turning in the middle

of the night: get out of bed and do a small calming activity, like a yoga pose, meditation, or a short walk. Herbal remedies include valerian root (for sedative effects) or ginseng (to stay asleep). Nonherbal foods that Oz recommends are things like Montmorency cherries (a type of sour cherry), pumpkin seeds, steamed dandelions, or occasionally the ancient Mexican liquor pulque (made from the agave plant), which has a very calming effect on the nervous system.

A well-known cause of a bad night's sleep is stress. As it turns out, that horrible feeling you have inside is more visible than you know. As Geoff Wright told the *Daily Mail*, stress tightens the capillaries, decreases the flow of nutrients, and causes "skin and hair to look dull." Stress also dries out the skin and the protective outer layer of skin cells break, the cells shrink, and the lipids between cells evaporate. Also, studies show that stress shortens the protein caps at the end of chromosomes called telomeres. If telomeres are too short, cells become permanently damaged or die, which visibly accelerates the aging process.

"The shortening of telomeres basically reflects the time clock that is ticking," writes Dr. Petrou, "and indicates how many more cell replications are possible. Decreased leukocyte telomere length is important because the leukocytes play a crucial role in immune function, and when the telomere length is prematurely shortened, that shortens the number of replications that [each] can undergo."

Stress directly exacerbates acne. A Stanford study from 2003 found college students reported their worst flare-ups during exam periods. Indeed, stress triggers the release of cortisol, which in turn drives the sebaceous glands to overload on producing oil. High levels of cortisol in the bloodstream also cause brittle nails, weight gain, and hair loss, which—when caused by stress—can take six to twelve months to reverse.

Chronic stress can take a toll on teeth, with more people unconsciously grinding away. Unmanaged stress also correlates with weight gain, as studies have shown that people are more likely to choose unhealthier foods when stressed, as well as form habits like mindless munching and eating on the go. We reach for foods higher in fat, sugar, and salt because they increase cortisol levels, which is partially how a Yale study in 2000 found higher levels of cortisol present in women with excess abdominal fat who were otherwise slender.

"Having a better handle on emotional stress and the role of psychological stress in aging is a new area of study [for dermatologists]," writes Petrou. While severe stress can cause hives, rashes, or fever blisters—and exacerbate conditions like psoriasis, rosacea, and eczema—these are not generally the issues dermatologists treat for stress. They tend to be focused on stress-related facial muscle tension (which brings wrinkles) and general dehydration.

Increased cortisol allows free radicals to build up and break down otherwise healthy cells, called "oxidative damage."

Ultimately, an environment that is stressful and unmanageable is chemically destructive, inside and out. These feelings set the body into survival mode, where all attention and energy goes to the most important functions.

At one point or another, we have all sacrificed sleep and endured stress for a loved one. Friends and family can have a real impact on lifestyle and appearance. Healthy relationships bring us joy and peace, embolden our individuality, and help us cope with issues of self-acceptance. On the other hand, some friends contribute to stress, and it doesn't take long to learn who they are.

According to the World Health Organization's Health Impact Assessment, "greater support from families, friends and communities is linked to better health." In 2009, Tara Parker-Pope reported for the *New York Times* that friends "help [fight] illness and depression, speed recovery, slow aging, and prolong life."

Healthy friendships also strengthen the immune system and decrease chances of getting a cold—as Parker-Pope noted in *O Magazine* in 2014. One study, in *JAMA: The Journal of the American Medical Association*, found "people were given nasal drops containing a strain of a cold virus,

[and] those with six or more types of social ties (including friends, coworkers, and fellow volunteers) were four times less likely to get sick than those with only one to three types of social relationships."

Parker-Pope also reported on a 2005 Australian study that found that "older people with a large circle of friends were 22 percent less likely to die during the study period than those with fewer friends." There is also a 60 percent increased chance of obesity among people whose friends had also gained weight. In 2008, Harvard released a study finding that "strong social ties could promote brain health as we age."

A 2006 study from the *Journal of Clinical Oncology* proved "women without close friends were four times as likely to die from the disease as women with 10 or more friends." A University of Virginia study from 2008 asked college students to climb a steep hill with a weighted backpack and asked them afterward about how difficult they felt the steepness of the hill was. "Some participants stood next to friends during the exercise, while others were alone. The students who stood with friends gave lower estimates of the steepness of the hill. And the longer the friends had known each other, the less steep the hill appeared."

Overall, good friends increase our ability to manage stress. "Researchers from University College London measured cortisol levels ... in individuals 30 minutes after the subjects woke up," reported *O Magazine* in 2014. "They found that the loneliest people had levels 21 percent higher than the most socially connected."

Nevertheless, the ways we connect socially have been changing. Despite developments in social media networks, studies show that maintaining relationships in person is beneficial for brain health. "According to one study, the more frequently people interacted with others, the higher they scored on cognitive tests," reported *O Magazine*. Also, the *American Journal of Public Health* found that "among older women, those who had daily contact with friends saw their risk of developing dementia reduced by 43 percent compared with those who had contact less than once a week." Most scientists believe social interaction improves synaptic connections in the brain, "staving off cognitive decline," as the magazine states. Healthy friendships not only help us manage stress, they can increase the chance of a better night's sleep. A study in *Psychological Science* looked at the sleep patterns of college students, and "those who reported feeling more connected to their peers fell asleep 14 minutes faster and spent 17 fewer minutes awake during the night than their more solitary counterparts."

As the saying goes, friends don't let friends do drugs. Regardless of illegal addictive stimulants, legal drugs can be addictive and harmful if abused or overused. "Bad" drugs are like trash in the grotto, not allowing that blue glow to spread. They disrupt normal body function, causing vast nutritional deficiencies. Cells that line the stomach and intestine will be damaged after repetitive drug use. This is just one of the reasons essential vitamins and minerals are unable to get into the bloodstream and give skin and hair what they need to be healthy. When the body ingests too many toxic substances, it becomes more difficult to filter out through the liver, so some literally filter out through the skin (one reason that drug users often suffer from dry, cracked skin or otherwise poor complexions).

Although we shouldn't set aside the risk of cancer tobacco brings, there are plenty of other negative effects of smoking, including poor skin and thinning hair. "Cigarette smoke has long been … associated with the breakdown of collagen and elastic fibers in the skin, resulting in the premature development of wrinkles and flaccid skin in individuals who smoke," explains Dr. Petrou in *Dermatology Times*. The impact, by the way, is not limited to actual "smokers" but also to those who are exposed to so-called "secondhand smoke" on a regular basis.

Dr. Petrou also cites a Mexican study, which found that cigarettes reduced blood flow in the face, "further underscoring the detrimental effects of cigarette smoke … The perfusion between smokers and nonsmokers was compared using Doppler ultrasound and found that the test subjects who smoked demonstrated a prematurely aged microcirculation."[a]

Aside from tobacco, all smoking inhibits the body from feeding necessary nutrients to the skin and hair. "Smoking chronically deprives the skin of oxygen and arterially supplied nutrients ... A prematurely aged microcirculation probably has just [as] big an effect on premature skin aging as do the nanoparticles that create reactive oxygen species that are inhaled or even touch the skin itself."[b]

Similarly, smoking, vaporizing, or ingesting pot results in an immediate increase in testosterone levels, Dr. Ariel Ostad told *The Huffington Post.* Testosterone allows oil glands in the skin to overproduce sebum oil, causing breakouts. "People who are chronic users of marijuana can also experience hair loss on the scalp or even excess hair growth in other parts of their bodies due to this testosterone jump," Rebecca Adams reports, also in *The Huffington Post.*

Getting high from smoking or ingesting even a small quantity of marijuana often results in sugar cravings, for high-glycemic-index foods that also irritate the skin, promote acne, and may heighten psoriasis and rosacea. Recent studies have also supported earlier theories that pot can age your skin in the same manner as cigarette smoke. "These hydrocarbons can inhibit cells that are chiefly responsible for making new collagen," thus aging the skin more rapidly, reports Adams.

It is guaranteed that smokers will not be able to look their best, but those who choose to drink in excess are also misguided in thinking that the effects will only appear on the inside and not the outside. Excessive alcohol dehydrates the skin and depletes nutrients that help it look its best. Those who drink often also tend to have unhealthy diets, which can cause the skin to look dull. "It may make us feel good, but alcohol is a hepatotoxin, [which is] a toxin to the cells that detoxify your body," Dr. David Colbert told *The Huffington Post.*

Although an occasional glass of red wine or clear liquor are least harmful, relatively speaking, "the less sugar you take in with your alcohol, the better for your long-term wrinkle risk."[c] Sugar can also exacerbate hangovers, says Dr. Jessica Krant in *The Huffington Post*, as well as cause sallow skin, bloodshot eyes, and irritated acne from spiking insulin levels.

Alcohol abuse has even further negative effects. Facial blood vessels can permanently dilate, with red spider veins in the neck or the face. Regardless, whatever the intake, "between the congeners, the liver damage, and the dehydration, it's clear alcohol does damage to our skin," says Dr. Colbert.

Although our cell phones might not be a drug, we can easily feel like we're addicted. As one doctor jokes, "just like alcohol ads, so should technology companies carry warnings on their products and in their advertisements. 'Text responsibly.' 'Don't surf, then sleep,'" wrote Dr. David Volpi for *The Huffington Post* in 2012. He references researcher Sara Thomée who says, "Public health advice should therefore include information on the healthy use of this technology."

Between 50 and 90 percent of people who work in front of a computer screen will strain their eyes and experience some form of eye damage. Common symptoms of eyestrain, dubbed "Computer Vision Syndrome," will include sore eyes, dry eyes, teary eyes, blurry vision, double vision, light sensitivity, difficulty focusing on images, neck pain, headache—or a combination of all of the above.

A common mistake: sitting too close to the screen. "This forces your eyes to work harder than usual as you strain to focus on tiny font sizes," Dr. Brian Boxer Wachler told CNN. Eyes must be twenty to forty inches away from screens when viewing for an extended period of time. Also, the screen should be in the correct position and angle. The top of the screen should be level with the eyes, Dr. Wachler recommends, so your vision is only slightly lowered onto the screen. The angle of the monitor should be set to reduce reflections. The less glare, the less strain.

As Jeffrey Anshel told CNN, use the three B's rule: blink, breathe, and break. Whereas people normally blink eighteen times per minute, the frequency lowers when looking at a screen or any digital device. "Correct breathing can relax the eye muscles," says Anshel, "so be conscious of your breathing" especially during stress, when people tend to hold their breath. Also practice the 20-20-20 rule: every twenty minutes, take twenty seconds and look twenty feet away.

Besides body pain, eye damage, and fatigue, overuse of technology has mental and emotional consequences. "The artificial light from TV and computer screens affects melatonin production," writes David Volpi for *The Huffington Post*, "and throws off circadian [sleep] rhythms, preventing deep, restorative sleep." Blue light from screens was studied by Rensselaer Polytechnic Institute, which found that the light from using a tablet PC for just two hours will lower melatonin production by about 22 percent. Most doctors recommend no blue light use during the evening or before bedtime.

Not only can mindless tech use prevent deep sleep, but it can also exacerbate stress. In a Mobile Mindset study by mobile security company Lookout, 73 percent of people admitted they would panic if they lost their smartphone, and 54 percent said they check their phone even while lying in bed. Everyone is susceptible, but young adults most especially. Researchers from the University of Gothenburg, Sweden, studied four thousand people between the ages of twenty and twenty-four. The data showed that intensive use of cell phones and computers is linked to increases in stress, sleep disorders, and depressive symptoms. Among all adults, heavy cell phone use showed an increase in sleep disorders in men and an increase in depressive symptoms in both men and women. Those who felt the need to always be accessible on their phones were more likely to report mental health issues.

We already knew that watching TV too frequently can lower self-esteem, especially in young developing minds.[a] In fact, a 2012 Indiana University study found that, for girls, "exposure to today's electronic media in the long run tends to make you feel worse about yourself."

Researchers at Stanford University found that heavy dependence on technology and multitasking directly inhibits social and emotional growth among "tweenage" girls. The study covered almost 3,500 girls from ages eight to twelve who were asked how much time they spent watching videos, listening to music, reading, doing homework, emailing, posting to social media, texting, instant messaging, talking on the phone, and video chatting—as well as how often they were doing two or more of those activities simultaneously.

"The girls' answers showed that multitasking and spending many hours watching videos and using online communication were statistically associated with a series of negative experiences," writes Stanford's Dan Stober. For example, comments included "feeling less social success, not feeling normal, having more friends whom parents perceive as bad influences, and sleeping less." Indeed, beauty, fashion, and magazine advertising continues to target these eight- to twelve-year-old girls in their most critical period for social and emotional development.

Still, it's not just girls who experience technological whiplash. In a study by the nonprofit Anxiety UK, more than half of adults who use social media reported the networks had changed their lives, and 51 percent said not for the better.

As *The Huffington Post* reported on the study, "Forty-five percent of responders said they feel 'worried or uncomfortable' when email and Facebook are inaccessible, while 60 percent of respondents stated 'they felt the need to switch off' their phones and computers to secure a full-fledged break from technology." About two-thirds of the people in the study had trouble sleeping right after using social media. 25 percent reported more difficulty in their relationships.

"Researchers at the University of Maryland," reports *The Huffington Post,* "found that people who used their phones more often were less likely to engage in 'prosocial' behavior, like helping others or contributing to the greater good."[b] After using a cell phone, "study participants were more likely to turn down volunteer opportunities and were less persistent in completing word problems, even though they knew their answers would provide money for charity."[c]

Balance is key. We prefer technologically efficient days, but "while we often think we can multitask by keeping one eye on our phones, one on our friends, [research from the University of Utah] reveals a very different reality: People who engage in multitasking perceive themselves as great jugglers, though data shows they are more likely to be *less* capable of focusing on multiple things at once than peers who don't make a habit of multitasking."

After the election in 2016, women had a spectrum of reactions, but at one end grew those who multiplied their calendars and tripled their waking hours to fight the glass ceiling that failed to break. It put Debora Spar's 2014 book, *Wonder Women: Sex, Power, and the Quest for Perfect*, in a new light. For all the delight that a cell phone, status update, or tweet can give, failing to understand how to keep technological use in strict control can have direct and visible impacts on our health. Although digital addiction's effect on our outward appearance may seem like a superficial cause for concern, stress, sleep issues, and obesity, for example, are far more serious. "New evidence is confirming that the environment kids live in has a greater impact than factors such as genetics, insufficient physical activity, or other elements in efforts to control child obesity."[d] Increased screen time is likely to be associated with larger waistlines.[e] Not only may there be a false belief that "tapping away on a computer can replace physical activity," but of more concern, "screens can lull you into unconscious eating."[f]

Despite how much technology keeps changing, some things stay the same. The benefits of a spiritual life have always been accepted, but now they are being proven to improve appearance – especially in their link to better sleep, better relationships, and less stress.

It may not be true that a little prayer is as good as a face-lift, however, new studies show that an inward commitment to meditation or an active spiritual life can have positive outward effects. According to Jade Dyer at Monash University in Australia, there is "little debate that spiritual beliefs provide psychological comfort for those suffering from illness or disability." In fact, studies show that spiritual activities are "associated with health-related quality of life." In another study, there were "42 independent samples investigating the association of religious involvement with all-cause mortality." The researchers found the odds of survival for people who scored highly on religious activity were 29 percent higher than those who scored lower in their religious involvement.

L. H. Powell conducted nine longitudinal population-based studies which found that, in one instance, there was a 32 percent reduction in mortality risk in elderly Mexican Americans who attended church once a week compared with those who never attended. Indeed, foundational lifestyle choices and environments are changed after spiritual activity is increased. "As social support has been shown to improve health and increase life expectancy, the social aspect of religious practice may contribute to decreased mortality rates in churchgoers," Dyer observes.

"Spiritual practices tend to improve coping skills and social support, foster feelings of optimism and hope, promote healthy behavior, reduce feelings of depression and anxiety, and encourage a sense of relaxation," according to University of Maryland Medical Center's website. "By alleviating stressful feelings and promoting healing ones, spirituality can positively influence immune, cardiovascular (heart and blood vessels), hormonal, and nervous systems."[g]

As the stress we feel on the inside leads to physical expressions of our struggles on the outside, the body can experience relief after spiritual activity. "A person's most deeply held beliefs strongly influence his or her health," according to the article. "Some researchers believe that faith increases the body's resistance to stress. In a 1988 clinical study of women undergoing breast biopsies, the women with the lowest stress hormone levels were those who used their faith and prayer to cope with stress."

People who attend regular religious services "tend to have better immune function," says a study from Duke University. In another clinical study of more than two hundred older adults undergoing heart surgery, "those who were religious were 3 times less likely to die within the 6 months after surgery than those who were not. Not one of the 37 people in this study who described themselves as deeply religious died." There are many reasons for why these groups of people also happen to be healthier; however, the university points to faith, hope, forgiveness, social support and prayer as all characteristics of a spirituality that do impact on health.

Meditation, mindfulness, and positive thinking can have overall health benefits. "Without [spiritual] hope—a positive attitude that a person assumes in the face of difficulty—many people become depressed and prone to illness. In a thirty-five-year clinical study of Harvard graduates, researchers found that those graduates who expressed hope and optimism lived longer and had fewer illnesses in their lifetime."[h]

Many religions have specific ways of exploring the process of forgiveness. Nevertheless, it is an important spiritual journey. "Another survey of 1,400 adults found that willingness to forgive oneself, and others, and the feeling that one is forgiven by God, has beneficial health effects. Some researchers suggest that emotions like anger and resentment cause stress hormones to accumulate in the blood, and that forgiveness reduces this build up."[i]

Prayer and meditation are not only strongly associated with recovery and abstinence from drugs, but they have a more interwoven role in medicine than we think, the article says. "In a 1996 poll, one half of doctors reported that they believe prayer helps patients, and 67 percent reported praying for a patient." Although we cannot know for sure the effect of distance prayer, "current research in coronary care units (intensive care units in hospitals devoted to people with severe heart disease, like those who just suffered a heart attack) suggests that there is benefit. Compared to those who were not prayed for, patients who were prayed for showed general improvements in the course of their illness, less complications, and even fewer deaths."

Spirituality has brightened lives for centuries—whatever the form, whatever the continent, whatever the language or tradition. "The act of putting oneself in the presence of or conversing with a higher power" is a healing process, according to researchers and authors Stephen Murgatroyd and Sarajane Aris. We have so many lifestyle choices to make each day, and yet—ironically—it is the balance of rational thinking and intuition that brings us to greatest health. We have to reach for the visible and the invisible. We have to trust science and our gut.

* * *

Ayurvedic practices of the science of beauty are at least 1,500 years old and belong to the Hindu rules of traditional medicine. As Melanie Sachs explains in *Ayurvedic Beauty Care*, "diet, digestion, air, and exercise" all impact on skin, hair, and body shape:

> Regular exercise is essential to health and vibrant beauty because it helps clear the channels of the body so that all the tissues

> can be thoroughly cleansed via sweat and other eliminatory channels and be well supplied with nutrients. Exercise is especially helpful for the skin because in order for the skin to renew itself and be fresh and clear it needs to be cleared of wastes.

She continues, "[exercise] strengthens the body's musculature, keeping it firm and shapely … strong muscles help support beautiful skin … [exercise] builds stamina and boosts heat in the body and the immune response." On a mental and emotional level, exercise "helps to reduce tension, reduce anxiety, and promote a sense of overall well-being … deep restful sleep … mental stamina" as well as "the energy boost needed" to create and sustain a "well-balanced and healthy self-care routine…"

These comments are echoed by the Livestrong Foundation: "We worked with Dr. Robert R. Provine, a neuroscientist from the University of Maryland, to identify non-fitness related traits associated with attractiveness, like healthy teeth, smooth skin, good hair, upright posture, and even confidence … While standards of beauty vary across cultures, youth and healthiness are always in fashion because they are associated with reproductive fitness," according to their website.

Sachs introduces the Ayurvedic method of choosing exercises according to skin type. Ayurveda proposes different workouts for oily, sensitive, and dry skin. People with oily skin (kapha) should aim for vigorous, high-impact aerobic workouts for up to an hour each day. Because of their innate tendency to retain water, they benefit from working up a good sweat.

High-energy people with sensitive skin (pitta), says Sachs, should choose fast-paced workouts to burn off excess energy and help them blow off some steam. Although they like to push themselves, they lack kapha's stamina and should limit their workout periods to avoid getting burned out. Sensitive skin types particularly enjoy competitive sports, and even if they choose solitary exercises such as running or swimming they might transform the workout into a training program or a marathon prep.

Dry skin types (vata) will benefit from regular routines like daily exercise. Although they jump into activity enthusiastically, they have limited physical endurance and lack psychological tenacity. Structured, low-impact, moderately paced exercise is best, such as ballet, modern dance, yoga, hiking, swimming, fitness walking, and so on. Sachs suggests they limit their workout to thirty or forty-five minutes per day.

Hatha yoga, as Pratima Raichur explains in *Absolute Beauty,* effectively balances body, breath, mind, and spirit. Yoga not only develops "physical flexibility, strength, and grace, but also enlivens the subtle energies, balances prana, steadies the emotions, and increases the vigor of the mind." Other all-encompassing practices like yoga recommended by Sachs include Sotai, Do-In, Taoist exercise, tai chi chih and callanetics.

Almost any exercise will have a direct impact on outward appearance. When you exercise, "nitric oxide is released from the linings of the arteries to allow blood vessels to move more blood more freely," explains Dr. Oz and Dr. Roizen in *You: Being Beautiful.* The smallest arteries open up, allowing more blood and important nutrients to reach the skin. Exercise, writes Jenny Bailly for *O Magazine*, "improves your circulation and oxygen capacity, it improves your complexion ... And raising your heart rate once a day makes your skin glow."

Collagen and elastin are two proteins in skin tissue that contribute to elasticity. Both are degraded by sun, stress, and chronological aging. However, as Livestrong reports, "[a] study by Bispebjerg Hospital in Denmark found that prolonged exercise stimulated collagen and elastin production and improved skin thickness ... The thinner our skin, the more prone it is to fine lines and wrinkles."

Exercise also stimulates growth hormone, something that mainly happens while you sleep. According to Oz and Roizen, the growth hormone revs up the production of collagen and elastin, renewing surface cells faster, and promoting fibroblast health. Dermal fibroblast cells are responsible for maintaining all the connective tissue in the skin, especially allowing the dermis and the epidermis to join together to form the top, visible layer of the skin.

As much as we complain, perspiration is a beneficial by-product of exercise. It not only helps regulate body temperature and balances electrolyte levels, but also serves as a cleansing agent. The body releases toxins through the skin all day long, but when the pores dilate during exercise, dirt and oil can reach the surface and be cleared away along with dead skin cells and bacteria.[a] Dr. Kavita Mariwalla, a New York-based dermatologist, tells Livestrong, "A study by scientists at the Eberhard Karls University at Tübingen, Germany, found that that sweat also contains a natural antibiotic that helps defeat certain bacteria—and bacteria on our skin is one cause of acne."[b] Opening the pores with heat before or after exercise can be beneficial, as long as it's comfortable. Sitting in dry heat or a steam room is good, because it's relaxing and therefore reduces stress for the skin.

Exercise can also alleviate acne by reducing inflammation and enhancing lymphatic flow in the face, which, as Dr. Mariwalla explains to Livestrong, "can help to reduce water retention in our bodies and improve under eye puffiness and dark circles"'

Exercise even regulates hormones. "The Texas Heart Institute reports that a person who exercises vigorously and regularly has lower levels of circulating stress-related hormones, which helps improve the health of the blood vessel lining," according to Livestrong's website. "This improves your skin tone and curbs sallowness," says Dr.

Mariwalla, and results in a clearer complexion with more healthy coloration.

Many exercises, yoga included, can greatly improve posture, increasing self-confidence. A study from Great Britain showed that regular exercise improves self-image. The study looked at people who regularly went to the gym and found they felt better about themselves—and had better health, overall, than people who stayed home.

Exercise can also strengthen the hair. Yoga poses, for example, where the head rests lower than the heart, can increase the circulation in the scalp. Breathing deeply in these particular poses will also help fight stress. During all exercise, though, circulation increases and the blood "delivers essential nutrients and oxygen necessary for healthy hair and hair growth," Dr. Mariwalla tells Livestrong. "Exercise also helps to reduce DHT," a hormone that specifically stalls hair growth, and similarly lowers levels of cortisol in the body, according to the foundation's website.

Working out can even brighten your smile. When circulation increases on a regular basis, it is easier for nutrients to get to the teeth and gum tissues. According to the Livestrong foundation website, the *Journal of the American Dental Association* reports that "researchers found that subjects who exercised and had healthy eating habits were 40 percent less likely to develop periodontitis, or gum disease … Another study conducted at the Jordan

University of Science and Technology showed that individuals who exercised regularly had far superior oral health than non-exercisers."

In *Ayurvedic Beauty Care*, Melanie Sachs emphasizes that "exercise during the day helps cleanse the body of adrenaline that builds up duc to stress and keeps the body tense and mind overactive," inhibiting sleep. Shawn Talbott, Ph.D. and author of *The Metabolic Method*, explains that "exercise reduces sleep-inhibiting cortisol in our bodies. Since cortisol is the 'fight or flight' hormone, it puts our bodies into a highly alert state, making us ready to duke it out or sprint for safety ... but that same cortisol can actually fuel our workouts."

When we work out on a regular basis, we must remember to always slightly increase the difficulty, says Dr. Oz. "More intense exercise preserves neurocognitive function by decreasing the expression of the Ap0E4 gene to help clear the beta-amyloid plaque that gunks up your power lines. [It also results in] increased telomere length," the cells which allow the mind to engage more deeply and with endurance. He suggests choosing an exercise once or twice a week that "requires not only your body to work but also your mind," such as yoga or a game of tennis.

Low-intensity and high-intensity exercises should happen at different times in the day. At low-levels, Oz and Roizen advise, "[t]alking and walking 30 minutes a day are the most effective strategies for treating and preventing depression." The authors suggest a ten-minute midmorning walk to stretch the legs and wake up the mind. They also suggest a brisk thirty-minute midday walk. Avoid working out for half an hour before a meal and for at least one or even two hours after eating, Sachs advises. Still, a ten- to fifteen-minute stroll after eating certainly encourages healthy digestion. With these general guidelines in mind, Dr. Michelle Copeland adds: "The key is going consistently … the most consequential action is establishing a daily ritual."

Your most intense exercise sessions should be close to the start of your day, according to Sachs. It is better to do main exercise in the morning when metabolism is naturally slow and the mind and body can benefit from extra stimulation. Too much exercise in the late afternoon leads to fatigue, and exercise at night leads to an overstimulated mind and insomnia. Low-intensity sessions like an exercise-band workout are okay, but harder workouts should not be close to bedtime. Livestrong and The National Sleep Foundation recommend exercising at least three hours before you go to bed to avoid disrupting healthy sleeping patterns.

There are some movements right before bed that can help sleep. "Exercise before bed by gently stretching the spine, neck, and shoulder areas where the most tension accumulates in the day," Sachs suggests. "One technique is to lie on the floor on your back and draw up your knees and clutch them. Rock back and forth on your spine to loosen the spine and increase even flow of circulation throughout the spine. This helps the whole body to relax."

Other Ayurvedic end-of-day rituals from Sachs:

> Practice skilled relaxation during the day or when you get home from work ... Relaxation-exercises condition you to develop increases of alpha brainwave stimulation. Do such exercises in a place not associated with sleep, but relaxation; i.e. not your bed, but perhaps a lounge chair, couch, or floor. Doing such an exercise before bed can settle you down so that you do not go to bed in an overly tired or mentally overactive state.

Although Saks endorses exercise highly, she encourages staying centered most of all.

> [We] use machines to exercise the body and dream of having abs, pecs, and buns 'of steel'—we want to *become* machines, as if we could outdistance or outsmart the aging process with technology. The only way to conquer aging and disease is to reduce stress and expand awareness. The technologies of consciences are the tools of the science of longevity. Machines wear out and run down; the intelligence of the bodymind is self-renewing. Exercise your

> biceps by picking up a baby or giving a massage to someone you love. If you want to press a couple of hundred pounds, hug some friends. A nurturing touch can undo a day's worth of tension and stress.

How the body is able to focus, stretch, move or exert itself is dependent upon what kind of fuel it has. In the same way that exercise is healing and strengthening from the inside out, food affects our health and, therefore, every aspect of our exterior appearance.

* * *

The experts agree: how you feed your body is how you feed your skin. According to Dr. Michelle Copeland in *The Beautiful Skin Workout*, "What you might not be aware of is that the foods you consume affect more than your waistline; they can also improve the appearance of your skin … Skin is an outward reflection of the internal situation … Eating is a regular part of every day, so making empty choices is simply 'a missed opportunity.'"

The Ayurvedic tradition agrees as well. Skin needs nutrition and digestion, says Pratima Raichur in *Absolute Beauty*. Healthy digestion and elimination of waste produces "[c]lear skin, bright eyes, glossy hair, strong nails, stamina, clarity, and a gentle and compassionate nature," she writes.

As light comes into a sea cave and dances around the walls, food comes into the body and gives us life. In *It's All Good*, Dr. Habib Sadeghi writes, "Food gives us its life-force ... food isn't an inanimate object, it's part of us." In the same book, editor and chef Julia Turshen explains the nutritional changes she made. "I decided then that my body wasn't an apartment I was renting, it was the house I would always live in."

In many ways, that house we live in is our skin—and food is essential for skin health "The Ayurvedic term for the physical body is *annamaya kosha*—literally, the food sheath," writes Raichur. "All body tissue is formed from the nutrients we consume. Is it any surprise, then, that the stale, processed lifeless foods create aged-looking lifeless skin? What we feed is what we get. Therefore, eat a diet rich in fresh foods, as well as enlivening thoughts and loving feelings, if you want to create the radiant look of absolute beauty."

"Food is many things," Dr. Sadeghi writes, "It's necessary, nurturing and healing," not—as we would like to think—just the next box on our to-do list. We have a tendency to rush through meals and overthink nutrition. We may be passionate, but "instead of using that passion to enjoy food, we do what we do with most things in life. We complicate it. We over-think it. We worry about whether or not a certain food is good for us, or whether or not it causes some health problem." Eat and run is not really feeding. "It's a sensorial experience. Food comes from the earth. So do we."

Feeding must be a feel-good experience—sensorial and positive—in order to be healthy. "Food must be a pleasure-filled, spiritual experience," says Sadeghi. "It builds our bodies through sustenance and nurtures our souls through sensation … A lot of people think great flavor is an afterthought when it comes to 'healthy' food, but if we are to be fully nourished by food, it needs to taste wonderful."

As Dr. Sadeghi explains, animals in a study who were regularly fed a diet full of nutrition but void of any good flavor eventually died from *malnutrition.* "It's clear that there is a physiological link between taste and health. If we don't enjoy the food we're eating, regardless of whether its broccoli or brownies, we're absorbing fewer of its nutrients. In order to be fully nourished by our food, we must take pleasure in it."

That principle is reflected in *It's All Good*, a cookbook authored by Gwyneth Paltrow and Julia Turshen. The pictures are cheerful, the layout is peaceful, and both women write that creating the project was truly positive. In Paltrow's case, they were "having the best f*@£ing time doing it."

They truly enjoyed cooking and drafting recipes, and the whole book exudes a relaxed pleasure. "Meal times should always feel happy," says Paltrow. "These recipes first and foremost pay attention to the emotional power of food—and also happen to be amazingly good for you," adds Turshen. "They satisfy our nearly embarrassing, totally nerdy love of great cooking, and they also take care of our bodies."

Ayurvedic principles match the authors' desire to bring positivity into each and every meal. "Food prepared with love and pure intention to benefit others is always better energy," writes Sachs. From her research, she also agrees that food needs to be pleasing: "All tastes and qualities should be present in one meal … be flexible and always try to enjoy what you eat."

Ultimately, how you eat and what you eat are equally important. While the selection is truly vast, a part of life we tend to take for granted, Sadeghi, Paltrow, Turshen, Copeland, Raichur, Sachs, and Oz all have several points on which they agree.

Good digestion is enhanced by intelligent selection and skillful preparation of foods, says Raichur. "The dietary principals for staying young and beautiful are universal," says Sachs. "Keep the colon clean and the digestion strong." She references Western nutritionist Paavo Airola: "Scandinavians favor rye and whey; Germans advocate mineral water, fermented foods, and the use of juice fasts; Mexicans cook with lime, papaya and hot pepper; Asians eat a diet low in fat and high in fiber rich grains. In theory, most of these regimens do help either to avoid constipation or promote digestion."

Although our food industry today tries to provide nearly an infinite amount of choices, Ayurveda suggests starting your focus on water and portions.

Similar to the beauty of a sea cave, water plays an integral role in the beauty of our bodies. "At least 70 percent of the skin's blemish and wrinkle-fighting hydration comes from the water we consume," writes Kat James in *The Truth About Beauty*. Most experts agree eight glasses a day is the healthiest goal but, as Oz writes, "drink as much water as it takes to keep your mouth and lips moist throughout the day." Water from a purifier is far better than bottled water (unless, of course, you're out of the country). And sipping warm or room temperature water with a hint of lemon or lime throughout the day and with meals benefits good digestion, says Raichur. Although tap water may be a challenge in foreign countries, keeping hydration up while traveling is important, writes Copeland, especially in arid climates where the skin cannot absorb as much moisture from the air.

Sipping water throughout the day not only allows the body to flush out toxins, but it also keeps the brain fully functional and better able to cope with stress—a universal skin aggravator. Valuing water and giving the body enough throughout the day is important, but the next step is to understand food groups and what foods to aim for, and in what proportions, for a healthy diet.

The Ayurvedic nutritional breakdown recommends a balance of "40-60 percent whole grains, 30-50 percent fresh fruits and vegetables, [and] 10-20 percent high quality proteins," writes Raichur. Whole grains provide energy throughout the day. Fiber helps maintain a toned digestive tract by providing bulk, helping to clear toxins and other excesses. Fruits and vegetables provide strong mineral and vitamin levels that, according to Raichur, are responsible for "that intangible radiance." Diets should be slightly lower in animal proteins than vegetable proteins, she says, because animal proteins "increase the toxicity of waste products due to slow transit time."

Keeping meals low in fat and low in salt also help the skin. Limiting bad fats and eating good ones helps to keep the blood clean and free of clogging. Good circulation means better skin because it's more nourished. Salt tends to increase signs of aging, especially around the eyes, like bags and puffiness.

Clever combining can also make a meal more appealing. The right combination of foods eaten together can minimize the glycemic impact. Foods with whole-grain flour or other complex carbs with protein fiber or fat all lower the glycemic index of a meal, James says.

Certain foods can be good for you but will create toxins if eaten in the wrong combinations. Avoid eating: very hot and very cold at the same time; raw and cooked at the same time; dairy products with animal foods (like milk and fish, or milk and meat); dairy with salty, sour, or pungent foods; and very sweet with very salty. A better way to combine foods is to mix flavors subtly, says Sachs. "Think of the opposite pairs of attributes and tastes: heavy and light; moist and dry; heating and cooling; sweet and bitter; pungent and astringent; and salty and sour."

While the Ayurvedic breakdown is a familiar balance, their idea of portions may be new to some. Eat only as much as would fit into two hands cupped together, says Raichur. "Cup your hands side by side, and imagine them filled with your favorite food," says Sachs. "According to Ayurveda, this is approximately the size of the total serving one should eat at each meal … in fact, it is only half a handful less than what fills the average stomach—and this is as full as Ayurveda suggests the stomach should get."

It is important that this portion be filled with a "favorite" food. Minding portions isn't the same as constantly cutting back. "Stop eating light and start eating well," says James. "Quality is far more important than quantity." Even snacking can be healthy. "There's a healthy way to satisfy each and every craving," says James.

Indeed, the serving of two handfuls of food must be balanced in different tastes. "Every meal should include all six tastes in proper proportion," says Sachs (sweet, bitter, pungent, astringent, salty, and sour). "One of the most common mistakes in diet is that we eat certain tastes in excess and never eat other tastes at all." Feeding healthily, rather, means intentionally choosing foods and "altering the proportion of tastes ... it doesn't necessarily mean eliminating foods from your diet completely." With change toward limited portions and a variety of tastes, says Sachs, "a little every day, you will end up with a perfect balance of tastes on your plate with little feeling of deprivation."

Seeds (grains, nuts, and beans), fruits, vegetables, and protein are helpful categories to begin with, but accurate categorization is a murky task: is a tomato a fruit or a vegetable? Depends on who you ask. For healthy skin, hair, and fitness, I suggest the following list of foods—some of which you may eat every day and others you may not have even heard of. These key foods can be balanced into a weekly diet, based on tastes and preferences.

***

GRAINS

Although studies suggest that 95 percent of the carbohydrates we reach for are refined, we should only reach for low glycemic index grains. They all have polyphenols and carotenoids, which slow down the aging process, and most are a good source of B vitamins, selenium, and magnesium. All regulate blood sugar, and all add great fiber to move toxins through the body and brighten skin.

Quinoa cooked and quinoa uncooked are like two different foods. When possible, choose uncooked recipes, because this form of the grain is truly a superfood, sacred in ancient South America as powerful fuel. It has more protein than any other grain, and is so loaded with antioxidants you would benefit from daily ingestion (these include: manganese, phosphorus, magnesium, folate, B vitamins, vitamin E, and as much omega-3 and omega-6 fatty acids as some fish—if not more). Uncooked quinoa increases elasticity in the skin and strengthens the hair shaft. Paltrow and Turshen also recommend quinoa flakes as a gluten-free protein-packed substitute for oats.

Rice. When you choose white rice instead of whole grain brown, experts estimate that you miss out on at least 75 percent of the antioxidants and nutrients that are removed in the production process. Medium-grain and long-grain brown rice are pretty similar. Although brown rice is more nutritious overall, wild rice is higher in protein, folate, and B vitamins, so it can be worked in throughout the week for variety.

Oats. For breakfast or a snack, reach for steel cut oatmeal with avenanthramide, an antioxidant that is particularly good for circulation and the heart. Oats moisturize the skin from the inside out, with natural lubricating fats and other antioxidants that form a protective layer over the skin against UV light. It has zinc, iron, magnesium, and potassium to promote healthy hair growth. Don't forget to choose brands without any refined sugar added.

Rye. According to nutritional research from the nonprofit Organic Center, whole rye bread has more nutrients than any other whole grain. It has four times more fiber than whole wheat and is packed with iron. Most commercially available rye bread and pumpernickel (made from rye) is made from refined flour, so make sure "whole rye" tops the ingredients list. Store loaves in the refrigerator.

Barley. Whole grain barley is a great choice for hair. However, whole-grain or "hulled" barley is much better than "pearled," because the bran and germ are removed. Hulled barley is a great source of fiber, as well as manganese, phosphorus, and thiamin. It also has selenium, which increases skin elasticity and fights photodamage. Barley juice, also called barley water, is wonderful for digestion and reduces bloating.

Bulgur, a main ingredient in tabbouleh salad, has manganese, magnesium, vitamin B6, fiber, and a lot of folate. It has even more fiber than oats or buckwheat. It's a no-brainer because it cooks fast and is versatile enough for any recipe.

Wheat Germ. Organic wheat germ can be sprinkled over anything, and just a tablespoon or quarter cup throughout the day provides a kick of selenium, manganese, zinc, folate, fiber, and a huge amount of both omega fatty acids. All of these are fantastic for skin and hair, especially B vitamins like biotin, which plumps up the fat in cells in skin and strengthens the hair shaft.

Buckwheat is not edible until the hull is removed, but afterward it reveals a triangular-shaped grain, or "fruit seed," that is healthier in darker colors. It is great for skin because it is a good source of magnesium, manganese, and rutin—an antioxidant that combats inflammation and damage. It's great for hair because it has all eight amino acids. Try it hot as porridge, flat as a pancake, or roasted dry (kasha).

FRUITS

Pomegranate is high in vitamin C, vitamin K, and fiber, and more antioxidant-dense than green tea or red wine. This means it keeps skin bright and wrinkle-free, as well as possibly reducing the risk of certain cancers. The fruit has both ellagic acid and punicalagin. Ellagic acid is a compound that fights free radicals; the second is a nutrient that helps skin cells preserve collagen. Dr. Oz explains that eating these seeds will thicken the epidermis and help fibroblasts (the cells which produce collagen and elastin) live longer. It also contains polynutrients, which accelerate wound-healing. Add about one cup of pomegranate seeds—not just the juice—to the weekly routine. Eat on days with higher physical activity, because most of the calories come from sugar.

Papaya. The Taíno word *papáia* became *papaya* in Spanish (although the Australian and Caribbean namesake, *papaw* or *pawpaw*, is more recognizable in the products supermodels use; like "Lucas' Pawpaw Ointment"). Papain, also known as the "Papaya Enzyme," helps digest proteins, but it can also kill dead cells and cure impurities, brightening the skin. Overall, this fruit is full of antioxidants, and just one cup of chopped cubes has more than 100 percent of the daily recommended intake of vitamin C and one third of vitamin A. One whole medium-sized papaya mashed (or about 300 grams) would give about a third of the daily recommended intake of folate, a fifth of fiber, a fifth of potassium, one tenth of pantothenic acid, and about one tenth of magnesium. Beyond that, the seed extract is high in flavonoids and alpha hydroxy acids, which is why it (along with the pulp of this fruit) is a basic component of many facial creams and shampoos. Gently rubbing the flesh of the fruit on the skin can tighten and brighten. It's a gentle exfoliator, because papain breaks down the inactive proteins of the dead skin cells accumulating on the surface of the face. It's also especially low in sodium, which helps lock in moisture for the skin and hair.

Kiwi. Many people think that the vitamin C value of oranges and kiwis is comparable, but just 100 grams of kiwi (or about one extra-large fruit) has 155 percent of the daily recommended value, whereas 100 grams of orange has only about 89 percent. The little green superfruit comes from California in November through May and from New Zealand in June through October. It has high antioxidant properties and can defend the DNA in cells from oxygen-related damage. Also, 100 grams of kiwi offers 50 percent of vitamin K, about a tenth of potassium, and a tenth of fiber daily recommended values. Vitamin K keeps blood from clotting, prevents bone fractures, and can protect against various cancers.

Berries (strawberries, blueberries, and blackberries). Berries in general are full of antioxidants and fiber, which work best against hunger pangs and in regulating insulin. **Strawberries** are full of vitamin C, and eating about eight medium-size strawberries per day would fill the vitamin C quotient. This boosts production of collagen and keeps skin firm. The ellagic acid in strawberries takes it one step further than most vitamin C foods by protecting the elastin fibers and preventing skin from sagging. In 2004, **blueberries** were highly ranked by the department of agriculture for their antioxidant activity (wild blueberries came in at #2, regular blueberries at #5). One cup of blueberries has a concentration of nine thousand antioxidants, and the same serving of wild blueberries has a concentration of thirteen thousand. Even half a cup every day "will help to prevent the cell-structure damage that can lead to loss of firmness, fine lines and wrinkles," according to *Fitness* magazine. On that same list, **cranberry** is #6, **blackberry** is #8 and **raspberry** is #10, so working any of them into a daily routine is great for skin. To avoid sugar, prioritize raspberries, then strawberries and blackberries tied, then blueberries.

Red grapes (including red wine). Dark seedless grapes (either red or black) "contain powerful natural chemicals and antioxidants that have been shown to treat inflammatory skin conditions," reports *Glamour UK*. Not only do grapes have carotenoids (like beta-carotene) and stilbenes (like resveratrol), but their antioxidant list is so unique it brings the total number well into the hundreds. While they all make for great skin, resveratrol in particular is good at increasing cell longevity. Red grapes are a great snack because they have a low glycemic index, protecting energy levels from peaks and valleys. Plus, pesticide residues can easily be avoided just by going organic. About twenty grapes throughout the day will offer a great dose of vitamin C, vitamin K, a few omega-6 fatty acids, and a refreshing energy boost. **Red wine** is an alternative way to incorporate these nutrients into the daily routine. Deep-color red wines are not only great for your skin, but they help prevent blood clots and may slow cancer growth, as well: the resveratrol especially has powerful cancer-fighting capabilities for lymph, liver, prostate, stomach, and breast cancers. Darker color, full bodied reds, like pinot noir, are more nutritious because antioxidants originate from the pips and skins of the grape at the beginning of the process, resulting in a higher concentration of antioxidants. Also, because of its melatonin content, just one glass with dinner will improve sleep.

Olives. Just an ounce of **olive oil** is full of vitamin K, E, and omega fatty acids. It is particularly high in omega-6 fatty acids, more than some fish. All of these antioxidants prevent premature aging, as does **safflower** oil, which is lower in saturated fats. The omega-6 fatty acids found in safflower oil moisturize from the inside out. The omega-9s in olive oil, however, contain oleic acid, which is particularly moisturizing and contributes to the longevity and effectiveness of other antioxidants. When Paltrow and Turshen aren't using extra-virgin olive oil, they reach for a more neutral taste like high-quality **canola**, **grapeseed**, and safflower oil—all of which are strong in antioxidants for the skin.

Avocados grow on trees, and although they look like a vegetable, they technically are a fruit. Half a regular sized avocado (about 100 grams) brings in vitamin C, vitamin E, vitamin B6, and pantothenic acid in moderate amounts; but is particularly high in folate, vitamin K, fiber, and omega-6 fatty acids. Many of these nutrients calm the skin, reduce inflammation, and increase fat cells in the dermis for a youthful tone. And yet, it is avocado oil that is often so overlooked. The oil itself is exponentially higher in omega-6 fatty acids. In fact, one tablespoon of avocado oil is seven times more packed in omega-6 than just the fruit. Vitamin E and other antioxidants in the fruit help with dry skin and UV protection, but nutrients in the oil really give collagen production a kick. Try it as an olive oil alternative, drizzled over seafood or incorporated into mayonnaise.

(Other highly alkaline fruits not mentioned: watermelon,

banana, fresh coconut, currant, lemon, lime, persimmon, and passion fruit.)

VEGETABLES

Beets are one of the best toxin cleansers and are essential for epidermal health and healing. They have a high concentration of betalains, which gives them their pigment (and which can be found in other foods like **chard** or **rhubarb stems**). Beets give the skin antioxidant, anti-inflammatory, and detoxification support because the concentration of betalains (in the peel and in the flesh) is higher than any other food. However, the betalains can be damaged by too much heat in cooking. It's best to eat beets raw or steamed for only about fifteen minutes or roasted for an hour or less. In addition to betalains, beets are an awesome source of folate (which improves cell production in the skin and hair); only two raw beets are great for manganese, potassium, and vitamin C. They also offer lutein and zeaxanthin, antioxidants that increase circulation, a wonderful plus for feeding nutrients to the skin.

Dark greens (like kale and spinach). Although they may not seem to be water-filled foods, they have a strong moisturizing effect, from the inside out, as their water molecules penetrate skin cell membranes. One cup of **kale** is loaded with vitamin C, vitamin A, manganese, omega fatty acids and a ton of vitamin K. **Spinach** also has wrinkle-fighting antioxidants (such as vitamin C,

A, and K). Both also have lutein, which makes eyes healthier and protects skin from UV damage. Research published in the *Journal of Agricultural and Food Chemistry* showed that 'Spinach stored in light for as little as three days had significantly higher levels of vitamins C, K, E, and folate," as well as more of the healthful carotenoids, lutein, and zeaxanthin. Three cups of either kale or spinach throughout the week is a minimum, but through salads, fresh squeezed juices, and omelets the intake could easily be higher. Another plus, says Dr. Oz, is that they "[s]low cognitive decline even more than fruits. Eating two or more servings a day (just two!) decreases the decline in thinking by 35 percent over six years." Smarts and skin, a winning combination.

Tomatoes. This salad staple can reduce the chance of getting a sunburn, says Dr. Oz, and its nutrients are best absorbed when combined with some lipids (fat cells), as found in a few walnuts. While fresh tomatoes can easily find their way into our daily routine, the best form for your skin is tomato paste. Lycopene, the red pigment in tomatoes, is absorbed better when it is cooked or processed, so include canned tomato sauce, tomato juice, and ketchup in your weekly meal plan. Lycopene stimulates the skin and helps keep it from turning red when in contact with UV light. Volunteers who consumed five tablespoons of tomato paste daily for three months had 25 percent more protection against sunburn, according to one study. (Note: lycopene can also be found in **pink grapefruit**.) Tomatoes both fresh and cooked are high in vitamin C and firm the skin by boosting the production of collagen. According to Paltrow and Turshen, canned tomatoes are a favored ingredient in many of their recipes "because they are already peeled and ready to go." Just remember: raw tomatoes are slightly more alkaline than canned or pasted.

Red bell peppers. Vitamin C is a wrinkle-fighting antioxidant and, like its bright red superfood-friend tomato paste, red bell pepper is powerfully nutritious for the skin. Only half a cup of chopped red pepper gives more than 100 percent of the daily recommended value of vitamin C. But it doesn't end there; that same amount gets you halfway to vitamin A and one fifth to vitamin B6 daily recommended intakes. All of these nutrients plump up the skin and keep the hair healthy. Paltrow and Turshen use a Korean red pepper paste in their recipes called gochujang, which is made from a mix of chili peppers and rice flour.

Broccoli is high in vitamin C, with only 100 grams offering 149 percent of the daily recommended value. That's a close tie with kiwi. Unlike kiwi, however, broccoli surpasses the daily recommended value of vitamin K, offering 127 percent for every 100 grams (a little more than one cup chopped). It has about 10 percent of vitamin A, 10 percent potassium, 10 percent manganese, 10 percent dietary fiber, and a little more than 10 percent of the daily recommended level of folate. These antioxidants are what increase the luminosity in the skin and restore damaged tissue. This veggie by itself has about half the omega-6 value of salmon, and these fatty acids, as well as calcium and folate, "support the healing process and aid the proper function of skin cells," *Glamour UK* reports.

Broccoli is also a boost for hair. Vitamins A and C will stimulate production of sebum, the oil secretion that acts as a natural moisturizer for the scalp and hair. Broccoli seed oil is particularly beneficial. It's packed with hair-nourishing vitamins, for increased strength and silkiness. The oil has a unique fatty acid composition similar to silicone in shampoos, an omega-9 fatty acid, also known as erucic acid, which gives the hair a smooth sheen without leaving the residue that harmful chemicals would.

Sweet potato. Beta-carotene converts to vitamin A in digestion, so the orange-colored sweet potato loaded with beta-carotene can do a lot for skin. Vitamin A helps cells renew faster and one derivative, called retinoid, is a staple in expensive skin products. A medium sweet potato has almost 400 percent of the daily recommended intake. It is also a good source of manganese, potassium, vitamin B6, and vitamin C. Eating sweet potatoes will improve circulation, which gets more oxygen and nutrients to skin cells. "The women of Okinawa, Japan (who also happen to be the world's longest living ladies), enjoy a purple sweet potato they call imo every day for breakfast, lunch and dinner," says Dr. Oz. This purple variety is still a sweet potato, but has 150 percent more antioxidants than blueberries.

Garlic. The allicin in garlic is capable of killing off many harmful bacteria, which is why it can help with acne and other skin infections. It will also increase circulation and bring more nutrients to the skin.

Artichokes. Boiled artichokes are a good source of vitamin C, K, manganese, and folate (which works against the formation of free radicals). Peptides can smooth fine lines, and the minerals may bring new life to dry hair. They can even strengthen the scalp and help with dandruff. Besides increasing circulation, they also reduce cholesterol, enhancing liver health (which in turn, keeps the blood clean and the skin luminous).

(Other highly alkaline vegetables not mentioned: turmeric root, ginger root, cayenne celery, kelp, seaweeds, parsley, watercress, asparagus, alfalfa sprouts, cabbage, cauliflower, squash, turnip, onion, taro root, lotus root, parsnip, arugula, endive, and mustard greens.)

PROTEIN (EGGS, FISH, NUTS)

Eggs. Egg yolks are full of selenium, zinc, and protein—all of which clear the skin and keep it clear. One study found that eggs help protect against lines, brown spots, and cancer because of two important antioxidants: lutein and zeaxanthin. Women in this study reported softer, firmer, and better hydrated skin. One medium-size egg (about two ounces) contains more than 10 percent of the daily recommended value of riboflavin, about 10 percent of vitamin B12 and phosphorous, and one fifth of the daily recommended value of selenium. It also has biotin, folic acid, and high levels of choline. Egg protein "[p]lays an important role in skin health by providing a source of amino acids," reports the Livestrong Foundation. "Your body uses these amino acids to generate new proteins within your skin cells. Some of these proteins—such as collagen and elastin—lend strength to your skin tissue, while others—such as melanin—contribute to your skin's color." Eggs even have 100 percent of the carotenoids essential for eye health, just an added bonus. For Paltrow and Turshen, locally farmed organic eggs are the favorite, either from chickens, ducks, or quails.

Fish (salmon, tuna, mackerel, sardines, and anchovies). Less than half a filet, or 100 grams, of cooked wild (not farm-raised) **Atlantic Salmon** has more than two thousand mg of omega-3 fatty acids and two-hundred mg of omega-6 fatty acids. "Omega-3s contain alpha-linolenic acid, which decreases dryness and keeps skin soft, smooth, and supple," writes Dr. Oz. All fatty fish, like salmon, tuna, or mackerel, reduce inflammation and keep the pores open, helping to prevent acne. Salmon also contains astaxanthin (the carotenoid that makes it pink), which along with omega-3 makes skin and hair appear younger, says Dr. Oz. Salmon also has selenium, which helps protect against sun exposure. Note: Paltrow and Turshen only use fish (of whatever species) that have been caught as close to the kitchen as possible, so talk to the local market to learn more.

Tuna. This is a bit slippery to pin down because there are so many varieties (at least fourteen, if you count all canned and cooked options). For canned, avoid white and choose light; more specifically, light tuna canned in oil and without salt. This canned choice offers over two hundred mg of omega-3s and over two thousand mg of omega-6, for every 100 grams—almost an opposite match to salmon. It is also high in selenium, niacin, phosphorus, and vitamin B12. For cooked tuna, choose fresh bluefin cooked on dry heat. This offers a higher ratio of omega-3s to omega-6s, similar to the balance of salmon, but levels of both are slightly lower than the canned option. Cooked tuna still has a lot of selenium, niacin, phosphorus, and vitamin B12 to offer, as well as more vitamin B6 than the canned choice.

Mackerel. Also a great choice for your skin, but avoid Spanish, Gulf, and especially king mackerel because of high mercury content. North Atlantic and Pacific chub varieties are best. Although Atlantic mackerel is higher in fatty acids raw rather than cooked whereas Pacific is higher cooked rather than raw (note, for the next sushi night), their levels aren't that different and are pretty high overall. Both leave you with "glowing, radiant complexion and spot-free skin," reports *Glamour UK*, and are loaded with, "eicosapentaenoic acid (EPA) and docosahexaenoic acid (DHA), both of which combat acne."

Sardines and Anchovies. Atlantic sardines canned in oil and European anchovies canned in oil are both great for your skin, but sardines get the blue ribbon. They are absolutely packed with omega-3 and 6 fatty acids, as well as selenium, phosphorus, calcium, vitamin D, niacin, and a ton of vitamin B12. Not only do sardines provide "key nutrients for skin health and disease prevention," but they also highly boost "skin thickness and elasticity," according to the Livestrong Foundation.

Oysters. Like salmon, oysters contain skin-clearing nutrients; however, oysters can be wild or farm-raised (with some benefits from each). Farm-raised are less likely to be infected with norovirus or salmonella, but wild oysters are full of natural nutrients from the ocean. "Unlike fish, oysters don't need to be fed," explains W&T Seafood on their website. "Instead, oysters act like a sponge, absorbing and filtering minerals and nutrients from the water around them." Again, there are several varieties, but raw emu oysters are relatively low in nutrients overall, so avoid that variety. Both wild eastern mollusk oysters and Pacific mollusk oysters are less nutritious eaten raw or cooked in dry heat and are best when cooked in moist heat. Farmed eastern oysters are better cooked than raw. All oysters are a good source of zinc, which aids in skin cell renewal and repair. In fact, this high zinc food combined with foods high in vitamin C increases elastin, creates collagen, and will even result in stronger nails.

Almonds. Commonly thought of as nuts, these superseeds can be paired with foods containing selenium to enhance antioxidant ability. Almonds and cottage cheese, for example, would be a supersnack for your skin. About thirty almonds (or 1 ounce) have over a third of the daily recommended value of vitamin E. Volunteers in one study consumed 14 milligrams of Vitamin E each day (about twenty almonds) and proved less sunburned than those who did not, *Women's Health* reports. They are also particularly high in omega-6 fatty acids, about fifty times as much as salmon. Almonds can help fight free radicals and even oxidative damage caused by pollution, according to a recent study from the Chinese Center for Disease Control and Prevention. Although it's not as nutritiously potent as the seed itself, Paltrow and Turshen use almond milk (plain unsweetened), almond meal, and almond butter in many of their recipes.

Superseeds (like chia, pumpkin, and flax). The chia seed is an oldie but goodie. An ancient grain used by the Aztecs as their main energy source, "chia can help restore energy levels and decrease inflammation because of its omega-3 fatty acids" says Dr. Oz. "Similar to corn starch, chia can be used as a thickening agent and as a substitute for whole grains." Only one ounce of Chia seeds has almost half the daily recommended value of fiber. They have three times as much calcium as skim milk. And they have ten times as many omega-3 fatty acids as wild salmon, improving skin because omega-3 fatty acids strengthen cell membranes by protecting them and providing moisture. "They're a sneaky diet tool, too: Since they absorb up to ten times their weight in water, they keep you feeling fuller longer," says nutritionist Keri Glassman for *Allure* magazine.

Very high in omega-3 fatty acids, **pumpkin seeds** also provide copper, zinc, and magnesium. Any deficiencies in these minerals have been linked to acne flare-ups—just another reason for why these seeds really help. **Flaxseed** should also be a weekly staple. Although quite high in minerals like selenium, copper, phosphorus, and magnesium, the tiny flaxseed is particularly high in manganese. They are also rich in omega-3 fatty acids (more so than chia or pumpkin), which work in the skin to diminish fine lines and spots.

Supernuts (like brazil or walnuts). **Brazil nuts** are large in size and can seem awkward to incorporate in meals at first, but just one kernel (or 5 grams) offers 137 percent of the daily recommended value of selenium. They do have a little saturated fat, but they are a healthy addition to any snack—especially when paired with foods high in vitamin E. Any deficiencies in zinc and selenium can exacerbate acne. **Walnuts** are also great for skin because they are rich in alpha-linolenic acid, an omega-3 fat that keeps skin lubricated and supple. Just half an ounce of walnuts would offer 100 percent of the recommended daily intake of ALA. One ounce (or about seven shelled walnuts) has half the daily value of manganese, one fifth of copper, and one tenth of phosphorus, magnesium, fiber, folate, and vitamin B6. Also, one ounce of walnuts offers five times as much omega-3 fatty acids as salmon and has more than one hundred seventy-five times as much omega-6 fatty acids. Researchers recently discovered that walnuts contain melatonin, a hormone that regulates snooze patterns.

OTHER

Green tea. Although both green and black teas fight free radicals, green tea is higher in polyphenols and antioxidants. Polyphenols give these teas their bitter flavor. The antioxidant value in both of these teas could be even higher than that of vitamin C foods. They are the best teas to choose because green tea leaves in particular are young and have not yet been oxidized, so they have up to 40 percent more polyphenols than black tea. However, "green tea has one-third the caffeine of black tea … [and yet] it's shown to yield the same level of energy and attentiveness" without the ups and downs associated with other caffeinated drinks, says Oz. Just don't drink it with milk, since "the casein in milk has been shown to inhibit the beneficial effects of tea." The caffeine in these teas kills ultraviolet-damaged skin cells (which could turn precancerous). The antioxidants in the tea start to degrade as it cools, so drink up when hot. A study in the *Journal of Nutritional Biochemistry* found that drinking two to six cups each day can reverse the effects of sun damage in cells as well as protect against UV radiation, making this drink a skin savior.

Dark chocolate. Flavonols in organic dark chocolate are powerful antioxidants and, among other things, heal rough skin and protect it against UV rays. In a study published in the *Journal of Nutrition*, women who drank cocoa fortified with flavonols reported improved skin texture and resistance to the sun compared to those who drank lower levels. Although just a few ounces per day is enough, the package should indicate at least 60 percent cacao in order for flavonol content to be effective. The same reason dark chocolate makes us smile is the reason it can increase cell turnover in the skin: it boosts endorphins and serotonin, two chemicals not only responsible for happiness but which also suppress stress.

TIMING

Breakfast. Ayurvedic scholars recommend foods from the sattvic or sentient diets early in the day, including: cereal grains, legumes, vegetables, fruits, nuts, unpasteurized and unhomogenized fresh milk, fresh milk derivatives (like ghee, butter, cream, cottage cheese, or paneer), yogurt (or lassi), raw honey … and plenty of water.

Lunch. Reach for dark leafy greens and, if possible, add wild Alaskan salmon to salad for improved skin elasticity. Salads should be loaded with key foods because, as Sachs adds, the largest meal must be midday when agni (or metabolism) peaks. In warmer months, make sure this time of day is an opportunity to eat foods high in water content, says Sachs.

Dinner. In the mellow evening hours, choose light, well-portioned meals such as soup, steamed vegetables, or whole grain breads. Be careful with hard-to-digest foods at this time of day, like citrus fruits, root vegetables, yogurt, and anything even lightly fried. Dr. Oz suggests one glass of alcohol, preferably deep color red wines high in resveratrol.

In-between. Snacks are key. They may be large or small, depending on your level of activity. For midmorning, Oz suggests fruit and nuts with a cup of green tea, or natural teeth whiteners such as carrot slices or apple wedges. In the slump period, which usually comes between two p.m. and six p.m., Sachs suggests choices based on skin type. For dry skin, choose roasted nuts or a warm bagel and light cream cheese with a cup of hot herbal tea. For sensitive skin, go for juicy cold watermelon in summer or a pear or apple in the winter. Finally, oily skin can choose grapes, pumpkin seeds, or sliced apple with cinnamon.

Throughout the day, think: more meals and smaller meals. It is better to eat lighter in warmer weather, when digestive fire is naturally weakest, and more heartily in the cold when agni (or metabolism) is at its strongest. Try to eat your main meals at the same time every day. Leave three to six hours between meals, and avoid eating at least two hours before actually going to sleep. Going to bed on a full stomach allows undigested food to produce ama (or toxins in the digestive tract).

Make food choices as local and as fresh as possible. Find foods that were grown within a four-hundred-mile radius of the area in which you live. "All stale foods and leftovers (more than a day old) lack prana," or life-giving energy, says Sachs, "and create toxins in the body."

Also choose foods that are seasonal and organic. All organic is richer in nutrients, especially trace minerals. Organic food is also a healthier choice because there are no pesticides, no growth hormones, no antibiotics, no irradiation, no sewage sludge, and no genetically modified organisms. (About that "sewage sludge": apparently, "[c]onventional foods in the United States can be grown in a mud-like by-product from sewage-treatment plants," writes James, "which, because it was considered hazardous, was banned by the government ... Industrial and domestic hazardous waste and chemicals survive the sewage-treatment process [and make their way into the food].")

Also, try to find food that comes from grass-fed animals. "Not all organic animals are grass-fed," says James. But those that are "have been found to contain healthy nutrients that have all but disappeared from conventional meats, such as omega-3 fatty acids and conjugated linolenic acid (CLA), which has been shown to promote fat loss and possibly prevent cancer."

While eating, watch out for patterns that will put peaks and valleys in your energy throughout the day. This can mainly be done by being sensitive to high glycemic index foods. Insulin normalizes blood sugar levels throughout the body. Insulin resistance is a condition in which the cells build up tolerance to insulin, making the body less effective at doing its job of keeping blood sugar levels stable. Foods and beverages containing any refined sugars can cause insulin resistance and, consequently, blood sugar spikes throughout the day.

"Get gorgeous by going low-glycemic index," says James. "High glycemic index foods are based on white flour or sugar, such as pasta, starchy vegetables (potatoes and corn, for example) and conventional candies, desserts, and baked goods ... The lower a meal's GI rating, the kinder it is to your body and skin, the more slimming it is, and the more stable your mood, energy, and blood-sugar levels." Plus, eating sugar and high GI foods induces glycation and collagen crosslinking—a process that causes wrinkles.

Avoid simple sugars at all costs, says Dr. Oz. They end in *-ose*: like glucose, sucrose, maltose, and dextrose (although not ribose), or syrups (another word for sugar), any grain except for 100 percent whole grains (since grains turn into simple sugar), and any saturated trans-fats. Sachs lists other foods that have an unbalancing effect: coffee, black tea, caffeinated drinks, very hot peppers and very pungent spices, iodized salt, too much alcohol (especially grain alcohol, such as vodka, whiskey, and rum).

Some major *don'ts* are agreed on by all the experts. These

are "toxic foods" or "foods low in pranic energy—that is, they are lifeless," according to Sachs. Never eat chemically fed, chemically treated, genetically altered, or irradiated foods, says Sachs. That also goes for chemically preserved, processed, canned, and frozen foods; artificial sweeteners, artificial coloring, and "no fat" or "low fat" foods made with fat substitutes. Avoid buying foods containing dye or MSG, and avoid deep-fried foods or those cooked in reused oils (hydrogenated oil, animal fat, shortening, or margarine).

Next ... spice up your food. Not just to improve taste, but to enhance nutrition. Start with spices that are slightly higher in antioxidants. According to Copeland, cumin, rosemary, and thyme are the most potent. Still, "just about every spice studied," writes James, "has been found to have unique health properties, including antibacterial and antifungal actions."

Her strongest suggestions include: cinnamon, cayenne, cilantro, and turmeric. Select organic, unprocessed cinnamon, which does not include sugar. It has antibacterial capabilities and can improve metabolism, according to a USDA study. Cayenne curbs appetite and makes you feel full before you are full. Cilantro is great for a cleanse; it grabs heavy metals and carries them out of the body. Turmeric has anti-inflammatory, anti-cancer, and liver protective benefits.

Paltrow and Turshen celebrate the ability of spices to bring out unique flavors in foods. Many of their recipes use Old Bay Seasoning, but they also include an interesting, lesser known product called Chinese five-spice powder: a mix of ginger, cloves, black pepper, cinnamon, and fennel.

Sensitive stomachs can be eased with a tea made from cumin, coriander, and fennel seed, which ease digestion. Post-dinner, try a mild, warm ginger tea. According to James, ginger improves digestion, eases nausea, improves circulation, and is being researched as a heart tonic. Consider finishing each meal with a lassi or yogurt drink with live acidophilus bacteria, which helps digestion. To improve good bacteria in general, eat plain yogurt and drink kefir (always unsweetened). Also incorporate garlic into each meal—it kills yeast and many bacteria.

Depending on whether you live on a farm or in the city, daily meals must be supplemented because, unfortunately, food isn't as nutritious as we think. According to Dr. Oz, a morning supplement should include one half of a multivitamin (a pill with at least 500 IU of vitamin D, 600 mg of calcium and 200 mg of magnesium); 600 mg of DHA (omega-3 fatty acids), either by itself or in 2 grams of fish/cod liver oil. Finally, take all with a full glass of water. The other half of the multivitamin should be taken at dinner (or around six thirty p.m.).

When choosing supplements, check the labels and look for as "natural" as possible, says Raichur. The more synthetic they are the more they will aggravate digestion. This is especially true for vitamin E, which must be bought in natural form. Sometimes an oil-based capsule is better for absorption, as in the case of Coenzyme Q_{10} (CoQ_{10}). Avoid the cheapest vitamins and generic drugstore brands, says James. They are the ones most likely to contain di-calcium phosphate, cellulose, or other fillers. And avoid "little pills that have 100 percent of all the Recommended Dietary Allowances (RDAs)," she says. "They're useless. One little pill cannot give you everything you need."

Taking EFAs (essential fatty acids) can actually help release fat from the body, says James. This would include flax, borage, evening primrose, and fish oils. About 2 grams per day of fish oil capsules is equivalent to 13 ounces of fish a week, says Dr. Oz. It is also possible to take smaller capsules of DHA, like 400 mg for women and 600 mg for men. These can come from purified algae (also called a vegetarian or plant source) because that's where the fish themselves get these oils.

If you're taking fat-soluble vitamins like D3, you need some fat in your stomach and intestines, so take DHA before the rest of your vitamins. There are also certain ways to take vitamin E and C that are better than others. Look for mixed tocopherols rather than just alpha-tocopherol (for vitamin E), says James. Look for bioflavonoids, like quercetin, rather than just vitamin C. Many people take probiotics, but check to make sure labels contain acidophilus or other strains of beneficial bacteria, says James. These are the ingredients that rebalance the good bacteria in the gut for better digestion and immunity.

Other supplements can enhance specific attributes or alleviate problems. To prevent oily skin and hair loss take GLA (gamma-linolenic acid), which inhibits the enzyme responsible for strong oil production and thinning hair. James also suggests zinc gluconate supplements for acne, or MSM as topical or supplement (a better utilized form of sulfur). For those working on weight loss regimens or resizing portions, hydroxycitric acid both curbs appetite and blocks the synthesis of body fat, says James.

Some of the best supplements are available as superfoods. Raichur suggests spiraling, blue-green algae, young grain powders, and sea vegetable tablets, for example. Green powder, suggested by James, includes barley grass, spirulina, and wheatgrass. Other supplements based on superfoods, says James, would be those with turmeric and green tea, or phytochemicals like ellagic acid, or a lycopene-lutein combination; or just superfoods themselves, like chlorella.

If you are totally stumped, bring back an oldie but goodie: chyawanprash. Some experts say it goes back two thousand five hundred years and others say ten thousand. Either way, this ancient vitamin comes from the Ayurvedic tradition and looks a bit like blackberry jam. Ingredients usually include a cooked mixture of raw honey, triphala, ghee, sesame oil, and berries along with other herbs and spices. Today, it is widely sold in India and works to prevent disease and truly strengthen the immune system. Consume one tablespoon per day either plain or stirred in with warm milk or water. The potency of triphala and alma fruit make chyawanprash a healthy beauty supplement.

HOW TO EAT

One reason why it's important to have a general understanding of these healthy choices is that we have to appreciate the boundaries and limitations of our own circumstance. "Practical strategies make all the difference," James continues. "Your best intentions will inevitably be affected by convenience and practical limitations imposed by your daily routines and environment." There are always logistics to deal with, so find affordable ways to slowly iron out change until it feels like healthy choices are a gradual evolution as opposed to a forced deadline.

Nothing should be forced. In fact, nothing should be negative. There are so many reasons for why feeding must include joy. Begin your meal with a blessing, says Sachs. If that's not your thing, or "if you are not comfortable with prayer, try just taking a quiet moment—the time it takes for two full breaths—to appreciate the beauty of the meal on your table and your own capacity to savor it.

"Actually look at the different foods on your plate before you pick up your fork," Sachs continues. "Use all your senses: smell the aromas, notice the array of colors and what is hot or cold, feel the steam, be still and listen to your breath. Bringing conscious awareness in this way to the simple joy of eating also helps to relieve compulsive eating habits, which are be definition unconscious patterns of behavior." Raichur suggests giving thanks before and after meals.

Remember to taste the food. "Let all your senses savor the meal," says Sachs. "Eat at a modest pace and eat with the whole mouth. Taste the food; notice its different flavors on the tongue (sweet, salty, sour, and bitter in order from tip to back); feel its changing textures; pay attention to changes in your mood and physiology; listen to your body. Eating this way is actually a remarkable experience. You will discover sensations you probably never noticed before, and a level of pleasure and satisfaction from your food that you probably never imagined."

Although it may be difficult to control, or even consider, unconscious behavior—the emotions involved while cooking, during eating, or even when serving—is all relevant to healthy eating. "Energetically, the emotions we carry into the kitchen to cook affect the food we eat as much as those we carry to the dining table," Sachs writes. "Thoughts get added to the mix like extra herbs and spices in a recipe: the cooks care and attention enhance the life force in food."

Never eat when you are upset, even just a little bit. "Take a few minutes before you sit down to eat to address your worries or upsets ... You do not necessarily have to resolve problems on the spot, but at least acknowledge them, decide on when or how you will address them, and then set them aside with the understanding that you will return to them, at the appropriate time," says Sachs. "When you bring your concerns into your conscious awareness in this way, you diminish their power to control you. You may discover that merely committing yourself to a time when you will resolve a problem relieves your mind of its weight. Then you are free to eat your meal without angers or fears eating at you."

For related reasons, this is why Ayurveda asks that you cleanse before eating: wash the body, wash the hands, wash the feet, or cleanse the mind with meditation. "We nourish the spirit while cooking by offering blessings for the food and love and benefit to those who will eat it. Choose a manner of doing this that suits you," she says. Find some prayers or meditations that flow with your cooking style, or "chant or sing as you work."

Without the dwarfs from *Snow White* in your head singing, "Whistle While You Work," try to let mindful meditations or rituals "increase the joy of the activity, not the burden of your labor. More than anything, it is a matter of your intention and the quality of your attention as you work." With all these thoughts, advisors, and texts to consider, what matters at the end of the day is our inner voice. In her own words, Sachs says, "Open your awareness to the bounty and beauty of nature as you handle and prepare her foods for your nourishment."

***

The word *cosmetic* comes from the Greek *kosmetikos*, meaning "skill in arranging." Back in the 1930s, when Jean Harlow's painted face was all the rage, she sported sculpted brows and platinum hair that (some might say) gave her the boldness to convince strangers she was the ultimate heroine.

And yet, diving deeper into the Greek origin reveals another definition. The root word *kosmos* means "order." The Greek mathematician Pythagoras used the word *cosmos* to describe starry skies. At first, the word *cosmetic* seems to refer to manipulating something original: hiding, covering up, or distorting our natural state. However, ordering nature can also mean taking care of nature. A cosmetic can be something that increases the appreciation of natural design (the natural structure of the hair follicle, the pleasant symmetry of facial features, and all other extraordinarily well arranged aspects of our physical reality).

Perhaps the real question is, do you want to be someone else or do you want to be yourself? For now, let's think of makeup as the former—a tool for making up a new identity, such as in performance—and instead liken cosmetics to skin care: or enhancing, protecting, and sustaining skin health.

Why do we need cosmetics or tools at all? Why not just leave nature be?

Unfortunately, almost nothing about our modern environment is purely natural. The body—including the skin and the hair—needs to be protected and nurtured. Otherwise, its health is too determined by an outside environment designed more for capitalism than for health. More people live in cities, says Sachs, and are constantly exposed to dirt, pollution, and stress. It's hard to effortlessly maintain health (or "natural beauty") when toxins are in most of our food, water, and air.

The skin is a living organ and so, like all others, it has scientifically defined "healthy" and "unhealthy" states. "Skin is composed of two layers," explains Copeland. "The epidermis (the part you see) and the dermis underneath." The dermis is the thickest layer of the skin and "holds you together." It contains fibroblast cells which make the collagen and elastin proteins that give skin its strength. Also, "dotting the dermis are hair follicles, sweat glands, and sebaceous glands, which produce the oily sebum that lubricates your skin and hair," Oz writes. The skin feeds through tiny blood vessels, bringing nourishment, while the main lymph nodes help to drain toxins away.

Although the epidermis is the body's main barrier, it's less than a millimeter thick, so only the smallest of molecules can get through. Skin renews itself every six to eight weeks, so the epidermis largely determines how fresh you look. The outward signs of aging are caused by the inward life of the fibroblasts. Although they produce both collagen and elastin, they are quite prone to damage from UV radiation. The skin also secretes fat, but these ceramides actually help protect the outer layer of skin for better hydration and lower susceptibility to irritation. We have to wash the skin gently because "washing with fat emulsifiers, like soap and alcohol," can alter pH balance too much and damage skin's natural protection, Oz adds.

This relationship between the dermis and epidermis is generally universal; however, race and ethnicity play a role. African, Asian, and Hispanic skins have greater amounts of subcutaneous fat tissue, so they often appear to be less wrinkled than Caucasians as they age, and are better at resisting the effects of UV radiation (to a point). Also, as Ayurvedic tradition states, it is important to identify your own unique qualities and understand your vata, kapha, or pitta skin type (dry, oily, and sensitive, respectively).

Skin care requires both self-evaluation and education on the products out there. We need to understand products too and, unfortunately, most companies don't make it that simple. Ingredients listed on skin care packaging is often indiscernible. While it is important to check for allergens, we also need to learn how to recognize irritants, dehydrators, carcinogens, and other compounds that sometimes do not accomplish what the packaging promises.

Why does it matter so much?

As Sachs puts it, "[I]f you were offered a meal made with acetyl alcohol, iodopropynyl butylcarbamate, sodium dodecylbenzenesulfonate, disodium EDTA, BHT, red dye #17, and yellow dye #10, would you want to eat it?" The skin happens to be one of the body's major organs for consumption. She continues, "[A]lthough we get most of our nutrition orally, the skin ingests nutrients as well. In fact, unlike the food we chew and swallow, which is broken down in the stomach before it is absorbed, creams and lotions applied to the skin bypass the digestive process and go full strength into the bloodstream."

There are multiple options for ingredients and products, but the Ayurvedic method is the most pure approach and calls for plant-based skin care products. "Skin is alive, and lifeless chemicals cannot give life back to the skin. Synthetic molecules lack intelligence, or what Deepak Chopra calls the self-contained 'know-how' of the building blocks in living organisms to preserve balance and internal stability."

Extracting plant nutrients and formatting them into an effective product is a process still under technological development, making most choices more expensive than the average drugstore cream. Nevertheless, Raichur provides convincing motivation:

> To be "alive," beauty products and topical remedies for the skin should be made purely of plants, or any of their parts or pure extracts, which are balanced by nature and full of the intelligence—the vibratory energy—that constitutes life. By plants we mean all forms of vegetation, including trees, flowers, fruits, vegetables, herbs and spices. Technically speaking, plants are differentiated from herbs by their woody stems above the ground. Plants also include spices, which comprise all *pungent* plant substances such as cinnamon and cloves.

Ultimately, the word cosmetics "perfectly reflects the ancient belief that beauty, indeed, is born of harmonizing your lifestyle as well as bringing order to the mind and inner workings of the body," writes Sachs. Better that we prevent a problem than react to it; as Sachs puts it, the healthy body "prefers routine over chaos." Here are the conditions and techniques for the healthiest possible skin.

***

UNHEALTHY

Alcohol. If it's near the end of the list on a product it's okay, but if it's in the middle or the top it will always be too drying.

Petroleum. Petroleum forms an occlusive layer over the skin; "nothing can get in or out," says Copeland. It can be an effective ingredient in a product for injuries or for stopping bleeding, but is misunderstood as lip balm, for example.

Silicone, Lanolin, and **Dimethicone**. Popular in anti-wrinkle and acne products, these ingredients are not actually healthy for the bloodstream, and dimethicone is a known carcinogen. Particularly in wrinkle-fighting products, avoid **alpha hydroxy acids**, **beta hydroxy,** and long-term **glycolic acid** use, says James. When applied to the skin before makeup, they can often cause the makeup to look blotchy. Also, avoid **Retin-A** or **Renova** because they are synthetic vitamin A derivatives and can be dehydrating, James adds. Particularly for acne, avoid **benzoyl peroxide**, **tetracycline,** and **Accutane** because they are too harsh for regular use.

Heptapeptides and **collagen complex**. They are often pricey and added to many plumping products as a "miracle" ingredient. However, collagen complex is actually a derivative of animal tissue and has "no effect on the skin's own collagen, according to medical experts," says Sachs.

Sachs has the best advice on how to discern the fine print. Summarized, she suggests avoiding:

> **chemical dyes** (FD&C colors, D&C colors, HC colors or peroxide dyes), **fragrances** (meaning synthetic fragrances, otherwise it would say "essential oils"), **detergents** (NDELA formed with either TEA, DEA, MEA, sodium lauryl sulfate), **petroleum** (paraffin, mineral oil), **bleaching agents** (hydroquinone), **drying agents** (phenols), **surfactants** (PEG-8 or polyethylene glycol), **emollients** (mineral oil, lanolin, silicones such as dimethicone, fatty alcohols such as cetyl alcohol, stearyl alcohol, myristyl alcohol, and triglycerides such as vegetable oil), **emulsifiers** (glyceryl stearates, laureth 4, beeswax, cetearyl alcohol, polysorbate 60 & 80), **preservatives** and **parabens** (such as methyl and propyl), **certain antioxidants** such as BHA, BHT or tocopherol, and **animal products** like lanolin or ceteareth 20 (made from sperm whale oil). The most dangerous and potential **poisons** are formaldehyde, propyl alcohol, tolune 2, 4 diamine and EDTA.

Sachs warns against this whole list in detail, but in general we can gather that they are all substances that clog pores, cause blackheads, cause metabolic stress, initiate baldness, interfere with vitamin absorption, are potential allergens, cause fetal abnormalities, and are FDA-suspected carcinogens or known carcinogens.

HEALTHY

Remove makeup. Regardless of how fast they are, avoid chemical makeup removers. Pure, plain vegetable oil on a cotton ball is enough. Try sesame oil for dry skin types and sunflower or safflower oil for sensitive and oily skin, suggests Sachs.

Wash (the face). Wash the face twice a day and always after exercise. The pores are most vulnerable when the body is heated—don't let sweat and dirt seep in and stay there. Wash with warm water at a comfortable temperature and then splash with cool. Warm water opens up the tissues and then a cool shower sends blood shooting to the skin's surface, making it best ready for nourishment. Water that is too hot dehydrates skin by removing too much inherent oil, says Copeland.

Avoid "average" soap. "Most [soaps] dry the skin and alter its pH balance causing it to become more alkaline." If the skin is exposed to too many drying products, it will begin to produce excessive oil—either an origin or exacerbation of acne. There is an acid mantle (like cellophane), says Oz, that forms a protective layer over the face and body to prohibit the growth of harmful bacteria, fungi, and so on. Introducing even ordinary soap results in losing that acidity.

If you do choose soap, Oz suggests picking "the simplest [because] … every added chemical increases the likelihood of skin irritation." The shorter the ingredients list the better. Specifically, he suggests "saponified olive oil, with a small amount of an essential oil such as lavender or peppermint."

The nontraditional, Ayurvedic option (as Sachs and Raichur suggest) is a soft herbal cleanser mixed with warm water or milk, usually in powder form, called an "ubtan." The powder mixes with the skin and moisture upon contact and makes a light, creamy lather. Ayurvedic recipes ask for only herbs and essential oils appropriate for the skin type.

Wash (the body). "Baths are holy," writes Sachs. "That is, they purify us and make us whole." Eastern philosophy aside, whether it's a bath or shower, bathe again in warm water or cool water, never hot and cold. Apply the same logic for body soaps. She cautions against harsh scrubs (like loofas or chemical powders) and suggests rubbing with a towel instead.

Exfoliate. Although most people don't need to exfoliate every day, every other day or a weekly routine is healthiest. The skin sheds at a rate of a million cells per hour, so whatever the skin type, we all need mild exfoliation to remove dead cells. Exfoliating stimulates the epidermis for new cell growth and prepares it for whatever nourishing properties can aid in cellular rejuvenation. The worst choice is a scrub made of jagged, uneven, or naturally shaped particles (like salt). Scrubs made with beads or perfectly spherical exfoliators tear the skin less. Ultimately, a chemical exfoliant is safest for weekly use, like glycolic acid. A glycolic acid wash, with few other ingredients, can successfully combine the steps of washing and exfoliating, depending on skin type.

Eye care. The skin around the eyes is especially delicate. Sachs recommends many healthy eye treatments, but one in particular is a wash made of fennel or eyebright tea. Once cooled, bathe each eye by blinking in the wash. To cure bloodshot eyes, dip cotton pads in slightly cool rosewater and place over eyes and lie down for ten minutes. For thicker lashes and brows, put on a touch of castor oil or olive oil nightly.

Tone. When the skin is clean and fresh, try a toner or mister. Oily skin types can tone with a mild herbal astringent applied with a cotton ball. Mists for dry or sensitive skin can be pure spring water, herbal tea, or water enhanced with minerals (appropriate details can be found in Ayurvedic recipes). Mists bring vitality back to the complexion, says Sachs, especially during travel or a stressful day at work.

Right after washing the face is the best time to treat acne, and the purest Ayurvedic treatments include ingredients from grains. Azelaic acid is a naturally occurring compound in certain grains and is sometimes prescribed for acne, says James. Similar are phospholipids, tea-tree oil, and essential oils like neem or neroli oil.

Nourish. Serums feed the skin best because their molecules are smaller than moisturizers so they can travel deep and deliver essential antioxidants effectively. For most skin, a serum is only necessary during the day. (At night, the steps of nourishing and moisturizing are combined. More on that later.)

Some Ayurvedic serums use fresh-cut fruits, juices, teas, and dry crushed leaves or powders to feed the skin, but pure liquid extracts (essential oils) are the most concentrated and refined. Essential oils, as Sachs puts it, are the "essence" or the active ingredient of the medicinal plant. They are commonly misunderstood to be "oily," but they are really just liquids distilled from leaves, stems, flowers, bark, roots, or other elements of a plant. Massaged into the skin, they help improve circulation and strengthen connective tissue, reducing wrinkles and protecting against infection, says Sachs. She writes that essential oils are 70 to 80 percent more concentrated than herbal powders, yet their molecular density is so fine that they penetrate the skin to the cellular level and produce effects 60 to 75 percent stronger than the herb taken whole.

Also, as the source of the plants' immunity, essential oils have natural antibacterial, antiseptic, antifungal, and preservative properties that help to heal wounds or infections. Positive facial oil ingredients would include cocoa butter or almond butter; olive, sesame, sunflower, or safflower oil; strong herbal decoctions; essential oils and rosewater. The best way to apply essential facial oils are the essences diluted in a base of vegetable oil or ghee, which can then be mixed slightly with water (for normal skin) or liposomes (for mature skin).

Moisturize. Moisturize and nourish when there is still a little dampness left on the skin from washing—for example, right after getting out of the shower when the skin is still moist.

All moisturizers can be broken down into two main categories: humectants and lubricants. Humectants draw water from the air onto the skin's surface, and lubricants wrap over the existing water in cells. Copeland prefers humectants because they won't trigger breakouts. Look for fragrance-free, hypoallergenic, and made with a natural base of squalene (from olives), avocado oil, walnut butter, or cocoa butter. In addition to these bases there should be antioxidants as well, which can sometimes come from essential oils, but there are lots of other options. "Look for products that list an 'active ingredient' and a particular concentration," says Dr. Oz. Vitamins and supplements in skin lotions usually have to be up to 10 percent of concentration to really do something, says Oz. The formulations also need to be pH balanced, and the active ingredient must be able to penetrate the skin. Vitamin A, for example, only works at a much lower concentration.

Although marine extracts, papaya, and licorice are especially good for wrinkles, they are not commonly found ingredients in moisturizers. To moisturize, with either a face lotion or a face oil, the healthiest common ingredients, according to Oz, are: **vitamin A** (retinoids), **vitamin B3** (niacin or nicotinamide), **vitamin B5** (pantothenic acid, panthenol), **vitamin C**, **vitamin E**, **Coenzyme Q_{10}** or **ubiquinone** (small molecule antioxidant), and **ferulic acid** (small molecule antioxidant). Each have different uses and purposes, and some are only effective in particular combinations. At nighttime, massage with warm ghee, almond oil, or olive oil combined with a few drops of rose or sandalwood essential oil, says Sachs. Dab pure *Rosa mosqueta* oil around the eyes at night to combat the deep wrinkling that will naturally appear over time, she adds.

Retinoids are relatively faster than all the other safe choices. Retinoids are just vitamin A derivatives that have been proven to boost collagen, reduce fine lines, speed cell turnover, and even smooth discoloration. They are available over-the-counter (as Retinol) or with a prescription. Put on a gentle moisturizer, let it soak in for thirty minutes, and then apply retinoid.

Niacin prevents injury caused by the sun and increases certain fats and proteins in the skin, Dr. Oz says. Although found as retinoic acid, retinol, retinaldehyde, or retinyl propionate are appropriate. The types that should be avoided are Retin-A or Renova. Retinoic acid decreases acne by knocking out bacteria and decreasing the thickness of the dead layer of skin and oils that clog pores. This decreases visible pore size. Topical vitamin A increases the stretchy elastin fibers, the hearty structural collagen, and the natural moisturizer (hyaluronic acid) in the skin. It also reduces dark pigmentation. Retinoids are really the only thing you can put on the skin to repair sun damage (resulting in smoother less-wrinkled skin) and they decrease actinic keratoses that can cause skin cancer. Light destroys vitamin A so, again, apply at night.

Vitamin C also needs special consideration. As one of the skin's main water-based antioxidants, it can increase levels in skin at least forty times by rubbing in at least a 10 percent concentration of L-ascorbic acid. However, it can break down with light and oxygen, so store it in containers in a dark place and use at night when it can stimulate collagen and elastin. It protects against sunburn and sun-induced wrinkling, knocks out free radicals after UV exposure, helps brown age spots, and will achieve better results if used with vitamin A than when used alone. In fact, L-ascorbic acid is the main type of vitamin C that actually penetrates the skin. If the concentration is kept at 10 percent, then it has been kept well acidic.

Vitamin E. This is a major lipid-soluble antioxidant, but topical vitamin E needs to be in the form of dl-alpha-tocopheryl acetate. The more user-friendly tocopheryl acetate is not as great as alpha-tocopheryl, and may hurt the skin. Vitamin E needs vitamin C to work, so it would be better if they were together (because C is water soluble and E is lipid soluble so they permeate different kinds of cells). The real vitamin E, dl-alpha-tocopheryl increases the effect of sunscreen, protects the immune system from threats, and slows wrinkle production. Because UV light degrades it, just like vitamin C, it should be applied with sunblock or at night.

CoQ_{10}. Although it helps prevent damage to the lipids on the surface of the skin, says Oz, the amount in products is often exaggerated. They usually have 90 percent less than advertised, so check consumerlab.com or look for the USP-verified symbol on the package to ensure ingredients are what they advertise.

Kinetin or Kinerase features the growth factor furfuryladenine, which can diminish wrinkles without irritation in the same way marine extracts rejuvenate the skin.

Plant phospholipids also act as a humectant, preventing evaporation. They carry nourishment into the skin cells and even create reservoirs of moisture deep within the skin, rare to find in other treatments, says James. Liposomes are made of lipids, says Sachs, the same substance that makes up cell walls. They carry materials through the cellular membrane and deposit them in the cell itself. They facilitate the absorption of essential oils into the skin—but don't try to make them at home, and search for ones made with egg protein or bean extract oil.

Other healthy ingredients to spot in the fine print are **alpha-lipoic acid**, **beta-carotene**, **carnitine**, Coenzyme Q_{10},

ferulic acid, **flavonoid**, grapeseed extract or **polyphenol** or **resveratrol**, **green tea**, **white tea, isoflavones**, **lutein**, **lycopene**, milk thistle, **silymarin**, **licorice**, **chamomile**, **aloe**, **rosemary**, **curcumin**, **Pycnogenol**, **hyaluronic acid**, **tocotrienols**, **selenium,** and **thiotaine**.

Protect from the sun. After cleansing, nourishing, and moisturizing (and before going outside), put on SPF. "Solar radiation radically alters your cells and DNA," says Copeland, and "triggers the release of free radicals which weaken the skin's collagen and elastin." UV light is a major cause of the outward signs of aging.

Choose a "sunblock" over a "sunscreen," Copeland says, because zinc and titanium oxide begin working right away whereas sunscreen must first be absorbed for twenty minutes. Always double-check for the label "broad spectrum," indicating that it protects against both UVA and UVB rays. Also, antioxidants like vitamin C, vitamin E, and green tea make more effective, mineral-based sunblocks resulting in anti-inflammatory effects. For an average workday, go for SPF 30 (meaning, the time it would take you to burn would be "thirty times longer than if you went outside with nothing on," says Copeland).

Hair. Regarding all hair products, protein is key. Hair is 97 percent protein and 3 percent moisture, says Sachs. As described before, start caring for the hair by eating for the hair. Increasing quality proteins, as well as minerals and vitamins, will result in a noticeable difference. Foods with iron, sulfur, zinc, B-complex, and vitamin C as well as essential fatty acids will directly affect the hair.

Wash. Both the brain and the scalp prefer to be kept cool, so even when washing the hair its best to use warm water and a cool rinse. Cool water is more efficient at removing soap anyway, as well as toning the scalp and refreshing the nervous system, says Janice Clarke.

Don't shampoo more than three times per week. Wash without foaming cleansers. Use natural, sulfate-free, ultra-gentle shampoo. Avoid sudsing agents such as sodium and ammonium lauryl sulfate, as they are too harsh and strip hair of its outer protein layer. Herbal cleansers wash away dirt without washing away natural moisture, so the hair isn't desperate for conditioner after the damage of "squeaky-clean" shampoo. Sachs gives guidelines for making simple shampoo at home of a strong herbal decoction. Depending on skin type (dry, oily, or sensitive), her recipe includes appropriate ingredients (like lavender, geranium, sage, or bay leaf).

If desired, rinse with natural color enhancers. Perms, coloring, and all permanent treatments are just as damaging as heat. "Perms and dyes chemically alter the shaft of the hair, often making it dry and brittle," says Raichur. "Herbal hair rinses are the safest way to highlight and enhance natural color and bring a glossy shine as well as strength and thickness."

Massage. Scalp massages are the real key to hair health. After washing, massage scalp with two drops of lavender or rosemary essential oil before drying. For added shine, follow shampoo with a hair rinse of half a lemon squeezed into a cup of water. "Cultivate resilient, strong hair via healthier scalp and hair follicles by feeding them from within and avoiding the very same stripping, irritating, and dry assaults that cause problems on the skin," says James. Brushes should have smooth or rounded-tip bristles to massage but not scrape the scalp. Wash brushes once a week, and never use metal brushes or combs. Also, never wear tight barrettes, pins, or bands that weaken the root, especially to sleep. "Often tension in the scalp or fatty deposits block circulation," says Raichur, "drying the sebum and thus literally starving the hair root. Massage is the answer for tension relief to improve circulation and freeing the hair roots of dry sebum … Massage with shampoo is good but, as with the skin, oil massage is better."

Massage the scalp with sesame, coconut, or pumpkinseed oil enhanced with amla, shikakai, neem, sandalwood, jasmine, or coriander essential oils (bhringaraj and brahmi are harder to find, but are even better for hair massage). Warm oil a bit before and leave on for twenty minutes, or even overnight if possible. For everyday rejuvenation, massage a few drops of rosemary or lavender oil with the fingertips and brush hair upside down fifty times. Sachs offers weekly scalp massage treatments in her book that are more strengthening.

Dry. Blot excess water as much as possible by squeezing with hands. Then air dry or, when necessary, use cold settings on an infrared or ionic hair dryer. "Just as drought and blazing heat quickly destroys a lawn, heat is most detrimental for the hair ... weakening the scalp and the roots," says Raichur.

Regrow. Changes in hair growth can depend upon age, health, hormones, seasonal changes, climate, trauma, stress, and anxiety, says Sachs. Avoid Rogaine (minoxidil) and Propecia (finasteride), says James. Instead go for DHT-blocking hair-loss preparations, like Hair Genesis (a non-drug formula containing a DHL blocker) use Viviscal natural hair loss product, or nitric oxide (NO) or NANO, which is a natural form of minoxidil. Essential oils are best, though, so a combination of rosemary, lavender, thyme, and cedarwood, and a few drops of each mixed with jojoba and grapeseed oil will block the autoimmune defenses causing hair loss. For extreme cases, try Shen Min, an herbal compound based on the Chinese medical herb *he shou wu* (or *fo-ti*) to treat hair loss.

* * *

After growing up in a metropolitan city, and having graduated from three competitive schools, I compiled this health information with my millennial peers in mind. My friends are underpaid, wish they had more time for exercise, refuse to swear off their favorite junk food, and have generally accepted that to be perfectly healthy (indeed, to adapt to all the advice in this chapter) would take the focus and energy of a person whose outward appearance their livelihood depended on (in short, a celebrity). Most of the chapters in this book offer wide-ranging reforms that industries would benefit from adopting in full over a gradual period of time. In contrast, the intention behind my research in this chapter does not value upending one's life. Rather, as many options as possible are provided to prove that beauty is a daily choice, an inward source, and not a receipt from a drugstore. We can cast away income (at a pay gap we constantly protest) to cover up eye bags, mitigate acne, and gloss our hair to its highest capacity. This research should only help, not command, us to save money and make-under as opposed to makeover.

Ayurveda products are hard to find, mostly because the ingredients recommend a homemade process. Ayurvedic practices are even more rare, because the time and energy required has been challenged over many thousands of years by a successful trend toward the more expedient capitalism. How many of us have been relieved to know that a pimple before a first date can be temporarily erased by a $2.99 stick at the drugstore? How many of us, roused by independence, stole away fifteen minutes to buy a turquoise nail polish our parents would hate? And yet, how many of us have run our own fingers through our rough hair only to know we'll probably pick up the flat iron again the next morning? It doesn't take ancient Indian oils, $200 designer creams, or the hottest book on Amazon to decide that your beauty is the best beauty attainable. Either slowly study the natural science behind preserving individuality, or let go of the perfectionism that ties you to a corporate market so barely acquainted with you. Beauty is far more than skin-deep. Most hard decisions are.

[i] Dr. Ilya Petrou, *Dermatology Times*, 2014
[ii] Dr. Zoe Draelos
[iii] Dr. Jessica Krant, *The Huffington Post*, 2012
[iv] Indiana University Study in 2012
[v] *The Huffington Post*
[vi] *TIME*
[vii] *Scientific American*
[viii] *The Huffington Post*
[ix] Ibid
[x] An article published by The University of Maryland's Medical Center and edited by Steven D. Ehrlich
[xi] Ibid
[xii] Ibid
[xiii] According to the Mayo Clinic
[xiv] According to their website

CHAPTER 5
MODELS

In a halogen-lit room, not far from the Trans-Siberian Railway, a pale Russian girl waits patiently in a bathing suit. Outside the ground is frozen, but inside she stands beside dozens of other girls in bikinis. When Nadya answered the casting call that day, she had no idea she would be profiled in an American documentary investigating the modeling industry worldwide. *Girl Model* was produced by P.O.V and distributed by Dogwoof in 2012. The filmmakers followed Nadya on her path from poverty to fashion model. The film opens on a bleak, snow-covered, silent Russia in a somewhat industrial but mostly empty area. We are shown a compound of buildings and, inside, a selection process is underway.

"Modeling requires grace, good communication skills, good manners," echoes a man's voice on the overhead speaker. "Who wouldn't want their children to possess these qualities? The first secret of a successful modeling career is to start modeling at 5 to 10 years old."

There is a bare roomful of preteen and teenage girls in bathing suits, heels, and no makeup. They're tall, likely over ten years old, but not by much. The walls of the room are covered in distorted mirrors. Take one step to the right, you're ten pounds heavier; take one step to the left, you almost disappear.

The door opens up to the backstage of a theater. On stage are more girls standing and posing in formations. On the sides of the stage are girls waiting in the wings. Their voices blend in a faint Russian hush.

The scout stands on stage. She gazes over a sea of almost naked girls who blink back at her. Like a Roman slave owner checking stock before an auction, the scout walks up to a few to stroke a neck, tap a chin, or finger their hair. The scout is Caucasian with brown eyes and brown hair. Nothing in her appearance is glamorous. We are told her name is Ashley.

"I'm looking for a specific kind of girl for the Japanese market," she says. "Everyone has their own vision of beauty … for Japan it is quite specific. So the girls have to be a certain height, not too tall, cute, young—young is very important. It's not entirely up to me. I make note of what I see today. It often is not what I believe is the best and, sometimes the girl that I think is amazing for Japan doesn't work at all. That's what's exciting about this business," she says, never smiling. "It's totally unpredictable."

She continues to walk the room, pausing in front of a few. "They love skinny girls in Japan. And she has a fresh, young face, like a prepubescent girl … The Japanese always want something new."

She approaches Nadya.

"Can you come here? Closer. Closer. Can you open your hair?" Nadya is as pale as the walls with dim, blonde hair falling past her elbows.

"Hello. My name is Nadya. I'm thirteen," she says, smiling at a scouting aid holding a camera. She speaks slowly in a thick Russian accent. "Ummm?"

"I'm from Novosibirsk," the woman with a camera prompts her.

"I'm from Novosibirsk." Nadya walks to the edge of the room, where her things are up against a wall, and tucks her head into a sweater.

Ashley and her team decide to offer Nadya a modeling contract and call her up to the stage with the enthusiasm of a *Price is Right* announcer. With loud music pumping, they present her with a teeny-tiny crown that's just the right size for a doll. They laugh and try to press it into her head. Down below, her mom smiles, holding back fresh tears. Overhead, on the loudspeaker: "Top models are not only beautiful and charming … but also rich!"

The owner of Switch Modeling Agency, which Nadya is about to join, explains that the process she will enter is actually quite difficult—not just for her, or for girls in Japan, but universally. "We also have problems in the

West. And it's also a difficult uphill battle there."

He tells the filmmakers that his agency will support the girls in all types of encounters. "The depth of the psychology involved, you know, we go very, very deep with the girl, trying to understand all her problems … At the end, [we] form a profile and we try to sort of replace those fathers for them and support them anyway we can."

Before Nadya leaves for Japan, we visit her home. It is a simple dwelling. Her relationships in her family seem loving and peaceful. Her father acts kind and supportive. She steps through a condensed but lush back garden with her grandmother, looking like a careful, delicate Bambi. Her skin is so iridescent and her legs stretch out so like twigs that she barely seems sturdy enough to tread earthly ground.

"For me, beauty is first and foremost in nature," Nadya says, holding out small berries in her hand toward the camera. "Human beauty for me is inward. The beauty of the soul. If a person's soul is compassionate, everything else follows."

Back inside, she prepares for another modeling meeting.

"I'm such a grey mouse," she says to the camera with a soft smile. "An ordinary country girl." She is trying to shape her hair with a curling iron. "I want something different in my life." She sticks the wire of the device into a dirty old outlet that fails to hold the plug in the socket properly. "I want for things to be good at home."

Nadya's grandmother adds, "The only thing I wish for her is independence."

"Girls want to leave Siberia because it's easier to make money overseas," Nadya mentions later on.

Nadya's mother is contemplative. "We are very glad for Nadya, but we are worried. This anxiety will always exist because she is our daughter, our flesh and blood. We'll be waiting for her to come back."

After the scouting, Ashley boards another train and presents herself on camera like a typical young American woman—although, because her accent is slightly off, her nationality is a bit of a mystery.

"I don't know," she begins. "The business of modeling is not something I feel necessarily passionate about, 'cuz it really has no weight … It changes, minute by minute and … it's based on nothing. If you start to look at all those girls, and you really look at each one, you bring them close to you, in their eyes," she says, leaning in, the silver light painting her face, "you can start to see their age, and their experience, and that business is *obsessed* with youth. And especially my business in Japan." She shoots a glance toward the camera and slips back into the shadow. "You can't be young enough. And youth is beautiful. Because there's a luminosity, there's something in the skin, there's something innocent. And that's what my eye has been trained to see from Japan. So I look at beauty and I think of young girls: 'beautiful.'"

She is candid about her process. "When I work with Japan, they don't know what I do, where I go, as long as I bring them the girls. I have no job description of what I do, or what I'm supposed to … bring them. They cover my expenses and I get a commission of whatever I bring them. So that is freedom. I can kind of get away with not really caring about this business that much."
Later in the film, Ashley continues to reflect. "The models that we meet in Russia are really little girls, just the babies. But they're not my children. I mean, I'm not at that point yet. I'm sort of in that precarious place where they don't really know, like, can they be my friend? I care about the girls a lot, but I don't feel inspired by … I don't know … No, I do really care about the girls, it's just, I don't feel [as if] I have some huge, big, big truth to tell them about this amazing business; that I'm going to change their lives and make them happy and be fulfilled because it's a very tough, very tough business."

Japanese immigration requires Switch Models to provide Nadya with paid work during her stay abroad. The agency submits paperwork to the government guaranteeing that Nadya will receive two jobs plus $8,000 in a contract.

Nadya joins up with another Switch girl, Madlen, who will

be her roommate (sharing a shoebox-sized apartment), and soon they go on casting calls where Nadya hopes to be hired for jobs. She stands facing a couch of squat Japanese women with heavy makeup. One purses her lips. "I am looking for a more cool and stylish girl."

In a different office, Nadya is getting ready to meet with another powerful agency owner, named Messiah.

"Tell him your name and age," Madlen tries to translate, "say you are fourteen."

The man with the camera adds, "You don't say you are fourteen. You are fifteen."

"He wants you to say you are fifteen," urges Madlen.

Another night in Tokyo, Nadya and her roommate go out to explore the city.

"Look, that's cool." Nadya points to an Asian woman posing in front of a Chanel store for a picture. The woman's silk dress blows up in the wind revealing her heels and her legs.

"I love Marilyn Monroe," says Madlen. "She's my favorite actress."

Eventually, a company hires Nadya for a photo shoot in a magazine, but never pays her. "I don't know where my photographs go," she tells the filmmaker. Nadya finds a newsstand and starts flipping through pages. "I am looking everywhere for the magazine that featured my work. But I can't find it. My outfit was a black wig. It concealed most of my face." She flips through pages and pages of girls like her in poses, but none of them are her.

One manager affiliated with the agency, Rachel, was a model for five years. She rides around in the car with the girls from casting to casting.

"A lot of times," Rachel says to the camera, "you do shoots and you never see the pictures in the end. The pictures can be sold to a magazine afterwards, and [the girls] won't make any money because agencies don't want you to know what's going on anyway. It's better for them because, if you don't really know what's going on—how much you're getting paid, what are your expenses—they can get more money out of you. You have to be really on top of everything. And a thirteen-year-old won't be on top of everything. She'll be like, 'Oh my god! I'm going to Japan! I have all those jobs booked! I'm going to make that money at least!' But they don't know that they're not getting those jobs. They'll just take advantage of her."

Despite Rachel's considerable experience, and given her current work in the industry, she feels someone is to blame but doesn't know who.

"There are a lot of thirteen, fourteen, fifteen-year-old girls. I mean, there is too in Europe. And they're saying no, no, no. In Europe and America, they don't use girls under sixteen anymore. [But] the girls [there], I see them. In the casting, I talk to them. [And] who is to blame? We can't blame the girls, because they're just being sent. We can't blame the families, because maybe they're in need. Can we blame the agency that takes them on because a client will take them? Can we blame the clients that will pretend or won't know actually how old those girls are? There's no one to blame. The whole thing, it's so wrong. They all play blind, really. And if they use thirteen, fourteen-year-old girls, that means they do not want any girls that are a shape of a woman."

We learn that Ashley, the scout, was formerly a model, but it takes time for her to open up to the filmmakers about her background.

"I never like to think of myself as an ex-model. I never like to bring that point up. But of course, it does bring a different insight … I was the person who hated this business more than anybody, and now I'm fifteen years in it." We see flashback footage of Ashley filming herself as a teenager. She's modeling in Japan. She's backstage at a show wearing, basically, a white bag for a dress. She's busy multitasking, so she's speaking to her camera, but she's doing other things to get ready for the show.

"This whole place is hurting me too much." She holds

the camera close to her eyes. "Even if I do ten jobs in the next two weeks, it won't be any money for me by the time I cover my expenses. Fashion is so boring to me these days. I hate … I don't even *like* to look at the magazines. I mean, I do. It's just all the same stuff, all the time. Anyone who does it must be an idiot. So what are you trying to say? What would you rather do? Pottery?"

She explains her beginnings. "I remember the birth, being a model, and I hated it so much. I've never been so down. I remember days where I just literally stayed in my apartment and stayed in my bed all day. I just couldn't even get out of bed. I just didn't know what to do with myself. I felt so depressed. All I would think about is, okay, what am I really going to do with my life? okay, why am I doing this? When can I go home?"

Later, she adds: "All the girls just want to get out [of their home country], so they try … [to] be athletes, they can be gymnasts. They can be ballerinas. They can be models. They can be prostitutes. Most of the time, they do a combination … I mean, often. Yeah. They do. There are certain agencies like, high-class agencies, who will help facilitate … If you have the experience of making money, if you are a model, you only know how to make money as a model. You're a beautiful girl who uses her body. So it's kind of natural to think, 'Well, I sell my body for the camera and what's the difference?' You know the DVD's I gave you? You can see sometimes the girl presented herself in a certain way. The castings in Russia, sometimes it was clearly like she was presenting herself as a sex object, sometimes she was just as a young girl. I mean, those tapes are widely distributed. Of course, the goal is that they get placed in modeling agencies, but the reality is that they get placed in other places too. And I don't have firsthand experience of these things. Obviously I'm not participating … It's just normal to be a prostitute. For them, you know. Maybe it's easier than being a model. I mean, in a lot of countries prostitution is not considered a terrible thing. I don't really acknowledge that it exists."

Besides prostitution, there are other illegal choices models often make that agencies have to deal with. The owner of the Switch agency explains his approach.

"Now [you have to understand] they're difficult girls. So to have a good effect of education, we take these girls to the morgue. And we show them these young girls or boys who did drugs and passed away. That has everlasting effect. And if the model is still too hard-headed, we have the autopsy done in front of them. Believe me, that affects them so strongly … You know what the worst part is? When they realize they could be in their place. And that has very, very strong effect on them. Believe me. Seeing a dead young girl in front of you has a really strong effect. With an open body …"

Although we never see Nadya inclined even remotely

toward illegal choices or behavior, money is a stress.

“Our family has financial problems. Not only prior, but also because of this trip. If I need to do any photos when I’m supposed to smile, it doesn’t come out well when I think of all this stuff … I think all this will be over soon and it will be okay and I will be home. Everything will be over.”

In the midst of endless casting calls, during which Nadya doesn’t receive any jobs, she sits down on the outside stoop and rubs her forehead. She dials home. She is calling Russia from Japan on a cell phone, and she can barely hear with a thin connection.

“Mom.”

“Whose phone are you using?”

“The filmmakers’ …”

She buries her chin in her neck, hunches over, and starts to cry. “I don’t know.”

“What’s wrong?”

Nadya gasps between sobs. “Home … I want to go home, Mom. I don’t know.” Her fingers dig into her hairline.

“I don’t understand. I thought you had two jobs in the

contract?"

"Me too." She takes a little breath.

"What have you been doing?"

"Yesterday, I had four castings. And today I had one. I have three more left."

"What about your two jobs?"

"I don't know. I don't know … I don't want it at all. I just want to endure this and get back home. That's it."

She turns slightly away from the camera. "What am I eating? Nothing at all. What about others? Others have money. My roommate Madlen has a credit card. Her parents put it there … You? Don't do it. Keep the money for yourself so you can eat."

A moment passes as she waits for a response over the phone.

"Mom? Are you there?"

In Ashley's time off, she goes to Paris fashion week. She hails a cab in skinny jeans, a gray beanie, and little white boots. She herds into the theater and sits several rows back, only the glow of the stage reaching her face. "It's more than short term, [this work], it's an addiction.

It really is an addiction. Then I stick with what I know because I'm sort of afraid to really try new things."

Back in Japan, Madlen and Nadya know that (according to their contract) if they gain any weight, their agreement will be canceled and they will be sent home. They break open a candy bar and furiously start munching. Soon enough, we learn that Madlen gained too much weight and is sent home. "I tried the modeling path. I don't want it and I don't need it," she says on the way to the airport. "It will be very difficult to be here alone … We were always together and now Nadya's alone."

Nadya tells the filmmakers, "I miss Madlen." They show clips of Nadya in Japan riding the subway alone, eating meals alone, going to newsstands alone and searching for her one picture. "I'm trying to keep myself together, but it's a struggle." Finally, the agency sends Nadya home. She is more than two thousand dollars in debt.

"Now I see the world through different eyes," she says to the camera. "I am more grown-up—but, I think, you shouldn't grow up too quickly."

* * *

I am certain that each model would have a different and personal reaction to Nadya's story. Some will say it's not so bad. Others will respond with caution, noting that some things must have been exaggerated in the documentary.

Nevertheless, Nadya's criminal exploitation and emotional dislocation can be studied.

All throughout the documentary, I couldn't help but wonder: how many like Nadya go on with their stories untold? Their reflections are hidden, their lives are in a pile, their headshots are secret, and their ages are lies. Without a doubt, the first problem of the model is that, ironically, we can barely see her. As in Nadya's case, sometimes she is even hidden from herself.

In combining Nadya's story with data from modern studies, we can see the imperfections across the industry: poor health, insufficient finances, indecorous lifestyles, as well as conceptual misunderstandings of vanity, audience, and the paradox of the muse.

When Nadya's mom asks her what she's been eating and Nadya answers, "Nothing," their exchange is exemplary. The average BMI of a model working in the United States is 16.9. That's similar to, but just slightly less than, the BMI of the average Bangladeshi girl living in the third most malnourished country in the world. Regarding runway models specifically, research concludes that most meet the BMI physical criteria for anorexia. The list of reasons why models are "unhealthy eaters" is endless. Some can't afford it. Some deal with psychological agony. And some don't know the science behind their nutrition choices.

Few modeling assignments require "health" beyond

demonstrating the ability to fit into clothes—and yet, how many understand the contrast between "to fit into" and "to be fit"? In extreme cases, they actually represent two opposing approaches to health.

When the personal chef working for Gisele Bündchen and Tom Brady revealed their household family diet—meals with extreme, if not unheard of, ingredients—people laughed at the "absurdity" of the value they placed on physical maintenance. And yet, when we're driven to a fork in the road (either Bündchen's intricate recipes or *The Devil Wears Prada* maxim, "When I feel like I'm going to faint I eat a cube of cheese") we still have to avoid the latter.

It is hard to understand the finances of a model because, as has been the case for thousands of years, so much comes free to those who are "beautiful." But have we asked: how much is taken? Perhaps we can assume that Nadya was allowed to cut ahead in line once or twice in Japan. Though such perks cannot compare to coming home two thousand dollars in debt.

Although it is not unusual for a model to walk ten to fifteen shows during fashion week, the vast majority of models are not *paid* to work, reported Jenna Sauers for Jezebel in 2010. They are "paid" with the privilege of grabbing the attention of a front row editor or with a gift of free clothes from the designer (otherwise known as "trade").

Being underpaid and taken advantage of are practically the same thing, given how hard models work. When Karlie Kloss was fifteen years old, she walked thirty-one shows and presentations in one week during the fall/winter New York Fashion Week of 2008. Sauers reports that this was the highest record known for catwalks per day.

Perhaps the highest earning models right now are a combination of entrepreneurs, moms, and party girls—but the highest paid does not always necessarily mean the top model (and for that matter, how many of those moms were party girls before they were moms?). "Top" models often aren't the highest paid models, they're just the hottest, newest, and most in demand.

When Cara Delevingne came on the radar in 2012, she got booked more often than others but became an "it" girl at the same time. While "the duchess of the catwalk" was booked in eight shows, according to *New York* magazine, she was also very busy doing other things. "When not at work, she 'took the thumping music' of Rihanna for River Island 'as an opportunity to grind up on any/all other British celebs in attendance,' helped Rihanna leave a nightclub the following evening after a fan threw an energy drink bottle at the pop star, performed the knockoff Harlem Shake, hung out with Harry Styles and Rita Ora, and fell down a flight of stairs at a house party." As Hilary Moss concludes, "She certainly sounds like a good time." Now, Delevingne's reputation as a model is marked by her individuality, irreverence, inclusivity, and her bold stance against inequality and injustice. It would have been more to her credit if the industry hadn't promoted her popularity over her personality.

In how many industries can you say that an intense workweek is also an intense party week? In 2013, *New York* magazine reported on Fashion Week and its link between a busy catwalk schedule and a busy hook-up schedule.

"To industry outsiders, Fashion Week can seem like an orgy," wrote Kat Stoeffel. "Models descend, champagne flows, hip-hop stars perform two a.m. concerts." It's like "Greek week with better booze," and it's "why fashion editors' straight male friends badger them for plus-ones."

Although she says that not everyone equates Fashion Week partying with more sex, she does have an interesting exchange with Harry Brant and Peter Brant Jr., brothers described as the "mascots" of Fashion Week.

"The models get laid at Fashion Week," Peter says.

"The professional ones don't," Harry interjects. "If they're a good model, then they're not. They have jobs."

"Okay, Harry, maybe not all models are nice girls," Peter says.

Later, a male magazine editor tells Stoeffel, "You have to wing it … You can't plan on it. If you make plans to get laid, things get too complicated."

"You go to the Boom Boom Room," another male editor agreed, "and you stay until last call."

There is a revolving door of "it girls" who model on the side. In order for models to be healthier, the idea of an "it girl" has to be healthier. If everyone swarms around you as you enter a room, you have the responsibility to check in with yourself and ask why. Because you have the fastest car, or because you just pulled up in the most eco-friendly car on the market? Because you always have mean things to say, or because you always have kind things to say? Because you are invited to the most parties, or because you are welcome everywhere you go? What if no one swarms you when you walk in a room? What if being popular wasn't the point?

Popularity and partying are a slippery slope for health. In 2013, Selena Gomez entered rehab, but not for substance abuse. In 2015, Kendall Jenner was hospitalized for exhaustion. Only a few months following, Cara Delevingne opened up about her struggle with depression and getting hit with a "massive wave" of anxiety. Ellie Goulding was vocal about her panic attacks and exhaustion in 2016. Another common thread? They are all members of what has become known as the new "rat pack"—Taylor Swift's twenty-first-century "girl squad."

Between the years 2000 and 2014, the World Heritage Encyclopedia reports that ninety-eight male and female models died prematurely during their careers. The causes included: drug overdose, fire, drowning, suicide, anorexia nervosa, brain hemorrhage, heart arrest, and murder—not to mention those who have paid high prices like depression and both mental and physical deterioration. Although each story and each life is precious, they prove that it is too easy to allow the myriad of unhealthy influences models experience to lower their quality of life.

* * *

A model's state of mind changes the way she works. If, for instance, she thinks there is an audience following her everywhere she goes, that is going to affect everything. Vanity doesn't just touch one's relationship with oneself, but each interdependent connection—including at work. In this case, knowing your "best side" before posing for a photo isn't vain (if your job is to be in photos.) A model's concept of audience reflects how she relates to her brand as well as how she relates to the reader.

It's not hard to feel that models are obsessed with audience, but vanity isn't the only fuel. In the corner whispers and conference tables of this industry, models are told: the greater the audience, the better the jobs. For the ancient Greeks, like Homer, you filled an amphitheater by telling a unique and compelling story. Models could do this, but instead they are trained on how to magnetize paparazzi. Given the number of tweets, snapchats, instagrams and other social media feeds models churn out hourly, one wonders if they have any time to feel at peace with their lives.

In the documentary *Objectified, New York Times* critic Rob Wilson offers some insight into our concept of "audience" and the role it plays in the process of shopping for cars.

> "When you own the car and you drive the car, and you're making decisions about, are you going to put a bumper sticker on it, there's an idea of an audience. I feel pretty strongly that this isn't just true for cars, but for almost everything we buy. The real audience is really ourselves, and the person that you're really speaking to when you're speaking about 'why me?' and 'this car, is this the right car for me?' you're making a statement to yourself about yourself. And in sort of an abstract way, you're thinking about what they might be thinking of you and whether or not they like your Obama sticker or your Christian fish or whatever it might be. But the crucial thing is the self;you are your own audience. The truth is, no one cares on the highway."

According to Wilson, the *idea* of audience is a powerful

psychological activity. If he observes car buyers inventing an audience in order to justify their choice in purchasing this or that, then a model is responsible for not only magnifying the objects she is selling (purses, hats, shoes) but for transforming herself into an object to be sold. Her physical attributes become the products of a brand to be invested in. When the model fantasizes that she is at the center of an audience, she objectifies herself past the point of fantasy.

Models try to justify a manifest audience when paparazzi appear. However, paparazzi and an audience are not the same thing. The fantasy begins when they leave their doorstep imagining an audience being dragged along like a robe behind royalty. Although the concept of paparazzi does not equate to an audience, it does reveal an "other."

However, a model's job changes when she is on the runway. The presence of lights, photographers, and actual people sitting in actual chairs all constitute the transition to performance. In a show, she is not there for the reader. She is there for the designer. Although most designers eventually intend (if not rely upon) their clothes to be bought, the show does not function as an active marketplace.

The way we look at models is no longer just for their appearance. We see every aspect of their life in a picture that is really, truly of them. Their social media presence combined with our technological window builds a new world of transparency, one that gives some clarity to their lives. It all affects the way we encounter them—not just *look* at them. How we look at them is equally as important as how they look at us.

The story a model creates in an ad or in a magazine, therefore, is one of reality and interdependence that can no longer be regarded as a one-way transmission of an aspirational invitation. In fact, there are three beings involved. First, the model and, inseparably, her own true story; second, her motive in the scene or, more frankly, the brand who is paying her to be there; and finally, the reader, with whom she is communicating and affecting in the scene of the photograph. So how do models relate to brands now, and how should they relate to brands? How do models relate to readers now, and how should they be relating to readers?

We have been "looking at" models in two professional categories: the "runway" and "editorial." Both seem relatively static, but there is indeed a much broader category—call it "spokesperson" (whether or not they are ever seen "speaking"). They pose for photos, they do video clips, TV ads, attend whimsical dinners.

To this effect, a model really is a "role" model. A role model can be a peer, someone like you who you admire, someone who would make a great friend; or a role model is someone who is not quite a peer but who acts as a leader. If the team behind a brand thinks they have something admirable to offer the consumer, then their model has to be special and admirable *herself*—hence the success of African-American ballet dancer Misty Copeland (named in 2015 by *Time* magazine as one of the "100 most influential people in the world"). If brands want to be leaders, then their models should be also. In print, TV, and/or personal appearance, Copeland has represented T-Mobile, Dr Pepper, Coach, Inc., Dannon, and Under Armour (in a campaign recognized by *Adweek* as one of the ten best ads of 2014 and as "the year's best campaign targeting women").

Another successful "model" (and role model) is Tina Fey's campaign for American Express in 2014. We "believe" Fey because she seems to be the same person in the ads that she is in real life. Her accept-who-you-are, happy-go-lucky outlook merges well with AmEx's (supposedly) lax rules and credit card fees. She's easygoing; they're easygoing. She accepts messes; they accept messes. She chooses more fun, less rules. It is a successful partnership because her portrayal is not only honest, it's relevant.

In contrast, Banana Republic came out with a "Mad Men" line of clothing in 2013—a spin-off of a hypersuccessful TV show about New York advertisers in the 1960s. The show was a seven-season sensation, and the culture of the show was well known beyond the details of its characters and plot points. In this world, Kate Moss would have been just another passerby on the street. Marilyn Monroe was queen, and not an inch of her was to starve.

However, when Coco Rocha (at 5'10 and approximately 119 pounds) posed in ads for the Banana Republic "Mad Men" collection, fans of the show were uncomfortable. She was an unrealistic portrayal of the real women fans had grown to love.

"Numerous commenters complained about how thin Rocha was compared to *Mad Men*'s curvaceous characters," explained *New York* magazine's *The Cut*. "People are objecting that Rocha doesn't reflect the hourglass silhouettes popularized by the show's costumes." According to the magazine, here are some of the comments on Banana Republic's Facebook page:

"That woman is too skinny to accurately portray the time in which *Mad Men* takes place."

"Not loving the bony girl! Have you people watched *Mad Men*? Nobody looks like that. Thanks preppy brand for once again reminding regular girls that they just are not skinny enough."

"I don't understand how you never show Christina Hendricks model likes, so we can see how a dress would look on a female with breasts!"

The Cut broke it down even further.

"One of the major reasons why everyone loves [*Mad Men*] designer Janie Bryant's taste so much is that she makes womanly figures like that of Christina Hendricks, who plays Joan Harris, look so fabulous. For Banana Republic to show Bryant's collection on a runway-size model, no matter how lovely and healthy she is in real life, seems like a wasted opportunity for them to market the collection to the women who want it the most—women who see Joan and Peggy and even Megan in those nip-waisted, curve-flattering outfits and think, 'I could look good in that, too!'"

This may have been a "wasted opportunity," but it is only one of many. Twenty years ago, the average fashion model weighed 8 percent less than the average woman. Now she weighs 23 percent less. The average model in America is: 5' 10" tall, 16.9 BMI, and 118 pounds. The average woman in America is: 5' 4" tall, 26.5 BMI, and 162 pounds. Open communication, healthy environments, and successful market penetration cannot occur under such vastly distorting standards.

* * *

In the documentary *Objectified*, design critic for the *International Herald Tribune* Alice Rawsthorn says, "The goal of industrial design has always been mass production. It's been producing standardized objects for production by millions and millions of people." Mass production and standardization are by no means modern or, for that matter, American. "One of the earliest examples" she says, "would be the first emperor of China. He was waging war to try and colonize more and more parts of what would eventually become China. And one of his problems was that each of his archers made their own arrows. And so if, say, an archer died, a fellow archer couldn't grab the arrows from his quiver and start shooting at the enemy because the arrows literally didn't fit his bow. So the first emperor and his advisors came up with a way of standardizing the design of the arrows so that each arrow would fit any bow."

What are the similarities between arrows and models? Are not most companies run by hungry executives, ceaselessly charging toward the frontier to capture or win over a new territory of customers? They may not look as scary as Qin Shi Huang on a horse waving a spear, but make no mistake, executives in the beauty, fashion, and magazine industries are just as valiant. Similar, too, are how the executive and the emperor use standardization to connect. Some companies insist that the height, weight, and even race of models be uniform because they assume aspirational economics is so reliable that *one size fits all.* Modern transparency is not a trend; it's the new normal. We see that models are like arrows being pointed at us constantly, threatening to pierce our individuality and personal confidence with manufactured attractiveness.

Although the widespread overuse of Photoshop has even been parodied on *Ellen*, some models actively and openly accept it. In speaking to *Fashionista*, Victoria's Secret Angel

Erin Heatherton says, "This is what happens when you do a photo shoot; retouching is an essential part of our job ... We're not selling reality; we're selling a story. It's all about creating this fantasy." Later, she says, "It's not a fair message, but at the same time ... Healthy body image is not something that you're going to learn from fashion magazines ... Photoshop makes things look beautiful just as you have special effects in movies." On the contrary, special effects in movies redesign cities, machines, and weird looking cars. In photography, all kingdoms of Mag World use Photoshop to redesign the human. This is a major hindrance toward allowing consumers to connect with models.

It's time for those in the modeling industry to make widespread healthy choices. So where do we begin?

First and foremost, models need to be *adults.* Anyone under eighteen is underage and should only be used if the context of the ad requires children in childhood. Selling certain foods, young clothing lines or toys, for example, would be appropriate. If young girls are to work as models, they should never conceal their age or be manipulated into posing as older figures. When Dakota Fanning was featured in a Marc Jacobs ad with a perfume bottle between her legs, it was rightly banned in the UK because she projected an unhealthy message for developing young minds.

Second, choosing models today should not be about the

"new now." This is a misunderstanding. As Wilson says in *Objectified*, "We tend to want new things. [Industrial designers] can do something that has a different look, a fresher look, a newer look, a new now, next now, kind of look. And the problem with spending a lot of time focusing on what's very *now* and very *next* is that it isn't very *forever* and that means that it doesn't last … There's someone else coming along trying to design what's *now* and *next* after that."

Fashion is about change, but people are about relationship. We have confused constantly looking for the "new now" with appreciating individuality. The more a model's personality and unique identity is communicated, the more unusual the story—and therefore memorable.

Individuality has a lot to do with authenticity. Choosing models for their individuality also means not asking models to be anonymous. They should not all look the same. They should not be standardized. That's too easy. The challenge in portraying a human story is rejecting anonymity. When we look at the model, we should be looking at the *person*.

People who are famous for being famous often fail to be successful models because they are not first and foremost *role models*. If their one goal is to be noticed, then they effectively only offer a contribution as social climbers. Their business is not the law, medicine, teaching, lobbying, painting, rowing, building, or firefighting because their business is about inflating themselves.

We should invite people from all walks of life to become models as representatives of brands. Entertainers are trained performers, more often expected to play a "star" than just be themselves. Where are the athletes, military personnel, doctors, executives, scientists, astronauts, dancers, teachers, real estate developers … and so on? Models should be healthy adults with a strong sense of individuality whose work, background, character, and accomplishments all help them communicate a healthy message.

Models need to be people who are comfortable with themselves, seeking more of a connection with reality than with fantasy. We need to choose models who own their identity so strongly that it would be unthinkable to want to "fix" them with Photoshop or excessive performance tools (like heavy makeup, wigs, shape slimmers, etc.). They are who they are. We should celebrate it, not redesign it.

We have made some progress in our intent to seek out "real women" for models. In 2005, the *New York Times* took note of a trend in advertising. "Madison Avenue is increasingly interested in using everyday women in advertising instead of just waifish supermodels," Stuart Elliott reported.

Nike's candid, fresh, and even humorous ads were just such an attempt to promote more relatable models. The campaign was "frankly glorifying body parts that until now were almost never seen in ads, much less celebrated," wrote Elliott. One ad declares: "I have thunder thighs, and that's a compliment because they are strong."

In 2006, Chicken of the Sea aired a television commercial showing a woman being ogled by men in her office. She gets in the elevator alone only to reveal, with a sigh of relief, that "she really has a more-than-ample stomach, which she had been holding in," Elliott reported.

A top female ad exec told him, "We've gotten tired of airbrushed pictures none of us can relate to or recognize." One consultant cited the introduction of reality TV, which meant that "your neighbors, everyday people, are the new celebrities." Some marketers began "to shift from depicting women who are unattainable to women who are attainable."

Experts also noted that millennials make different choices than their parents. "Younger women have a different perspective," a Nike executive told Elliott. "They're more personally independent about who they can and should be." Nike is a leader now because they decided then to be "honest in how we communicate with our target consumer."

Back in the 1960s and 1970s, magazines were trying to find a way to introduce the first black cover girls. In 1968, *Glamour* ran a "Top 10 Best Dressed College Girls" competition and selected regular girls with cute style and personality. Katiti Kironde was an undergraduate at Harvard at the time, and in the end she was awarded the highest honor. The daughter of a Ugandan diplomat, Kironde was featured very much as herself, her individuality and personal identity shining through in her photos. In addition to her cover-worthy smile, she sported little makeup or trimmings, and appeared quite as we imagined she would strolling to class.

The editors at *Vogue* took a different approach when they put Beverly Johnson on the cover in 1974. Her eyebrows were thinned, her cheeks were rouged, and she was dressed up with gold earrings. Her name did not appear on the cover; she was presented as another anonymous model.

This pivotal choice is also a good example of how healthy messages can be financially successful. Kironde looks like herself, in her element, natural, and the picture on the cover assures us that we will learn her story. The issue sold so many copies that it still ranks as *Glamour's* single best-seller, ever. In *Vogue*, Beverly Johnson looked too much like another performer.

Regardless, the magazines blew open an important door and put a focus on diversity—a fourth and equally important factor in choosing models. Many assume that diversity means counting the number of nonwhite faces on a runway. To be sure, among the nearly 4,500 runway models who were chosen to strut in New York Fashion Week in February 2013, Jezebel reported that less than 20 percent were "women of color," which they defined as black, Asian, Latina, or "of some other ethnicity" (not quite all "women of color").

However, diversity in modeling is far more than an "ethnic audit." All voices must be present in a diverse community: physical traits such as hair, height, skin type, skin color, and bone structure, as well as socioeconomic background, sexual identity, religion, etc.

Why is diversity so powerful? The word *pluralism* has its roots in the political philosophy of Isaiah Berlin, that the recognition and affirmation of diversity within a political body permits the peaceful coexistence of differences in interests, convictions, and lifestyles.

Governments who adopted this way of thinking, Berlin once wrote, "[made it] possible for ourselves to know men as they truly are, by listening to them carefully and sympathetically, and understanding them and their lives and their needs." Those who turn from this practice resort to extremism, or "adhering solely to one value … refusing to recognize others as legitimate."

The Oxford-educated Russian was not the only one to realize the importance of pluralism. One of our own Founding Fathers made it a crucial seed in forming the identity of our new country. To avoid factionalism in the US, James Madison wrote, many competing factions advocating different primary principles should be heard, to prevent anyone from dominating. Each time the status quo changed, he said, the influences of groups are shared, and no one institution presides in dominance.

Modeling examples lacking in diversity are everywhere. At Victoria's Secret, for example, the average Angel "retires" at the age of 28.5 years—which, as it happens, was the life expectancy at an average person living in Ancient Greece eight thousand years ago. Tall, skinny models are a weak choice for their singularity, for their reflection of an extremist point of view, and also for their obvious disconnect to the world around us. Highlighting individuality and diversity in an ad renders a more successful image because it communicates more effectively. If there's anything we still know to be true about America, it's that we fought long and hard to become *united,* not standardized. A country founded on harmonizing differences can only continue through its people. A new generation of young women in this country cannot inherit such a Mag World if we want our America to not only survive but also thrive.

* * *

How we choose models is also how we employ them. Labor laws for models have endured slow, healthy development. In 2008, model Sarah Ziff was fed up with the industry. She had only worked for a few years, but during her career runway models ranged from fourteen to seventeen years old and most were sixteen to seventeen. They were too young, but they were also too unprotected. Ziff teamed up with Ole Schell to direct and produce *Picture Me*, a 2009 documentary film inside the modeling world introducing Ziff's visionary reforms for the industry.

More personal video diary than anything else, *Picture Me* takes us on her ride from unknown to well-known. Briefly preceding the release in 2009, Ziff also released a three-part film series for *New York* magazine continuing to expose the poorly represented rights of models. After these two films, Ziff founded Model Alliance and continued to shed light on educational options, health care, and compensation conditions.

Based in New York, Model Alliance is a nonprofit labor organization aiming to protect and advocate for the rights of models. In 2010, Ziff argued for their position as independent contractors but without some of the basic protections of those in other industries. She criticized nudity policies, break provisions, sexual harassment recourse, and visa sponsorships, among other things. Ziff also arranged a clinic for models to visit her group and talk about what they would need from such an organization. Finally, the Fashion Law Institute at Fordham Law School, in hand with Model Alliance, called upon Congress for laws allowing models under the age of eighteen the same legal protections as child performers.

In 2013 Ziff, alongside New York State Senators Diane Savino and Jeff Klein, authored a bill in which minors would require permits and employers would be required to apply for a general certificate of eligibility. That fall, the bill passed and included guidelines such as:

> A responsible person must be designated to monitor the activity and safety of each child performer under the age of 16. All employers must provide a nurse with pediatric experience. Employers must provide teachers and a dedicated space for instruction. Employers must provide safety-based instruction and information to performers, parents/guardians and responsible persons. A trust must be established by a child performer's parent or guardian into which an employer must transfer at least fifteen percent of the child's gross-earnings.

I support Ziff in her candor to isolate this community and change it intelligently. For all the girls with the ambition to model, she surely chose the road less traveled. While Ziff's work represents headway in New York, they also stand in contrast to significant legal progress made by other countries.

Israel, for example, has chosen to hone their legal regulations down further to the issue of the image of the model. Their regulations take into account not only the health of the model but also the health of the reader, who is most directly affected when the model is unhealthy.

In 2012, Israel passed legislation banning the use of "underweight" models in local ads and publications. Models must actually prove that their BMI is higher than the World Health Organization's indication of malnourishment (18.5). Furthermore, all local publications must notify readers when images have been altered digitally, especially in efforts to make a person appear thinner.

Although Israel is a small country with at most three hundred working professional models, France is not only larger but is highly entrenched in the fashion industry. In 2015, the French government passed a law banning excessively thin models and finally, in 2017, it has gone into effect. Not only do models need a doctor's certificate to prove they're healthy (BMI will be requested), but agencies that allow models to work without proper certificates face six months of jail time or fines upward of $80,000. In October of 2017, a disclaimer will be published on any digitally altered picture, labeling it a "retouched photograph."

"Exposing young people to normative and unrealistic images of bodies leads to a sense of self-depreciation and poor self-esteem that can impact health-related behavior," said Marisol Touraine, France's minister of Social Affairs and Health. The government hopes this legislation helps its youth "to avoid the promotion of unattainable ideas of beauty and to prevent youth anorexia." Perhaps it is no surprise that the reforms finally settled in, given that similar laws had already been passed in Italy nearly ten years earlier.

This movement is not only a legal reformation of images and practices but also an ideological renaissance. More than two hands are needed to lift the heavy weight off these delicate shoulders, and it should be our own two hands that do the work.

CHAPTER 6
PHOTOGRAPHERS

In a world full of spark and spectacle, the photographer is the one who stands outside the light. Shining beams cast down upon various reflective objects, but this person remains just inches behind in their own soft shadow.

The photographer is both the viewer and the creator. They are both drawn to beauty and at once immune to it.

I am not a photographer. Images are not my native tongue. I seek to tell the photographer's story from a distinctly limited point of view. I only ask: what is the photographer's life like now, and how ought it be within the beauty, fashion, and magazine industries?

Some click after the same star. Some shoot stock photos before a blank canvas. Some are invited by royalty into their homes. So what is a photographer?

A photographer takes a photograph. Their job is to position a camera and to press a button. Obviously, the camera has no idea what should and should not be photographed, so it's the photographer's job to decide. In that sense, the photographer is the participant *and* the witness. If they do not participate, they will not know what is important; if they forget that they are a witness, they miss the opportunity to take the photograph.

Not only is there much to consider in deciding what should be photographed, but few people can develop the mental skill to be in a given moment and outside of it at the same time.

"Photography carries a power," said David Griffin from *National Geographic* to a TED audience back in 2008, "that holds up under the relentless whirl of today's saturated media world because photographs emulate the way that our mind freezes a significant moment."

What is a significant moment?

Choosing a significant moment is a skill Griffin calls "flash bulb memory": or, "when all the elements [come] together to define not just *the event* but [also the photographer's] *emotional connection* to it. And this is what a photograph taps into when it makes its own powerful connection to a viewer."

Can a photograph possess emotional power? Indeed, in its purest form, a photograph is a simple object developed by a machine. A photograph is an image created by light falling on a sensitive surface. As light falls, the lens in a camera captures the visible wavelengths. It makes a reproduction onto film of exactly what the human eye would see. All photographs begin with light. Light is even present in the beginning of the word, the Greek *phos*.

There is only one moment in that process in which the photographer is relevant: reproduction. Why would anyone want to make a reproduction of a physical, real, transient moment? Why would there need to be a copy? Is a photograph a copy? And if so, what will we do with that copy? How do we treat that copy differently than the way we treat the memory of the moment itself?

Griffin insists that a photograph possesses emotional power. I would venture to say it doesn't matter what the emotional content is, or how forcefully it is present. That the moment is emotional is exactly what makes it worth sharing. This is not because an emotional photograph is more important than one that isn't, but because emotion is universal. Outside of context, outside of time or place, the emotion a photograph has to offer is a language that can be understood by anyone.

A photograph shares a moment with others who, for whatever reason, could not share in it themselves. Sometimes we take a photograph for a friend because they could not be there that day. Sometimes we take a photograph for ourself, for our future self, because we do not trust our memory to do the story justice. After all, in the best stories, the details matter.
This is the job of the photographer. They must jump into

a story, even if no other human is around, and discern which pieces of that story should be reproduced in order to construct a cohesive narrative to share.

This is the life of the photo*journalist*.

As Griffin argues, cstablishing an emotional connection is the first job of the photographer, but there's more. "To be a great photojournalist you have to have more than just one or two great photographs in you," he said. "You've got to be able to make them all the time. But even more importantly, you need to be able to know how to create a visual narrative. You need to know how to tell a story."

Journalism is storytelling. Photography is storytelling. Photojournalism is a special kind of storytelling in which the truth is preeminent, honesty is effortless, beauty is accidental, and adventure is always the goal. All photojournalists tell true stories about life, in fragments large or small.

In pointing out one photojournalist's collection of work, Griffin says, "He created understanding and empathy." Griffin reiterates that photojournalism must not only be moments that can establish a connection (and can be grouped together in such a way that they form a narrative), but the narrative itself must be coherent enough to be universal. Photojournalism must create more concord than discord.

"It is these kinds of stories, ones that go beyond the immediate or just the superficial, which demonstrate the power of photojournalism," says Griffin. "I believe that photography can make a real connection to people and can be employed as a positive agent for understanding the challenges and opportunities facing our world today."

How do great photojournalists, like those at *National Geographic*, come to know their readers so well? How can they be in some cave a million miles away from subscribers and yet "touch them deeply"?

The same way Homer did when he told one story and touched the lives of multiple civilizations. The same way Shakespeare did when he wrote one play which could be performed throughout the centuries. These photographers well understood that there are basic and powerful narratives at the core of human existence, and they portrayed those themes in the clearest way possible. Betrayal. Hope. Forgiveness. Homecoming. Pride. Bravery. Patience. Loss. These are the threads at the spine of *Romeo and Juliet* and *The Odyssey*. These are the themes that will be relevant to humanity forever, whether in plays, books, newspapers, or magazines.

So, what is life like for the photojournalist today who works for a women's or fashion magazine?
There are five main ways photographers of women's

and fashion magazines do their work that should change. Solving these five problems would not only improve their quality of life but their work and our quality of life as well.

The problem of the photographer begins with their economics: they are not always on staff and more often must freelance. Their work doesn't have a set home; they are given no set office, satisfactory salary, or benefits. Of course, each publication is different and the details of these conditions vary. Nevertheless, the consequences are that all but a handful of photographers in this industry lack real financial security.

The second problem of the photographer is that the equipment they are expected to use is expensive. "We have too many unnecessary things everywhere," said Dieter Rams, the former design director of Braun Kronberg, in the documentary *Objectified.* And this could not be more true for photographers in women's and fashion magazines. Coming to work each day requires bells and whistles galore. Most of the time, the equipment (beyond the camera) is optional and sometimes it is necessary (but it is not always true that the more expensive it is, the more efficient it is).

The third problem of the photographer is that, in women's and fashion magazines, they are expected to sell an object instead of tell a story. Of course, this is not their fault.

You can't blame them for doing what they are paid to do. Nevertheless, if all photographers refused to grant this bidding, the business would have to change.

The fourth problem of the photographer is that, in women's and fashion magazines, they not only have to sell an object but they have to sell perfection. They have to digitally edit their work to create norms and ideals outside of reality. They do this knowing that the message they push will be carried far further than one glossy page (due to the scope of twenty-first-century digital media).

Finally—although this is not true for all—they are involved in seduction at work because they are taught that sex sells.

The life of the photographer working for a women's or fashion magazine doesn't have to be like this. They can be given studios and more economic opportunities; they can be expected to use only the equipment necessary to tell a true story; they can be encouraged to use tools that only supplement skill (not the other way around); they can be required to submit a story proposal; they can be required to answer story arc questions such as plot, motive, and character; they can work toward revealing products within stories, not the other way around; they can kill perfectionism or any other unnatural expectations that allow a societal agenda to trump environmental exposition; they can stay on the street and maintain reality through fresh details; they can capture change; and they can leave sex far behind in exchange for news, style, and mindfulness. After all, a terrific story arouses the brightest liveliness in us all.

So how does a photojournalist begin to do all these things?

Chris Bangle, the former design director of BMW Group, had this to say in the documentary *Objectified* about making a simple industrial hunk of metal transform into a tantalizing experience:

> "Car designers are making extremely dynamic, sexy objects, in theory. But in reality, they're bending metal, plastic, glass. This isn't like a woman coming down a catwalk where she's swooshing the dresses and showing a little bit here and really getting your eyes to goggle. Uh uh. This thing is frozen in time, which means we have to create it in a way that you the observer look at it and you put the motion into it by the way you scan it, because that car has to be a reflection of that emotional energy that you want to see in it."

In this instance, the role of the industrial designer is not far from the role of the photographer. They are in control. They are responsible for communication. They are the ones who need to assess "what emotional energy is present here."

According to Bangle's perspective, if a photograph is just an object (a slimy two-dimensional piece of paper) how can it tell a story? First of all, it is difficult to tell a story on a sterile magazine set. It is also difficult to tell a story while being told that you need to sell a product. The truth is, products in photographs sell when storytelling comes first and a strong, positive connection is established. Right now, negative connections are usually established. It is as if they want us to feel jealous, unequal, or unsatisfactory. We tend to buy things in photographs aspirationally. This dynamic existed even before the hashtag #FOMO. However, the truth is that the emotional energy of a product ties to the motive in the story, and in order for the story to be successful it must be healthy.

As Anthony Dunne said of industrial designers in *Objectified*: "We use design as a medium to try and explore ideas, find out things, question. You've got cinema, fine arts, literature, craft—every other medium seems to have a part that's dedicated to just reflecting on important issues, yet design is the thing that's responsible for so much of the built environment around us."

How can photographs in women's and fashion magazines "reflect on important issues"? By accomplishing photojournalism. Unfortunately, they can't begin to reflect on important issues, let alone tell stories, if the photographs aren't *real.* Photoshop and other digital editing devices erase key elements of our physical reality and the very story that the photographer is trying to communicate. Sterile sets, poor research, aggressive product pushing, repetitive models, and models that—as subjects in stories—do not provide us with much to connect to, are all unsuccessful (albeit common) choices.

Digital editing and the use of Photoshop is so debated that the essentials of the situation have become crowded by nuance, and the reader is left hardly knowing what to think. *Do I care that all these photographs are Photoshopped or not? Is it a big deal to me? Does it really affect me? It's not as if I don't know that nobody's arms look like that. Not even* her *arms look like that. I know, because I see her arms on Instagram every day, and that's not how they look.*

Erik Johansson can untangle these questions. Although not a photojournalist, Johansson's keen understanding of how Photoshop can successfully tell stories is instructive. According to his biography on TED's website, he is a self-taught photographer who learned how to retouch photos to make impossible and extraordinary images. "Growing up with a grandmother who painted and a penchant for escaping into the other worlds of video games, he naturally blended the two into a technique using computers to generate images that couldn't be captured by a camera."

In discussing his process for taking pictures that he plans to Photoshop, Johansson points to some differences between his work and photojournalism. When a "true" photojournalist decides to take a picture with a camera, he says, "the process ends when you press the trigger." Photojournalism, for that reason, is about "being in the right place at the right time."

When he is in the moment ready to take a photograph that he plans to Photoshop, he says, "it's more about capturing an idea than capturing a moment." In fact, unlike photojournalists, who begin their process in real circumstances, Johansson's photographs don't start with a moment in time or true event, but rather with a sketch of an idea.

Creating a Photoshopped image that looks like it could be real is not the same thing as a reproduction of a true moment. "I just see [my work] as a puzzle of reality," he says, "where you can take different pieces of reality and put them together to create an alternate reality." In fact, for Johansson, Photoshopped work "[is] just really about combining different realities."

Unknowingly, Johansson stumbles over one of the only things photojournalism and his work (or any highly stylized and edited image) have in common: their unifying theme of a successful narrative. In Johansson's case, the narrative is fiction because his photographs are impossible; in the photojournalist's case, the narrative is as factual as a written piece of journalism would be.

"To achieve a realistic result, I think it comes down to planning," Johansson says of his work. For him, the process isn't in the recording of the true event, but rather "the process was in the planning [of the events themselves] instead." To be sure, as with journalists, photojournalists must plan to know their environment if they are to construct a narrative that coherently expresses that world.

However, while planning may be another rare similarity between Johansson and the photojournalist, the presence of illusion is one point on which they totally diverge. When Johansson says his photos (although impossible) "retain a level of realism" and "pieces of reality," we have to remember that the discussion of any image in terms of *levels* of realism is a departure from photojournalism altogether and enters art.

He describes the *level* of realism in his work, and really of any highly stylized image, as an illusion. In creating illusion, he says Photoshop and programs like it, "can create something that still looks three dimensional [or realistic] like it could exist, but at the same time we know it can't. So we trick our brains because [while looking at it] our brain simply doesn't accept the fact that [the picture] doesn't really make sense."

As Al Seckel said to a TED audience back in 2004, "in the best illusions, our expectations are violated in some pleasing way ... We can violate your expectations in a whole variety of ways: about representation, about shape, about color and so forth. And it's so primal." This very mental trickery is the ceremony of witnessing and accepting illusion; a ceremony in which an idea overtakes reason, and the mind surrenders what it knows to be true in order to subscribe to a lie.

Johansson says a piece of art, like a Photoshopped picture, can come close to reality under three conditions. Multiple realities can often be merged if they have the same perspective, if they have the same type of light, and if it is impossible to distinguish where one begins and the other ends. It has to be seamless.

"Sometimes, the perspective [in the photograph] is the illusion. But in the end, it comes down to how we interpret the world. *And how it can be realized on a two dimensional surface.*" Johansson emphasizes the power of the mind in this way. Our perspective, our mind, our limits on what can be real are what allow us to either buy into an illusion or not. It's an illusion if our mind overrides what it knows to be true. It's a lie if we simply refuse to accept it in the first place. For Johansson, an image that is Photoshopped is only "realistic" or believable if our perspective and our worldview are aligned in such a way that our values link up with the message in the picture.

In either case, the devil is in the details. Johansson values details very highly, and says his work would not be successful if the details weren't the priority. "The things that make a photograph look realistic [are] the things that we don't even think about. The things all around us in our daily lives ... They're really important to consider because otherwise it just looks wrong somehow." The things we don't consider, the things we tend to ignore, the things we assume are there because they *normally would be*, so we don't tend to *look* for them. They are the very key to making any photograph or group of photographs a successful narrative. Johansson's work proves that every detail of reality is crucial to every reality, either fiction or nonfiction. As detail is crucial to reality, detail is crucial to illusion, detail is crucial to photography, and detail is crucial to photojournalism.

So how does a video gamer turned digital artist have anything to do with a woman when she sits down to read a magazine (presumably) published for her? Indeed, how does the discussion of illusion even belong in the magazine publishing industry or in any journalistic discussion?

Seckel said he often gets asked the same question over and over. People want to know if men and women possess different abilities to process and react to illusion. "'Is there any perceptual difference between males and females?' [they ask] … and I say no."

If there is no perceptual difference, then why are so many more illusions published in magazines for women than magazines for everyone else? Why is there heavier Photoshopping in women's magazines than in men's magazines or in news magazines?

From an industrial design standpoint, understanding the superficiality or depth of an object is crucial in determining how much value it will bring to the user. As Dutch industrial designer Hella Jongerius says in *Objectified*, "If you look at art, you're touched by something. It can change your life … because in that moment it moves you, you have an emotion. You hope that an object will also do that to someone … And because you use objects in your home they become part of your family and you'll want to inherit them … Those are the stories you want with objects. That's what's fun about it. People have a lot of memories which makes it possible to give layers of meaning to the material." How can publishers and editors make a magazine in a way that ensures they are giving "layers of meaning to the material"? Largely, by printing photojournalism as opposed to digitally edited art.

Of course, well-written stories carry several layers of meaning with them—infinite, perhaps. But a magazine is not just a journal, a newspaper, or a university term paper that, usually being composed of words, must be successful literally. A magazine contains photojournalism. It must have ads, but it also must tell true stories with photographs. It makes no sense to publish a story in a magazine where the only photographs are ads. It also makes no sense to publish all the stories in a magazine without words. This unique medium is a marriage of both words and pictures, a utilization of both with deep and complete respect for the power of both.

Magazines *are* journalism. The words must be factual. The pictures must be factual. The stories must be factual. Not a detail, not a word, not a microcosm can be false. Not a detail, not a freckle, can be Photoshopped in a publication claiming to offer truth.

The possibilities for journalism (and photojournalism) in women's and fashion magazines are endless. Indeed, the best results of *not* using Photoshop is the preservation of "layers of meaning in the material," layers of meaning in the face, the landscape, the shoes, even the kneecap if need be. Keeping it complex and keeping it real are not only the same thing, but are the only effort worth offering the reader—who herself is both complex and real. How can we give layers of meaning to the material if we use sterile sets for photo-essays, as opposed to meaningful, connected environments? How can organic storylines come about if something as biologically sound as skin is altered and edited digitally all the time? How can we claim to publish in a spirit of support and camaraderie if, for example, the words of our stories are saying curves are beautiful but the pictures of our stories hold up an entirely different standard? No successful photojournalism exists in any women's or fashion magazine where comprehensive digital editing, product pushing, or poor reporting and planning are all the ingredients of a "hard day's work."

Some say the justification for sterile sets, superficial planning, and free use of Photoshop in these publications is essential to their business of *selling stuff*. However, once again, if you are in the business of selling stuff, you are in the business of publishing a glorified catalogue, not a magazine.

Incidentally, thoughtful planning for photo-essays and rich, uncontrolled environments for sets all help toward marketing a product. If one is interested in marketing (not product pushing), one allows the product to take its place in the market. To compete fairly, we must let the consumer choose. Product pushing, at least in a magazine, causes everyone involved to take the product so seriously that it is the first priority. No decisions and no choices can be made if that particular item isn't looking its best. Indeed, it has to look even better than its best, given that it will often be presented in an alternate reality (supposedly "better" than the one the reader exists in).

Sometimes the "product" the photographer is required to

be "selling" in a photograph is an object an advertiser has produced, making photo-essays in magazines quite similar to the ads themselves. Other times there is no product present, and the photographer is still selling *something*: perfection.

Nothing is perfect. Not even models. However, editors from all departments directly and indirectly decide that there is a "perfect." They hold their images and their photographers to that standard unforgivingly. It's not difficult to discern what these editors think is perfect—look at any collection of ads or images from one of these publications: eye bags aren't perfect, natural hair isn't perfect, large pores, moles, types of body fat—a variety of things have been declared "ugly." I know these editors think this because I've seen them hide their own versions of these attributes when they walk through the office door in the morning. "I wish I could Botox my thighs," one editor said to me as she sat down at her desk one morning. I will never forget it.

When Naoto Fukasawa, a designer in Tokyo, studied classical Japanese poetry, he discovered a new kind of beauty. "A very important turning point for me," he says in *Objectified*, "was the term 'obsessive sketch' by Takahama Kyoshi, the haiku master. When the poet's sentiments are overly visible, the audience may become uncomfortable. Japanese ritual is the opposite. By writing simply and only about what is there, the audience is drawn into the poet's world. Their imagination is stimulated, and a silent connection is established. I believe this is where the most important aspect of the Japanese sense of beauty lies."

Overloading the photographer with excess lighting, technical props, controlled environments, and so on is not allowing them to enter a simple journalistic process. In these publications, every end-result picture looks like an obsessive sketch. Nothing looks in the moment. Each hair looks like it has been put in place. Each nose looks like it has been powdered. Everybody looks like they are sucking in their lunch. Perhaps everything they ate that day was measured to achieve a slimming effect for that photograph.

In photojournalism, like *National Geographic*, we are drawn into the world in which the photographer is a guest. It is not his world; he does not control or dictate anything in it. He visits it and participates in it to learn what is intimately special about it. The simple images produced speak so much for themselves. Nothing is forced. Everything is lively. Our imagination is stimulated because we think we can hear the rumbling of that cart on the road, or we can feel the soft breeze as it coats the fields of tall grass. Like in Japanese poetry, a "silent connection" is established in great photojournalism because the action of the photograph is raw, uncorrupted, and tied not only to a clear and present motive but to a well reported theme.
Fukasawa believes that simplicity lies at the heart of

beauty. Photojournalism is incomparable to the charade of a thousand glossy covers. A Japanese sense of beauty in poetry is not only a natural sense of beauty but also the belief that hard work and restraint are required because any beauty worth capturing is already present, if only we stand back to let it rush in.

It may seem odd to produce a photo-essay by learning about an environment or community and then standing back to let the story unfold itself (as opposed to setting a stage). However, this is what journalists do every day. Each subject has a motive, each motive has an action, and each action a consequence. Photographs must always begin with the subject and end with the connection offered to the reader.

"When I first started the company," says David M. Kelley, industrial designer and founder of the firm IDEO, in *Objectified*, "the role of the industrial designer was primarily about the aesthetics or the cleverness around function. But it was always a minor piece. The company was in charge of doing the major piece of everything and we were [the] 'hired guns' to complete some aspect. As we grew, it became clear that companies were happy for us to do more and more of the actual design of the overall product … [they] do analytical thinking, we do [the] innovative or design thinking, where we're more focused on … user centered ideas [and] stuff that will resonate with the people who are going to actually use the product. We kind of come in from the point of view of 'what do people value? What are their needs?' And it just results in different products."

Put the autonomy in the hands of the photographer so that, like Kelley, they can be trusted with "more and more" of the "overall product." Let them decide. Let them experience, taste, smell, and walk in the story. In Kelley's business, they chose to be focused on user-centered ideas because they knew those concepts and experiences would allow the connection with the user to become the priority. They wanted to make "stuff that [would] resonate with the people who are going to actually use the product." Throw perfect out the door. Throw anything forced, placed, or manicured out the door. Begin with nothing and then become the reporter and report. What do these readers value? What are their needs? How can a photograph in a magazine tell that story?

"People need to demand that design performs for them and is special in their lives," Kelley continues. "These objects that they buy—you can't make your GPS thing work in your car—there should be *a riot* because they're so poorly designed. Instead, the person sits there and thinks, 'Ugh. I'm not very smart. I can't make this GPS thing work.' I can't make the things work—this is my field, and I can't make them work!"

If one photograph causes one reader to think for ten

seconds, "I'm not as pretty as her," "I'll never be that thin," "I can't get organized enough," or anything condescending whatsoever, then one massive failure has occurred. Do you think there has been one massive failure or millions?

* * *

Healthy examples set us in the right direction. Bill Cunningham's work as a photojournalist, fashion reporter, fashion enthusiast, and lover of beauty stands as a lesson for all of us to learn from. In the 2010 documentary *Bill Cunningham New York*, our eyes are opened to the details of his personal and professional choices. Although he passed away in 2016, he is still a superb teacher.

Bill's home was completely inconspicuous. He lived in a studio that was so small it could only fit a bed, several filing cabinets for old photographs, and space to walk in between. He used a bicycle almost daily, a small common hallway closet to store it in, and a common bathroom. When his rain poncho ripped, he had no need or inclination to buy a new one. "I know this embarrasses everyone," he said about piecing it back together with duct tape. "It doesn't embarrass me."

Despite Cunningham's wide success, acclaim, and profound respect around the world, he was happy to stand in the shadow. The spotlight was never on him (that is, until this documentary was produced). His life was unadorned, because the greatness he sought was not for himself. Amid his home and his personal choices, there was no sense of self-importance. Only simplicity.

"It has to be done discreetly and quietly," he said of his work. "Invisible, I think is the word." Becoming an expert doesn't mean grasping the limelight for yourself. He appreciated that, given the way a photograph works, the light shouldn't be around him but rather on his subjects.

There is one thing, however, he did unabashedly: capture the moment. He would run, jump, leap, slide, bike, and so on to seize and secure an image. Cunningham had such a high respect for "the important moment" that he sacrificed almost anything to position himself as best he could.

"He used to run after me on the street," said coeditor of *Paper* magazine, Kim Hastreiter. "He's like a war photographer in that way. He'll do anything for the shot. I've been in deep conversations with him when he would just run from me 'cuz he sees somebody. If he sees something that's amazing, he has to go shoot it."

As it turns out, for a man with a sunny disposition, he was a big fan of "bad" weather. In going over pictures that he took in the rain, Cunningham said, "when the wind blows a bit … oh isn't that fun. See, the ones you get in the rain? When it rains, it's a whole different scene. Or when there's a blizzard, that's the best time. *Things happen*. People forget about you. If they see you, they don't go putting on airs. They're the way they are. They have to be wearing what you're photographing. And then you're in business."

In bad weather, Cunningham found a clear motive for why people wear what they wear and for how they choose to wear it. Because his goal was photojournalism, he benefitted from these environments because the motive, actions, and consequences were all so direct and easy to communicate.

"He's caught me on a rainy day jumping puddles," said the still, poised, silver-headed Carmen Dell'Orefice, a fashion model with a sly eye turned toward the camera. "The same way I did for Avedon, but"—she finally laughs—"it was much less painful when Bill photographed me—and much more natural."

Cunningham's running and jumping, his interest in weather and the mess it creates, was reflective of how much he loved action. Action, motion, life, motive, moving, turning, changing—it all created an opportunity for a story to unfold. Clothes are only a part of a story as much as they are a part of life.

Running on curbs and having fun in weather is very important to his work. First, it is as if weather was a favorite of his because it became a plot device adding more action and complicating an already wild story right before his eyes. Second, it showed us how well he knew his environment. He is a street photographer: the street is his office, he has to be an expert of the street, a walker of the street, a natural on the street—both a participant in and a witness of the street.

"If you examine his pictures, he is always focused on some detail or some narrative … that he's documenting" said Harold Koda in the 2010 documentary, a curator of the Costume Institute at the Metropolitan Museum of Art (Met). "So his photographs, rather than paparazzi shots, are really evidence of what fashion is in any given moment in the world. His archive is really not an encapsulation of fashion, but of New York life."

For Cunningham, the story was important because the reader was important. He considered the reader and the service he owed them sacred. "You try to show the reader what was really new," he said. He understood the importance of serving the reader on their schedule and in their medium. "You have to be able to give the reader in a flash on Sunday news and excitement about what it was."

"I mean, is he horsing around, throwing a bunch of flowers in front of you? No. He's not that. But that's what he wants to be. I think he photographs life," said philanthropist and socialite Annette de la Renta.

Her comments remind us that photography of a staged set in a fashion magazine, overrun with stylists and their assistants, is not the same thing as a photojournalist reporting the fashion of true life.

Cunningham was a natural in his environment because he knew his beat. He knew the value of hustle—whether on a busy sidewalk, a gala dance floor, or at a fashion show.

In going over the raw images from his camera film, when he saw a bunch of stale, boring shots, he started to become impatient, waiting for the action to kick in. "Wait a minute. Come on. Let's get snappin' and crackin.'"

Cunningham not only had a clear understanding of why the street was an important setting for action, but also why the street plays an important role in telling the story of fashion. He recognized that fashion is a part of life, and life is not an illusion; its fabric is only as rich as it is real.

"He catches you crossing a street in boots and blue jeans … and he's so happy," said Annette de la Renta. "And he's much happier when you're in this looking terrible and ratty than he is if he saw you in something incredibly elegant and smart." He was interested in "the reality of how people dress," said Koda. "The best fashion show is definitely on the street," said Cunningham. "Always has been and always will be."

In a separate interview from 1989 referenced in the film, Cunningham said, "It doesn't happen like in a day or in an hour and that's it. I run around and photograph all people with holes in their sneakers. It's not that at all. Suddenly, I see something, then I see it again and I think 'ah, there's an idea.' And other times, I'll see it and I'll think, 'wow, that's an idea,' and then I'll look for it. But I'll be doing 10 other ideas all at once." The "idea" he has is not one occurring to himself on his own; it's an idea that he hears echoed from the street. A trend is born from a united idea, a united choice, made by the minds on the street who are themselves unconsciously united by some condition, need, or quest they experience in tandem.

"See, I don't decide anything. I let the street speak to me," he said in the documentary from 2010. "In order for the street to speak to you, you've got to stay out there and see what it is. You just don't manufacture in your head that skirts at the knee are the thing … you've got to stay on the street and let the street tell you what it is." In a city where anything can be available at the click of a button, "there's no shortcuts" in fashion journalism, he says.

He also appreciated rarity. "I would come into a place," said fashion icon Iris Apfel, "and he would say 'Oh! Thank God you're here. Everybody here looks so boring. Everybody looks alike.'"

"See, a lot of people have taste," said Cunningham, "but they don't have the daring to be creative. Here we are in an age of the cookie cutter sameness, there are few that are rarities. Someone who doesn't look like they were stamped out of 10 million other people looking all the same."

Despite the rare beauties, fashion, said Cunningham, is not about giving us pretty things to look at. Anyone trying to portray that story is mistaken.

"The wider world," said Cunningham in 1960, "that perceives fashion as, sometimes, a frivolity that should be done away with in the face of social upheavals, problems that are enormous. The point is, in fact, that fashion … it's the armor to survive the reality of everyday life. I don't think you could do away with it. It would be like doing away with civilization."

To understand his beat, he had a three-part method: shows, streets and evening events—three communities in one ecosystem. "You have to do three things. You don't get the most information from anyone. You have to photograph the collections. You have to photograph the women on the street who have bought the things and how they're wearing them. And then you have to go to the evening events. You can't report to the public unless you've seen it all. People just go off and say what they think. Well, it isn't really what I think. It's what I see."

Cunningham tracked the patterns of fashion trends through a cycle. Although it is a circle with no definitive beginning or end, he plotted two points: the show and the street. He went to the show where he witnessed art. He went to the street to witness the art come to life during the day, and he went to the galas to witness the art come to life at night. To complete the revolution, he tracked the choices and the style generated on the street and at galas to check for their reappearance back on the runway again. And so the cycle restarted.

"Looking at these collections, I look for what I think a woman could wear, would wear, and whether it would fit a human body—other than the model. I'm very attune to that. If it isn't something a woman would wear, I have no interest in it." The wearing is the action, is the verb. Getting dressed is the first action that begins a whole day of actions, a whole day's narrative.

Many in the industry were impressed with the way he understood his environment. "I sometimes will look at his pages in the *Times* or online," said *Vogue* editor Anna Wintour, "and just be so amazed that he and I and all my team and all the rest of the world were all sitting in the same fashion shows, but he's seen something on the street or on the runway which completely missed all of us. And in six months time, that will be a trend."

He noticed some differences between his method and the way things are done in the industry. "The photographers at the shows, they're all in the back. So they get a clear photograph with *nothing disturbing.* They get a plain wall. It's all fun. But they're getting everything straight on. Well, fashion's not that way. You have to know in an instant, 'Oh, the angle is *this,*' and 'the detail is *that.*' And it's not straight on. I just like [to sit] on the side so I can get a front, a back, a profile … Most of the time I miss it, but I try." He appreciated that fashion's greatest use is for the generation of style, and that style is at the center of every story.

As much as he understood the industry, he did not serve it. He served the reader. "If you don't take money, they can't tell ya what to do, kid. That's the key to the whole thing. Don't touch money. It's the worst thing you can do … They don't own me. That's the important thing, never to be owned. Money's the cheapest thing. Liberty, freedom, that's the most expensive."

"Bill's fingerprints are all over everything he does 'cuz he's never, ever, ever sold out on anything," says Kim Hastreiter from *Paper* magazine.

Despite his experience, skill, and wisdom, it was Cunningham's humility that shone brightest. "It's not photography. I mean, any real photographer would say,

'He's a fraud.' They're right. I'm just about capturing what I see, and documenting what I see."

At one point in the film, he encountered the hassle of moving to a new apartment. "I'm not going to worry. I have more fun going out photographing. I suppose it will bother me at the time, but, so what? It's inconvenient but otherwise … you can't interrupt your life with that nonsense."

He remained professional in every degree. "He's incredibly kind. I don't think we've ever seen a cruel picture done by Bill. And certainly, he's had an opportunity to really have done it. And he's chosen never to do it," said de la Renta. He also completely avoided taking advantage of people by using sex to monetize his work.

He was so humble that if someone ever alluded to him having an audience, he would say the *New York Times* has readers, but otherwise it's all in their head. "I've said many times that we all get dressed for Bill," said Anna Wintour. "It's one snap, two snaps, or he ignores you, which is death. You know? But he's always doing it because he has a point of view."

"I just try to play a straight game. And in New York that's very—almost impossible. To be honest and straight in New York, that's like Don Quixote fighting windmills. Shut up, Cunningham," he smiles. "Let's get this thing on the road. Get up and work."

On speaking of the particular joys of his job, he said: "It's always the hope that you'll see some marvelous exotic bird of paradise."

For a guy so interested in change, he exhibited very little personal change himself. It's as if he believed that the stiller and quieter he was, the sooner he'd hear that bird emerge. It was all about the people, the beat, the reader; not about him. He never once imagined that he would have any reason to be in front of the camera, and for that his work only gained in strength.

In 2008, he was awarded the Officier de l'Ordre des Arts et des Lettres by the French Ministry of Culture. After receiving his award from the president of the French Federation of Couture, he said, "This is such an honor for me … I don't work. I only know how to have fun every day. It's not work. Jean Luc is a professional photographer, but for me, it's just that I've always loved Paris. The people of Paris. The women of Paris. They are the subjects of the photographs. It's not the photographer himself, it's the ladies. When I photograph, many people think, 'He's crazy! He only photographs the clothes!' But that's *what we're here for.* I'm not interested in the celebrities with their free dresses. It's not *important.* Look at the *clothes.* The cut, the new cut, the lines, the colors, that's everything. It's the clothes, not the celebrities, and not the spectacle. It's as true today as it ever was: he who seeks beauty will find it."

* * *

What can we learn from Griffin, Rams, Bangle, Dunne, Johansson, Seckel, Jongerius, Fukasawa, Kyoshi, Kelley, and Cunningham? How should the fundamentals of their practices affect work in the beauty, fashion, and magazine industries?

First, from their collective example, we see that photojournalists must do their best to stand outside the light and leave behind their personal preferences and agendas for the stillness of allowing the story to unfold in front of them.

Second, the photojournalist must learn to be both the viewer and the creator, both the participant and the witness, so as to learn from a scene but capture it more than they contribute to it.

Third, the photojournalist must learn to identify the "significant moment," or an instance in which the elements come together not just to define the event but the potential for emotional connection. The emotional power of a significant moment must be such that it speaks in a universal language and such that it creates understanding and empathy.

Fourth, photojournalists working for women's and fashion magazines must tell true stories; otherwise, they must be required to announce when their work has been digitally edited so that we know it is, in fact, not a true moment.

All untrue moments, or all art to be published in a magazine, must be secondary and less than the photojournalism. For example, if editors and stylists want to put together a whimsical shoot where models are anonymously playing dress-up and digital editing is used, then these photo-essays must not only be clearly labeled as opinion pieces (where the editors and stylists are expressing their ideas about fashion as opposed to reporting fashion), but also these opinion pieces must claim less space than the photojournalism. Otherwise, a publication filled mostly with art and untrue photographs is not journalistic. Publications only interested in publishing art must indicate on their cover what their intentions are.

Fifth, photographers should avoid carrying unnecessary equipment or weighing themselves down with tools that hinder the natural reporting process.

Sixth, photojournalists should refrain from taking a photograph with the intention of selling an object, even if they are shooting an ad, because the story comes first. Only with a successful narrative can empathy be established, a reader engaged, and interest in the products generated.

Seventh, a photojournalist should not conjure or communicate perfection or that there is a "perfect" body type, hair type, skin color, boyfriend, job, address, etc.

Eighth, photographers should never use sex to sell an object, because sex is not a story in and of itself. It is an action within a larger and more valuable narrative. Succinct storylines and pure adventure are the only arousing narratives that are valuable because they are the only ones with significant moments.

Ninth, Photoshop and all digital editing devices should never be present in photojournalism. Digital editing may only be used to replace or fix what a camera captured poorly. It is a tool to supplement incomplete work, not to enhance work by adding untruthful characteristics. For instance, if a sunset was pink but it came out orange in the picture, Photoshop may be used to correct the technological mistake. But, if the sunset was orange and the photographer, editor, or someone else wanted it to be pink, digital editing cannot be used without a clear label or sign indicating that the photograph is no longer real.

Tenth, photojournalists should report and research photo-essays by building evidence into a narrative. Planning is appropriate when it supports reporting truth.

Eleventh, photojournalists should not perpetuate gender stereotypes, tell unhealthy stories, or provide scientifically impossible messages in any way.

Twelfth, photojournalists should try to preserve the complexity of subjects in order to sustain layers of meaning in the material.

Thirteenth, photojournalists should embrace the Japanese value of finding beauty in simplicity.

Fourteenth, photojournalists should retain autonomy and have a say in photo-essay planning. They should be allowed to function as reporters driving the story at the will of the evidence as opposed to the will of the editor.

Fifteenth, photographers should be user-centered, or reader-centered, such that the viewer can recognize themselves or some aspect of their lives in photojournalism or in the narrative.

Sixteenth, photographers should never underestimate the value of running, jumping, swimming, dancing, or silently stepping their way toward a shot. Agility allows reporting to be natural and helps photographers avoid having to recreate environments on sets because they were unable to exist in the original environments themselves.

Seventeenth, photographers should remember that where there is action there is narrative and to savor devices like bad weather and other ways people are tossed into story lines.

Eighteenth, photojournalists should report the news. Their work should contain evidence of fashion choices and answer the question, Why should I care about this now?

Nineteenth, fashion photojournalists should be expected to know their environment. If it is the street, they should make the street their office.

Twentieth, photojournalists should "let the street speak to them" or allow trends to arise organically from what they see over a broad spectrum reporting from an objective standpoint.

Twenty-first, fashion photojournalists should seek innovative subjects, "rare birds," or those people who drive style change in order to report the news.

Twenty-second, if fashion photojournalists are reporting on fashion, they have to respect the narrative and should not trivialize clothes or the people who care about them. Fashion is "the armor to survive the reality of everyday life"; there is nothing trivial about it, and those who dumb down the people or the choices are missing the real story altogether.

Twenty-third, fashion photojournalists should do their best not to interrupt the cycle of style flowing from the shows to the street and back to the shows again. They should respect the interconnectivity of designers and those who get dressed. They should also recognize when news is coming from a driven industry and when it is coming from a natural ecosystem, because the context changes the story.

Twenty-fourth, fashion photojournalists should make real women their subjects because real women are their readers.

Twenty-fifth, fashion photojournalists should secure economic stability in order to preserve autonomy. They are the reporters, they are the objective bystanders, we have to trust them, and therefore they cannot be "owned" either spiritually or financially, because money is not as valuable as liberty and freedom.

Twenty-sixth, these intentions should enable the photojournalist to liberate, not confiscate, as story; to widen fashion journalism, not to narrow it; and to diversify the reader experience, not control it.

CHAPTER 7
EDITORS

We may think our women's and fashion magazines are unhealthy now, but back in 1923, Walter Lippmann noticed unethical standards among the news industry of his time. In *Liberty And The News*, he cites malpractice among the editors:

> But now that men are critically aware of how their purposes are special to their age, their locality, their interests and their limited knowledge, it is blazing arrogance to sacrifice hard-won standards of credibility to some special purpose. It is nothing but the doctrine that I want what I want when I want it. Its monuments are the Inquisition and the invasion of Belgium. It is the reason given for almost every act of unreason, the law invoked whenever lawlessness justifies itself. At bottom, it is nothing but the anarchical nature of man imperiously hacking its way through.

Do I see women's and fashion magazine editors today exhibiting blazing arrogance, catering to special purpose, demanding immediacy through vanity, and leaving behind a fragrance of imperialism? On occasion, yes I do. Is now the time for a ranting blame game? No, it is not.

I'd like you to picture yourself surrounded by the mean girls at school. If you were a follower, it was probably true: when they wore pink, you wore pink; when they cut their hair, you cut your hair. You might have gotten tattoos, gone tanning, gained weight, lost weight and done a million other things to *follow the leader*. This atmosphere couldn't be further from how a magazine ought to feel. Stepping into the office, you shouldn't feel jumpy anticipating who is going to embarrass you that day or wonder whether or not you are going to have a seat at *that* lunch table. Certain women's and fashion magazines harbor an atmosphere of cliques and trite power plays, and publishers cannot afford to prioritize their black bottom lines over harsh psychological conditions.

When I think of how to describe the change I see in American women (on account of the perfectionism and standardization these magazines propel), I can't help but think of an old graffitied church in my father's hometown. Imagine a church that, whatever your religious point of view, has been made sacred simply by the care and community surrounding it. Imagine a place so loved that it never offered dusty sills or muddied carpets. Its soot-stained candelabras shine. And then imagine a storm of all kinds of cultural change happening outside: economic income drops, society rejects prayer, a loyal generation dies only to be supplanted by newcomers more interested in malls than worship. As values shift, the building has taken on a new meaning to its community: it isn't a church at all; it's just an open, lifeless, concrete canvas for those in possession of a paint can.

Growing up in Washington, DC, I've seen more than my fair share of inspiring graffiti, but anyone who has lived in a modern metropolitan city eventually learns the difference between art and vandalism.

Why do I see the negative effects on readers' lives by a (relatively small) group of unhealthy editors as a type of cultural vandalism? While there are some visible, outward signs of the effects of unhealthy editors on modern women, the superficial is only the beginning. From our outward physical reality to our mental health and our emotional intelligence, these editors have set a powerful, and sneaky, example that has reached quite far from Madison Avenue.

In the fifth and sixth centuries, an eastern European tribe displaced by the Huns became known as the Vandals. They barely numbered over a thousand altogether, but fit the bill of the lonely outsider. Once their shipbuilding skills gained them power, their appetite for oppression grew so much that, eventually, they conquered Rome.

Every time I see a junior fashion editor post a Kardashian pout on Instagram, I can't help but feel as though they look at me as just another potential uptick in their follower count. Is social media about community building for them, or about community conquering? It is not hard to imagine the "forever follower" landing a magazine job, tasting a bit of new attention, and then stampeding through her friend group, the cool circle, and eventually the psyche of strangers just to make sure her particular brand of pseudo-celebrity stayed as buoyant as it is glossy.

Who in the women's and fashion magazine industry has set a healthy example for you? Other than their closets, what personal qualities and values do you admire about your favorite editors? Here are the healthy editors who inspire me to not only survive but to thrive, to persevere rather than expire, and to value my individuality over the whitest of spotlights.

* * *

Cindi Leive made "glamour" possible for everyone when she took over the Condé Nast title in 2001. Although Leive's work sometimes slipped in conscientiousness, resulting in critics calling the magazine tone-deaf, she has set a healthy example as a boss and an executive. When the enormous, insensitive magazine brands failed to resound with millennials, smaller titles with savvier business and technical reporting emerged. Even titles with more respectful and wholesome views on body image rose up. Imran Amed of *Business of Fashion* (alongside Sarah Dubbeldam of *Darling* and Chelsea Sonksen of *Bossladies*) opened these niche doors and connected with millennials more directly. Elaine Welteroth brought diversity to *Teen Vogue* never seen before. Historically, Diana Vreeland was *Vogue*'s most spirited editor. Her bold choices, whimsical style, and grand embrace of color and change allowed her legacy to be marked more by freedom than by control. In the balance of all of them, Stella Bugbee created *The Cut* with sharp business and political reporting, as well as a wide vision for the spectrum of fashion (not just the thrill of the front row). Bugbee's mentor, Deborah Needleman, has always drawn intelligent writers toward her, keeping the work at her style magazines within newspapers as crisp as it is inviting. All of these editors create a chorus that, once familiar, can sink in with us. Their healthy examples can be researched in further detail—more detail than this chapter can offer—but, to be sure, the best way to get to know each woman is through copiously studying the work they sculpt.

Cindi Leive was an English major at Swarthmore College in Pennsylvania, but she minored in religion. Leive's career has been marked by her ability to take a holistic approach to journalism work and executive management, also influencing her role in the International Women's Media Foundation (IWMF). The organization works to elevate the status of women in media internationally. They advocate for press freedom and petition international governments to broaden the role of women in journalism. In 2013, Leive hosted the Courage in Journalism Award ceremony where recipients were honored at the Beverly Hills Hotel. One of them, Edna Machirori, was the first black female editor of a newsletter in Zimbabwe.

"Editor-in-Chief Cindi Leive Wore Flats and No Heels

For a Week" posted *Glamour* magazine in April of 2016. "I'm 5'2" … And for the past 15 years, I've lived my professional life pretty much completely in heels … [but] as a feminist, I'm all for anything that allows women to move more freely through the world." She walked into Condé Nast Monday morning "feeling a little anxious, in a pit-of-my-stomach way." As the week progressed, she stuck it out but noticed some surprises: "I gamely stayed in my flats—but actually had to reintroduce myself to at least two people I'd met before! Did I look that un-editor-in-chiefly? The 'short girl' part of my identity took umbrage."

This little experiment flew through social media and landed Leive on *Good Morning America* discussing her "heels detox." It's not just her heel height that's come down a notch. Throughout Leive's time as editor, *Glamour*'s headlines have relaxed a bit (at least in comparison to the condescension of other titles). Her reputation of being a down-to-earth boss reflects her work ethic at the magazine. She started as an editorial assistant for then editor Ruth Whitney and, after eleven years, was appointed deputy editor. After working her way up, Leive served as editor-in-chief of *Self*, which drew off of fashion and poured its readers into wellness. She grew its circulation by 11 percent, finally rejoining *Glamour* as editor-in-chief in 2001.

Leive gave *Glamour* financial success, but her wise touch was sometimes spread too thin. The readership grew to a base of 2.25 million, but those readers have not been shy to protest. In 2009, the November issue of *Glamour* featured a plus-sized photo shoot that unhappy plus-size readers called the "naked fat girl extravaganza." After Leive unveiled the image on *Ellen*, one reader, Kate Harding, responded on *Jezebel*, "[I]t's a good effort … But let's not kid ourselves—this isn't a revolution. *Yet*." Later, Margaret Hartmann for *Jezebel* wrote, "Rather than a full-length fashion spread, all the models are crammed together into one shot. They're also naked, which solves the problem of finding 7 designer ensembles bigger than a size 4."

Also in 2009, Jenna Sauers reported in *Jezebel* that *Glamour* editors "hammer out every detail of the stories they're going to print before they've even assigned writers to the pitches." According to her tipster, editors were "notorious for dispatching writers to find sources who exemplified predetermined characteristics and narratives … 'First they decided what the "story" was, then we found ways to make the "facts" suit that agenda.'"

In 2011, one staffer infamously left messes in the bathroom. Despite laminated signs asking employees to "remember to flush," an anonymous letter appeared referencing three a.m. work nights, an entire department quitting, and "a crumbling edifice caused by an environment so dysfunctional that job searches take place in the open and 'happy dances' occur whenever someone has decided to leave." Condé Nast's ethos, writes Sauers, "has long been to throw as much money at its self-appointed geniuses, simply trusting that however tyrannical the top brass, the cash would keep flowing in … [With] Cindi Leive's Midas touch fading, how long will it be before Condé questions the edit-side wisdom of its biggest cash cow?"

Most recently in 2016, Amy Schumer was featured in *Glamour* labeled as "plus-size." "Plus-size is considered size 16 in America," Schumer stated in an Instagram post liked 90,000 times. "I go between a size 6 and an 8. [*Glamour*] put me in their plus-size-only issue without asking or letting me know and it doesn't feel right to me. Young girls seeing my body type thinking that is plus-size?"

To be sure, Cindi Leive replied thoughtfully to Schumer in multiple tweets immediately following and apologized. In the spring of 2016, *Glamour* initiated a partnership with Lane Bryant with the goal to "change the conversation" about plus-size fashion. The partnership between the two companies eventually resulted in two plus-size-focused special *Glamour* editions, a Glamour.com video series based off Lane Bryant's "I'm No Angel" campaign, "Styled by *Glamour*" in-store vignettes at Lane Bryant retail locations, and a *Glamour* x Lane Bryant clothing collection.

Simone Kitchens published "The Year I Saw Myself on the Runway: More Women of Color in the Shows Is an Undeniable Do" in 2016. In 2017, the magazine congratulated Chrissy Teigen for her strong words on diversity in the modeling industry: "I want it to be a normal thing to see Asian models, and I think Asian models are really underrepresented in the industry, especially on the runways or in magazines." In February of 2017, Leive decided on a "shake-up" where "from first page to last, every photo we commissioned was created by women: photographers, stylists, hair, makeup, everything ... And *Glamour* plans to continue to increase our representation of women in creative contributor roles." This announcement not only had historical precedence in Condé Nast but reflected astute and transparent business acumen.

Business of Fashion has done great work to expand fashion reader horizons by offering economic and technical reporting. Imran Amed was appointed Member of the Order of the British Empire for his role as founder and editor-in-chief. He never thought he would work in fashion growing up, reporting for the *Guardian* in 2016, but was inspired by one television show hosted by Tim Blanks. He worked for McKinsey & Company after receiving his MBA from Harvard but left shortly thereafter to start a blog called *The Business of Fashion*. He would consult for fashion brands during the day and wrote "from his sofa at home in London in the evenings," reported Amy Verner for the *Globe and Mail*. His seed-funding campaign in 2013 allowed him to hire a full staff.

Social media and new technology irreversibly changed fashion style and production. New markets in China, India, and Brazil expanded in influence and complexity.

The financial crisis of 2008 warped consumer decision-making and values. Nevertheless, Amed trained his team well until they became known for their sharp interviews exploring "the key drivers of an industry undergoing unprecedented change," according to their website. Today, "the website, which aims to bridge the sometimes cavernous gap between business and fashion, has become a must-read for business insiders," reports *Vanity Fair*.

Recently, Amed has led *Business of Fashion*'s political coverage. In October of 2015, Nordstrom pulled Moschino "drug-themed" clothing accessories from their shelves, which Helena Pike covered in a post called "Social Goods." "The vote to exit the EU wasn't really about the EU, it was a protest vote of people who were left behind," argued Amed in an op-ed article from June 2016 following Brexit. Also in June of 2016, Lancôme shut their main Hong Kong stores after protesters accused them of bowing to China. In January 2017, Maybelline appointed their first male ambassador, quickly responded to with protests from Bangladeshi garment workers. Also in January 2017, Amed published an op-ed shared almost four thousand times pointing out the ways the fashion industry remains silent in the face of Trump's immigration ban. Finally, the entire *Business of Fashion* team passionately argued on Inauguration Day 2017 for reform, insisting that fashion must defend globalization in the face of Brexit and President Trump, given both pose an indirect threat to the highly globalized industry.
Amed is not the only editor to promote business and

political coverage of fashion news. Chelsea Sonksen founded *Bossladies* magazine in January 2016 and already she has gained 58,000 followers on Instagram. "Top Negotiation Tips from Ladies Get Paid," "The Secret To - And Price Of - Success With Jen Gotch," and "How Jihan Zencirli Of Geronimo Balloons Avoids Burnout" are just a few of their most popular articles. After the 2016 election, Sonksen posted an op-ed, "Our Post-Inauguration Reality," providing suggestions on what "women who are deeply concerned about how this new administration will influence our lives can DO in the weeks and months to come." Her final encouragement? "Stay vocal, stay optimistic, stay active."

Millennials have also received healthy encouragement from Sarah Dubbeldam at *Darling* magazine. Their mission statement: "*Darling* magazine holds the modern mold of woman up to the fire to evoke a discussion … [and lead] women to discover beauty apart from vanity, influence apart from manipulation, style apart from materialism, sweetness apart from passivity, and womanhood without degradation."

In March 2017, Victoria Sowell for *Darling* found over thirty free online personality tests on Google. "Why did I type the words 'best personality test' into Google search in the first place? I think it is because the person I see in the mirror can sometimes still feel like a mystery and I want to know her better than I do." Instead of giving trite reviews, Sowell concludes, "what we need and how we're inclined as human beings is just as important as how we treat others and the ways we extend ourselves and embrace change. Take hold of the tools offered to you in life, but every now then [sic], feel free to put them back in the shed and get out and live."

After the 2016 election, *Darling* magazine was one of the only publications to cover protests from both the right and the left. And while many other columns feature quick guides or how-tos, they cross serious subjects like, "Overcoming a Shopping Addiction: How to Quit Impulsive Purchases For Good."

In January of 2017, Theresa Miller Archer also wrote an article in *Darling*, "Finally, Clothes for the Modern Outdoorswoman." She profiled the evolution of Woolrich from its production of blankets for soldiers during the US civil war to their newest collaboration "Woolrich x Westerlind," which Archer calls "the future for all women's wear." Nowhere on their site does *Darling* reference the need for magazine cover girls to break the mold of model or entertainer. Archer does not interview "soldiers, sailors, engine drivers and dock laborers" in her profile of the modern outdoorswoman—all women Virginia Woolf wished were more visible, as she wrote in *A Room of One's Own*. And yet Woolf, as fond of walks as she was, might have been grateful for the fashion tip.

Although Edna Woolman Chase steered *Vogue* through the Great Depression and two World Wars (the only editor to serve longer than Wintour herself), Diana Vreeland is truly responsible for the magazine's history of vibrancy and spirit. She may have only been thirty-eight years old when Virginia Woolf died, but her kicks for independence and rallies for individuality must have echoed her soul sister across the pond.

When commenting on the former leader in a documentary about her life, André Leon Talley says the former chief was "never negative." Another member inside Wintour's network, Lauren Bacall, called Vreeland "up-side-down original." She was full of joie de vivre, and you could see it in her biopic. "It hadn't crossed my mind to work," said Vreeland of her own beginning, with a smile, "because I'm really basically quite lazy."

In August of 1936, Vreeland was hired by *Harper's Bazaar* to write a column, "Why Don't You?" It was full of out-of-the-box ideas and fabulous fanciful things women could do. This was in an age when women were told all the time what they should do rather than encouraged to imagine an alternative. The column was romantic, easygoing, changeable, fun, and Vreeland wrote it herself.

When once asked if there was anyone or anything that most epitomized great style for her, she paused for a second and answered, "A racehorse" because it just had that "little extra pizazz."

Vreeland's answer is not only symbolic but prophetic. She

does not pick a ballerina, for example, with a needlelike frame only bent on perfection. She picks a beast: unyielding, robust, with enough muscle and power to conquer anything on its own legs. Indeed, had a stricter editor with a flare for fear captained the publication through one of America's most tender eras, *Vogue* might not have enjoyed the economic and financial prowess that it struts globally today.

Vreeland believed that anything romantic was great, and this transferred into her personal life. Vreeland's mother called her "the ugly little monster," but Vreeland's love and eventual husband, Reed Vreeland, was the yang to her yin. "Reed made me feel beautiful no matter what my mother made me think," she reflected in her documentary. She was loud and bold; he was quiet and soft. They shared a faithful and mutual respect and love, a bond they nurtured for most of their lives.

Faithfulness, humility, and humor are qualities of a modern editor who, perhaps, might not have directly intended to inherit from Vreeland. Stella Bugbee, *The Cut's* editor for *New York* magazine, keeps us on our toes in her own special way. Bugbee led *The Cut*'s relaunch in August, 2012, after she served as its consultant while it was a vertical on *New York*'s website in 2011. Bugbee had come from the *New York Times Magazine*, *Topic* magazine, and *Domino* magazine, where she was creative director.

"The very unusual thing about Stella," Adam Moss said

to *Surface* magazine, "is that she has this big, important editorial job and has never been an editor before … What we saw then was that she was a natural editor—with a crystal-clear vision, an incredible sense of story, and great news judgment." Not for nothing, Bugbee's touch had an impact. From 2011 to 2012, Omniture metrics reports that *The Cut* was *New York* magazine's "third most highly trafficked web vertical with an average of 1.7 million monthly visitors."

Style.com had a monopoly at the time on raw, direct runway photography, so Condé Nast's appeal to the online fashion reader was already partly cemented. But by 2011, *Vogue*'s online website hadn't yet received sophisticated curation. Condé Nast's leading fashion content—their articles, op-eds, party stories, and wild fashion features—were best accessed in print. Wintour herself had been blamed for allowing her staff to turn up their noses at the notion that online readership could be equally if not more powerful than print.

In perfect contrast, Bugbee read *Slate* and Twitter voraciously and showed an appreciation for online journalism rare even among the leading publishers at the time. "I haven't really found [making the jump from print to web] challenging," she said to *Coveteur*. "I love it. The potential for your audience is infinite and you really get direct feedback about what's working, what's not working … You listen to it with varying degrees of seriousness. You … see what went viral. Do I then chase what's goes viral? Not necessarily ... A lot of things I believe in may or may not have a big audience, but I love knowing. I love having that knowledge of what people respond to. User feedback is just fun."

Bugbee's unique recipe for *The Cut* mixed *Vogue*'s sophisticated voice, *The Times*'s quick reporting, and Style.com's luscious access into the world of the runway. Her final secret ingredient? A pinch of snark. *The Cut* said things Upper East Side *Vogue* girls only mumbled when drunk, and it made their coverage both addicting and more on-point for millennial readers. "The site balances intelligence and a sense of humor, drawing on *New York*'s signature DNA even as it stakes out a space all its own," observed *Surface* magazine. It became known for its "smart, wry and candid voice," said *OKREAL*.

"I've always had this sense of talking directly to an audience," Bugbee told *OKREAL*. "That was one of the things that appealed to me about design: that you could make people feel things or identify with a scene. A punk poster communicated something completely different than something with preppy type—and you were actually talking to people that way. I think it's all about tone."

Bugbee steered *The Cut* away from "The Cutest It-Bags Under $50" and let her readers' curiosity flow into politics, sex, injustice, advocacy, sports, mental health, and unflattering fashion criticism. Even in the 2016 election, *The Cut* didn't just focus on the good, the bad, and the ugly of what everyone wore. They allowed their readers to experience grit and grace side by side, recognizing a need in women for real news that, perhaps unconsciously, echoed Woolf's plea that womanhood stop being a protected occupation.

Putting her in the greatest contrast to editorial magnate and consigliere, Anna Wintour, Bugbee never lost her focus on the integrity of the reader when she transitioned from consulting to the role of editor-in-chief. "We are in a really exciting moment where the audience is super smart and they want to be spoken to smartly ... [She, the reader] wants to know about politics and trends and shopping, and read a super personal essay about someone's mother. Treating people like whole people—I'm hoping that's the trend," Bugbee said to *Coveteur.*

Vogue earned a reputation in the '80s for maxing out glamour and spurring women to believe that bigger was always better. When asked, in 1986, what she thought was most important to her readers, Wintour (then at *British Vogue*) told the *Daily Telegraph*: "There's a new kind of woman out there. She's interested in business and money. She doesn't have time to shop anymore. She wants to know what and why and where and how." American women have changed a lot since the '80s, and the American economy is only one reflection of it. Debora Spar, one of the first female professors at Harvard Business School, published a book in 2014 featuring a woman in a pantsuit holding an upside-down headstand while miraculously continuing to type on her laptop. "Having it all" (Wintour's '80s mantra) is one of the ideals Spar debunks in *Wonder Women: Sex, Power, and the Quest for Perfection.* Chucking life to win at work was a mantra crumpled up and burned for incense by Elizabeth Gilbert in 2006 when she decided to start over again and relearn how to eat, pray, and love.

Bugbee's *The Cut* makes the reader feel deep respect and familiarity as opposed to top-down condescension. "I am the ideal reader," she said to *Surface.* "Everyone on my team is. It's a woman who doesn't like a lot of bullshit, who takes herself seriously but really likes to laugh. She likes high, she likes low, she's a real person with real goals and I never, ever want to talk down to her, no matter what." Thanks to the mentors in Bugbee's career, she knew how to stop a psychologically painful chain of command. Of her former boss Debra Needleman, Bugbee says: "She was a fantastic mentor. I learned a ton from her about asking hard questions, about service journalism, about perfectionism."

Bugbee's respect for her reader is translated to her respect for her team. She avoids performing the role of pseudo-celebrity, skips vain social media narratives, and from this she's drawn the best in the business to her. In a short amount of time, Cathy Horyn, Rebecca Traister, and *Allure* founding editor Linda Wells all joined Bugbee at *The Cut.* "She's that rare combination of a solid news editor and a focused yet very human manager," Cathy Horyn said to *Surface.* "Stuff just doesn't get under her skin—or, anyway, she doesn't let it show."

"Humor is of course one of the biggest things that we're looking for [in employees]," Bugbee said to *Coveteur*. "I look for very smart, very funny, irreverent types. A really good sense of humor and a willingness to play. To be super smart, but don't take everything super seriously. I would look for a great deal of ambition within a person—[who] has a sense of ambition to their writing and they want to do bigger, better things all the time for themselves."

"I'm surrounded by women, and thinking about women's issues all day long,"' Bugbee said to *OKREAL*. "'I'm even more keenly aware how being a woman impacts all the choices we make and affects all the success we have or don't have. And how important it is for women to be in positions of leadership, so we can help others achieve things and be at the table for important decisions. Otherwise we will get left out."

This humility is unusual among editors in the fashion industry, both in New York and abroad. And yet, Bugbee's priority for innovation coupled with her strong leadership helps us see that she would never be the type to waltz in and out of meetings interspersed by parties and exclusive dinners. "I've always needed to play a part in the end result of what I'm working on—so if I'm unhappy with the end result I only have myself to blame," Bugbee told *OKREAL*. "A non-negotiable for me is working with people who value innovation. I work best with a process where creativity is highly important and where good ideas are developed democratically. I believe good ideas can come from anybody, and believe in a pretty flat hierarchy for most organizations."

This sense of accountability allows her to joke about herself. She seems to have deliberately avoided a reputation for being out of touch. "I don't exercise as much as I need to, I don't get enough sleep, and I don't pay enough attention to what I wear even though I work fashion … I just recognize that you die trying to have it all," she said to *OKREAL*. "You have to pick the things that are most important to you, and work is one of the most important things to me, so I prioritize it. Balance is great if that's what you're into, but I also think it's something that can trip you up. It sets another impossible standard. I'm probably really imbalanced, but I'm fine with it. I do my best … You have to focus on the things you want to get really good results from and that is the only way to get better at those things. Sacrifice is part of that."

In 2008, push came to shove in journalism, and publications dangled on the choices of their leaders. In Bugbee's case, it is her devotion, humility, and commitment to sacrifice that has brought *The Cut* to the strong ground it stands on today. As Bugbee said to *Coveteur*: "I actually firmly believe that really good content does get the audience it deserves … I think mostly about making sure that I'm proud of what we're making … It's not a matter of high or low, it's more just, does this make me laugh? Does this push the boundaries in some way?"

In 2009, R. J. Cutler directed *The September Issue*, a ninety-minute documentary about the internal structure of *Vogue* and the process behind producing their fattest issue of the year.

"It's like belonging to a church," said Candy Pratts Price in the documentary.

"And Anna is the High Priestess?" asked Cutler.

"I would say she is more like the Pope."

Both "pope" and "devil" are names that have become synonymous with powerful magazine editors, if not with Wintour herself. Yet Bugbee has earned a very different name. "The idea is to stay fresh, try new things, and Stella is the driver," Horyn said to *Surface*. The image of a driver connotes control but also agency, intelligence, studied skill, earned strength, and a concrete understanding of the force you are operating. Bugbee's impact has made the magazine industry healthier and even made her own publication more lucrative. We are lucky to have editors who believe that our own happiness will always keep them in the black.

CHAPTER 8
FASHION

It's five a.m. I am sitting on my couch in sweats. Throat Coat tea is brewing on the stove. And I'm here to talk to you about fashion.

What could possibly be so important about fashion, you ask, that I should have woken myself up with (what feels like) two gumballs forming at the top of my neck?

I was lying in bed and a voice said to me, "This is it." Not "This is it!" like a mother points a finger to a child. "This is it," like a warm, clear announcement that it was time for us to talk.

Instinct, voice, purpose, action, intention, goal, and conversation are all vital organs to fashion.

Even in the dawn, with my body fighting an infection, I was sensitive to *instinct.* Even before getting out of bed, with "Be Prepared" from *The Lion King* running through my head, I could hear a *voice.* Over pain, I chose *purpose* (the purpose I've been choosing for five years to write this book). I *acted* on my choice. I'm not writing in a diary, I am *intentionally* speaking to you. My *goal* is to communicate a unique and substantive message. And we're already in a *conversation.* (Yes, books are a conversation: my thoughts, to my pages, to your pages, to your thoughts. Even in receipt of your own reactions to my message, you have participated in a conversation.)

Many people say that fashion is about self-expression. I do not disagree. Many say fashion is about identity—and this, on a grayscale, is true. What is certain? Fashion is about vocation.

I say vocation and you immediately think: religion, nuns, nuns wear habits, black and white may be a "thing," but *habits* are definitely not *fashion*.

Vocation is a term so rubbed into religious discourse that it rarely gets a chance to dry off and step out on its own once in a while. Let's consider a different definition of vocation.

From *Google*, *Wikipedia*, and *Merriam-Webster*:

> 1. A strong feeling of suitability for a particular occupation.
>
> 2. An occupation to which a person is specially drawn and for which they are particularly cut out for, trained or qualified.
>
> 3. An occupation regarded as particularly worthy and requiring great dedication, passion or personal investment.

4. A summons or strong inclination to a particular state or course of action.

5. And the Latin origin: *vocare* "to call" or "summon."

What is the most important training you need in order to get dressed in the morning? The dedicated practice of mindfulness to not only "know thyself" but love thyself. We should be drawn and look forward to getting dressed—not burdened by the obligation to follow someone else's rules. We should have a strong feeling of suitability and ownership when we face our closet. It's not a performance wardrobe with costumes to transform you into some kind of muse. You are the most qualified person to dress you.

We should get a strong feeling of suitability when we first try on clothing. It should connect with us in more ways than one. Perhaps you feel in tune ethnically or culturally with the designer. Perhaps it's cheap and affordable and that frugality represents your desire to save for bigger things. Whatever your clothes communicate to you, they should be "particularly cut out" for you—not you for them.

Now, let's take the secular meaning of vocation and overlay it with the spiritual. According to Christian belief and *Wikipedia*:

> God created each person with a specific set of gifts and talents oriented toward their own purpose and way of life. Since we have a divine call to serve one another, love is the fundamental and innate vocation of every human being. The use of one's personal gifts in their profession, family life, friend life, civic commitments, and so on—for the sake of the greater common good—is the energy and activity of vocation.

It is not for me to discern whether or not there is a "divine" call, but I can break down that last line. Healthy communities are indeed based on service and standing up for one another. We all have a specific set of gifts and talents. But is it true that being a good listener or designing a great skyscraper are talents that contribute to the greater good as much as matching polka dots or putting together a great outfit for yourself? *Surely, if I design a skyscraper, I am contributing a lot more to the world than dressing well each morning.*

How often do you look up? When you walk, how often do you look down into a phone or look forward at the people walking at you? How often do you work in a skyscraper, pass by a skyscraper, or live in one? Is it as often as you see another human with clothes on? Depending on where you live, I'd wager that we see clothed people more often than we send emails in a day—and, some days, it feels like that's all we do.

There is no such thing as a bad outfit, a quiet outfit, a meaningless outfit, or a thoughtless outfit—no more so than there is such a thing as an invisible person or a meaningless person. All clothing is seen, all clothing communicates, all clothes have meaning. What if someone read a novel and told you there was no characterization, or saw a painting and said there was no symbolism, or heard a song and said there was no message behind the lyrics? Art has layers of understanding. Just because you don't see it or feel it or notice it doesn't mean it isn't there.

So why is mindfulness key to fashion? Why is self-love key to style? What's the difference between self-love and vanity? And when does fashion serve a greater purpose toward a common good?

***

I want to approach the grayscale I introduced a few moments ago: is fashion about self-expression or is fashion about identity? The basic framework behind the argument that "fashion is about self-expression" is that fashion is a *choice*. You don't grow clothes. They don't magically manifest on top of your skin. You choose them, or you choose the person who chooses them for you.

But is every piece of clothing a piece of the self? Certainly not. This is why the latter statement exists on a grayscale.

Character and identity are not the same thing. If you have a piece of wood and you hack at it twelve thousand times until it becomes a perfectly smooth baseball bat, you have gradually, habitually formed a shape. One day it's a block of wood, and a few weeks later it's a baseball bat. Now, if you drop your bat down a flight of stairs, leaving a one-inch gash across the surface, it is still a baseball bat—it is not a "gashed piece of wood."

Identity can be influenced by mood—but character cannot. Character is who you are, slowly formed over time. Getting dressed each day is a routine honed by many, many small decisions much like tiny chisels into a piece of wood. If I have always been blonde, you would try to identify me walking down the street by my hair color. If I dyed it brunette, you might not recognize me right away, but you would eventually adjust. If I have always been friendly and I passed you on the street and said hello, it would be familiar because you know me to be an engaging person. If I passed you on the street, kept my sunglasses on, continued typing into my phone, and didn't stop to greet you, you would pass me and immediately wonder: was that her or someone who just looked like her? Identity may undergo superficial tweaks (our hair color, our contact lens color, even our name); character, however, cannot be quickly flipped. Character is more related to self-expression because "self" is the most intimate contact we have, and characterization is the self's slow development through life. Identity can be changed as quickly as a spy putting on a different wig.

Accepting fashion and style as necessary tools to form character brings up the highly contentious element of authenticity (contentious, especially among those who follow the fashion of Hollywood). Carrie Bradshaw, for example, was keen on mixing and matching; it would be a leopard tube top one day and a pinstripe pencil skirt the next. Sarah Jessica Parker's ballet body gave a graceful yet strong carriage to these outfits, allowing her character the alacrity necessary to engage with such a diverse and lively wardrobe.

Nevertheless, it is not true that Carrie loved "costumes." She was not randomly and unnecessarily grabbing loud and outrageous clothes. Carrie's closet expressed her character in two ways. First, as a journalist, it was her practice to enter and exit the richly varying lives of New Yorkers, and for this transit her closet reflected a chorus of voices—not unlike the panoply of quotations you would see if you flipped through her portfolio of columns. Secondly, Carrie's closet did have high-octane pieces she would mix in from time to time because Carrie herself lived a very intense life. Her entire column was about seeking both the thrill and the intimacy that sex can offer in a city so cavernous it seemed unending in its possibilities. An alarming orange jacket or a pink ballerina skirt vibrated with a particular energy because Carrie wore her heart on her sleeve, and there was nothing mute, coordinated, or classic about it.

If we can consider Carrie's wardrobe to be natural for her, as opposed to a random exercise of costume parading, then we can understand why authenticity—not performance—is so key to fashion. I grew up a ballerina. My father loved opera; my mother loved the theater. I've seen my fair share of costumes. They are irresistible pieces of art and sometimes brilliantly simplistic (enter: Annie Hall). But there seems to be this great gap between couture and The Gap, between the runway and your sidewalk, between a purse and Chanel. To be sure, the Costume Institute in New York would vehemently agree.

I do not argue that there is no difference; rather, I challenge both the importance we misplace as well as the flow of influence we misidentify. How can it be that costumes are more important than clothes? How can it be that the more whimsical piece from a runway predominates evolutionary style hierarchy over the clothes we see down the street? Is it always true: the rarer it is, the more important it is?

Allow me to answer by picking a bone with the fictional Miranda Priestly—the "devil" who wore Prada and the figure more people know than Anna Wintour herself. Priestly explained a trickle-down artistry that exists from designer to designer. In one icy monologue to Andy Sachs, Priestly says that when runway designers feature a color (and because the runway has such a premier and exclusive vantage point) that color—trend, fabric, pattern—then trickles down through lesser designer collections, eventually department stores, and finally into the "bargain basements" from which most people like Andy shop.

Priestly has skipped a step in her chain, and to illustrate I call upon Stefano Gabanna's mother. Stefano Gabanna is active on Instagram. He posts pictures of his mother all the time. The woman is always smiling, always seems happy, looks well moisturized, coiffed, and generally adorable. I don't know anything about her, but she must be one remarkable woman for Gabanna to celebrate her so often.

It is not impossible to imagine that a designer as prolific as Gabanna didn't just "dream up" an amazing outfit but actually saw elements of it in real life. There are no new colors in the world—it was in nature before it was on a runway. We must start seeing the runway as the culmination and ourselves as the origin. Our bodies, our shape gives designers their mold. Our hair, our eyes give designers their hue. Our laugh results in a thread of gold. Our tears result in a strip of black. It's all in us—and in the animated world around us. It's all from us, and our friends, and our sisters, and our mothers. We are the great creation, the life-giving, choice-making, free beings for whom fashion is made and without whom fashion would cease to exist.

I do not seek to undermine any designer; I simply seek to pull back the curtain on the real people—real people like you and me—who actually cause those ideas, and colors, and shapes to come down a runway. We should not feel so little in their eyes or in our own. We should not crouch so small in their shadow. We exist for a reason, and that reason is not to be a blank canvas (and that reason is certainly not to be a hanger with legs).

I would not be surprised if more than one high-level fashion executive was laughing at me right now. How vain, how stupid, how amusingly proud I must seem. So I am in the perfect position to ask: what is the difference between self-love and vanity, between confidence and arrogance—and how can we maintain both self-love and confidence while interacting (on a daily basis) with an industry far more interested in money?

You just do it. You ignore the noise. You start by finding places where you can be yourself. From peace grows self-love, and from sustained self-love grows confidence. You're in the territory of vanity if you're exhibiting two factors: obsession and objectification. If you're obsessing over every little split end of hair, you're indulging in vanity. If you're always being made up and puffed up and slicked down and painted on, then you're objectifying yourself. You possess self-love if you are generous with yourself. And you are confident if you are able to feed yourself love again, and again, and again—even when you think, *Why bother?*

So how can a demonstration of self-love (like dressing well each day) translate into changing the world for the better?

Do you not share the street? Do you throw trash on the sidewalk, spit on people's jackets, and glare at strangers? When you walk down the sidewalk, do you stomp in leaps or do you walk directly, leaving room for someone else to pass you? This is called looking out for yourself and another at the same time. It is as true in traffic as it is in dressing—you can love yourself and give love to the world through an outfit.

Perhaps you think the reason I'm arguing this is because I live on some posh, broad boulevard of Washington where everyone dresses capitally when you step out the door. To be safe, I do, but only for the last month of the five years of writing this book. If you dress comfortably, and identify yourself as someone who *really has better things to do than focus on and shop for fashion*, then you are indeed participating in self-love through dressing well. Comfy clothes aren't bad style, they signal a recognition of certain limitations and one's humility toward those limitations.

So why is it that a person who "dresses up" does the world a greater good?

Because excellent outfits are simply a more efficient reminder of self-love. Whether it's a pink dress, a polka-dot purse, or zebra boots—whatever unusual or unnecessary thing you choose to wear—we are delighted because we see it as a choice *from* you *for* you. Imagine if, one day, each person you passed on the street stopped you and said, "I did something really nice and pleasant and generous for myself today. I treated myself because I love myself"—and then proceeded to walk on. Wouldn't you find that odd? Wouldn't you start to wonder? *Who are these friendly people? What are they smoking? Why don't they stop talking to me? And … have I treated myself today? I love myself too, right?* Excellent fashion is award winning, but its greatest reward is on the street when we are reminded by each other that we deserve to be loved, even by ourselves.

***

Some leaders in the fashion industry exhibit self-love all the time. Some designers purposefully speak out or use their collections to demonstrate the value of self-love. We would see a recharacterization of the fashion industry if their behavior and routines were our example.

Christian Siriano was born and raised in genteel Annapolis, Maryland. Although he was able to transfer into the Baltimore School for the Arts, he was rejected by the Fashion Institute of Technology. Siriano traveled to London to continue his studies at the American InterContinental University of London. Instead of climbing the ranks of Burberry or Temperley, Siriano interned for Vivienne Westwood and Alexander McQueen. The former was always known for her high energy, but she also demonstrated the joy of being different. The latter harbored deep respect for roots and history but knew the fashion of the future required a commitment to imagination.

Siriano did briefly intern for Marc Jacobs, but only before he auditioned for "Project Runway." During the fourth season, he won more challenges than any other contestant, finally earning the chance to show a twelve-piece collection at New York Fashion Week in 2008. Although Siriano's collection on the show drew from Victorian times, his NYFW looks "came more organically, from nature," said Amanda Kwan for the *Seattle Times*. "The theme of a stormy night was repeated in dresses covered with layers of chiffon circles like groups of dark rain clouds. A one-shoulder mini dress made from diagonal tiers of gray and neon yellow chiffon strips looked like a rainy sky lit up with lightning bolts."

Siriano's recognition of the beauty of nature is one of many healthy beliefs that influence his inclusive point of view. In 2015, Christian Siriano custom-designed a wedding gown for plus-size fashion blogger Nicolette Mason. More than a commentator on cute clothes and clever accessories, Mason demonstrates commitment to self-love, healthy body image, and giving voice to her LGBTQIA peers. "Ali and I had the most spectacular, whirlwind, pink-and-glitter filled celebration of our love for each other," she posted in May 2015. "Christian Siriano's NYFW show was a body-positive triumph," exclaimed Maeve McDermott for *USA Today* in February 2017. "Unlike many top designers who ignore the fact that 67 percent of American women are plus-size,"

McDermott continued, "[this collection was] another celebration of diversity, body positivity and political unity." After the Trump inauguration, Siriano joined a chorus of designers who voiced sympathetic, thoughtful, and compassionate opinions on how fashion should continue to be welcoming. "I dress people I can support," Siriano told *Time* magazine in April 2017. "[Melania Trump] is representing what's happening politically and what's happening politically right now is not really good for anyone."

Marc Jacobs comes from an earlier generation. He is twenty-three years older than Siriano, and he has also fought battles that, to some degree, made Siriano's career possible. Men and women in fashion have always found Jacobs's particular dash of irreverence sexy (which should make his professional and personal relationship with Kate Moss unsurprising). But despite his loudness, his brand message has been tone-deaf at times. In the end, even if his irreverence was so strong that unhealthy consequences surfaced, it is that same strength that knocked down doors and will continue to do so in the future.

No matter what tone Marc Jacobs strikes, it's heard round the world. Marc by Marc Jacobs has over two hundred retail stores in eighty countries. All designs from the iconic Louis Vuitton between 1997 and 2014 came from his desk as creative director. He was one of *Time*'s "100 Most Influential People" in 2010 and named one of America's fifty most powerful gay men and women in an issue from

Out magazine back in 2012. Despite this success, Jacobs's start wasn't without challenges. His father was an agent at the William Morris Agency but died when Jacobs was seven years old, and his mother remarried three times, suffering intense mental illness.

"I don't have any problem with what people refer to as sexy clothes," Jacobs told *New York* magazine back in 2005. "I mean, everybody likes sex. The world would be a better place if people just engaged in sex and didn't worry about it. But what I prefer is that even if someone feels hedonistic, they don't look it. Curiosity about sex is much more interesting to me than domination." Jacobs gave this interview only four years before he would become engaged to his longtime partner, Lorenzo Martone, and ten years before the US Supreme Court would rule gay marriage as legal. Throughout his career, Jacobs has worked to allow men's fashion to have many different faces and to allow men in fashion design to break rules for the sake of pure artistry as opposed to making noise as prejudiced critics of the early 2000s would have believed. In 2008, Marc Jacobs wore a plaid Comme des Garçons skort to take his bow at the finale of his collection. "It's not really a kilt," Jacobs said to *New York* magazine. "It's kind of like a kilt and a short ... I discovered how nice it felt to wear. They're comfortable, and wearing it made me happy, so I bought more." While this clothing choice had straight men on social media swearing the trend would never spread, Jacobs's comments on his own style had less to do with his intention to shape gender norms and more to do with his success at setting a healthy example. "I wear now mostly Prada pencil skirts," Jacobs told *Racked* in 2011, and—whatever he was wearing—the fashion community breathed a sigh of relief to know that such a powerful designer embraced the freedom of making his own rules.

Sometimes, Marc Jacobs's irreverence helps him push healthy boundaries out of the way. And other times, his irreverence demands that his vision exist regardless of the unhealthy messages in its wake. In 2013, Dakota Fanning defended Marc Jacobs for her controversial perfume ad in which the flower bottle pointed upward from her thighs. The ad was released in late 2011, and Fanning was only seventeen years old. "If you want to read something into a perfume bottle, then I guess you can," Fanning told *Glamour* magazine. "We considered that its position was sexually provocative," said the British Advertising Standards Authority in a statement at the time. "The ad could be seen to sexualize a child … The ad was irresponsible and was likely to cause serious offense."

In 2016, Jacobs's use of faux dreadlocks in his Spring 2017 runway "provoked vociferous debate," reported the *New York Times*. The "bouquets of towering multicolored yarn" fueled "a continuing conversation about the relationship of cultural appropriation and creative inspiration that has grown increasingly heated," the *Times* stated. Twitter user @keikei_xo posted, "An unknown black man/woman has dreads, it is assumed they smoke and/or are unprofessional. Marc Jacobs has a model with dreads, it's boho chic."

In both cases, Jacobs challenged the status quo. Without the fact at hand, I feel confident most seventeen-year-olds today are sexually active. Jacobs's ad was not shocking because it implied sexual awakening at that age, but because it went against the maxim that most children are told: "wait until you are ready," "wait for someone special." Even advice like this might seem like a limitation to Jacobs—not because he actually is a hedonist, but because he seems to use fashion the way Oscar Wilde used writing to confront the prejudice of the day. "There is no such thing as a moral or an immoral book. Books are well written, or badly written. That is all," wrote Oscar Wilde at the beginning of *The Picture of Dorian Gray*.

Jacobs and Wilde share the belief that art can be for the sake of art and nothing else. Indeed, looking at a Comme des Garçons or Vivienne Westwood runway would leave you thinking just that. CDG has shown consistent leadership (and continues to do so under the direction of Rei Kawakubo) in offering wearable art. Although Kawakubo's line operates "according to an unconventional ethos rooted in raw creativity," reports *Business of Fashion*, "she has grown into a business turning over $220 million a year." Never having formally trained as a fashion designer, Kawakubo "has always followed the beat of her own drum, both commercially and creatively," continues *BoF*. In their words, she is "exalted by the industry as an icon of modernity."

Although girly by nature, Vivienne Westwood's eccentricity reveals a similar reverence for wearable art. In the first *Sex and the City* film from 2008, the protagonist Carrie tries on a plethora of wedding gowns—frills and sparkles galore—but she lands on an architectural piece with two points at the chest, a silhouette more forceful than innocent. Throughout her career, Westwood's joyful punk has given women a kind of "pussyhat pride" even before the knitting. Her anti-fracking protests back in 2014 bear attractive resemblance to the characters (and the fashion) of the 2017 protests following Trump's inauguration.

Before the Trump administration, Michelle Obama thought to use fashion as a way to reinforce the belief that being inclusive is very American. Jason Wu, the Canadian designer, was born in Taiwan but moved to North America at the age of nine. Although he shares giant artistic talent with others in this chapter, Wu's sewing didn't begin at a prestigious university. "At 16, he developed the Jason Wu doll," reported the *Los Angeles Times* in 2008, "a Barbie-esque figurine that Wu designed from head to toe, hair and makeup and of course, clothes." He was creative director at Integrity Toys before he attended Parsons School of Design, never graduating.

After becoming a finalist of the CFDA/Vogue Fashion Fund in July 2008, André Leon Talley introduced Wu to Michelle Obama. She first wore one of Wu's designs during an interview with Barbara Walters that same year. Now, the white, asymmetrical inauguration gown he made for her hangs in the Smithsonian Museum of American History. Part of their campaign posed the Obamas as outsiders, above the Beltway fray, so some might have thought Obama reached for Wu because he wasn't part of any establishment trying to make her into something she was not. Indeed, I don't know the depth of understanding between Wu and Obama or why their partnership grew the way it did. What I do know is that, when the First Lady made surprising fashion choices (Wu, J.Crew, other anti-elite companies) people got excited. Not even Comme des Garçons can reinvent the wheel coming down the runway; for the foreseeable future, humans have and will have two arms and two legs. It is strength, in its infinite shades, that makes something new. When Wu and Obama became friends, they showed the strength that America needed—a kind of strength America hadn't had from fashion in a long time.

It is not political fluff to say that the remaining examples of the strongest designers—at least in the example of this narrative—are women. Just because I am a woman does not mean I personally benefit from naming them as such. Nevertheless, Jenna Lyons and Sarah Burton have set a healthy example mostly due to their strength.

Alexander McQueen and Marc Jacobs were in the same generation that broke open conservative norms in the fashion industry. Where Jacobs's strength showed irreverence, McQueen's strength showed reverence toward heritage, mysticism, and warriors. His tragic death in 2010 allowed his namesake company to experience strong leadership once again under the steady hand of Sarah Burton.

"To say the show was highly anticipated is an understatement," reported Britt Aboutaleb for *Elle* after Burton's first full collection for Alexander McQueen in 2010. "But with the anticipation came a fear of what such a visionary brand could turn into—not to mention the fact that the house's wounds are still fresh." Indeed, Burton must have known what she was up against.
Nevertheless, her bravery showed through. Other designers use intimidating sunglasses, leather accessories, a stern expression, and untouchable rhetoric, but Sarah Burton, in her white blouse, jeans, and ballet flats, gained recognition for her *real* strength. "Succeeding Mr. McQueen is a difficult undertaking," said Cathy Horyn for the *New York Times*. "She was modest about what she chose to take on; some references to the McQueen craft and drama are [necessary], but her choices reflected a gradual transition … Over the next few seasons, she should feel more confident to bring out her own ideas. Craft is important but so is a mood or an emotion … The response in the room was enthusiastic." We can presume that this resilience did not affect the way Burton drew or enhance her ability to calculate color. Rather, this experience would have allowed Burton to take hold of a company that was fragile for all the wrong reasons;

namely, tragedy instead of ignorance.

"While most retailers have been suffering through this millennium's version of the Great Depression, J.Crew is having its golden era," reported Leah Bourne for *Forbes* in 2010. "Jenna Lyons has taken on fashion icon status comparable to the likes of superstar designers like Donna Karan and Miuccia Prada ('Jenna's picks,' which are updated monthly on JCrew.com, often sell out)."

As Bourne was quick to point out, the company was not enjoying a bump in sales due to celebrity endorsements. The steady and strong financial growth perfectly mirrored Lyons's promotions within the company. "J.Crew's recent success is more than just hype. The company reported 14 percent revenue growth for the third quarter of 2009 over 2008 and strong holiday sales … Drexler knows that his company's success isn't thanks to a celebrity endorsement or the latest wash of jeans. It has to do with consistency," reported *Forbes*. "Jenna Lyons was named president of J.Crew yesterday. The news arrives after several consecutive raises and bonuses for the creative director … Jenna's been working at J.Crew since the early nineties, and while we're sure she's had plenty of offers to work for other designers and retailers, she's stuck around, slowly moving up the ranks," wrote Lauren Sherman for *Fashionista* in July, 2010.

Lyons has been developing many ways to be strong since childhood. She was born with incontinentia pigmenti, "a genetic disorder that led to scarred skin, patchy hair, and lost teeth, requiring dentures as a kid," reported Danielle Sacks for *Fast Company*. "Her gawkiness (she's now six feet tall) didn't help. As a result, she was subjected to almost constant bullying." "I loved fashion, because it can change who you are and how you feel, and that can be magical," Lyons said to Sarah Harris of the *Guardian*. "She took a home economics class, learned how to sew … One Christmas her grandmother bought her a sewing machine and a subscription to *Vogue*. 'That was when I knew I wanted to be a part of it in some way.'" In no short measure, 2008 and the following recession gave Lyons the highest of challenges. In 2017, she announced her departure from the company that had been her home since 2003.

Football players have strength. Cheerleaders have strength and flexibility. But ballet dancers have all those qualities plus grace. Alessandro Michele is not a ballet dancer, but these three qualities make him the final healthy example in this list.

Michele started in knitwear. He joined Les Copains after studying at Rome's Academy of Costume and Fashion. He first flexed his strength while working under Karl Lagerfeld and Silvia Venturini Fendi at Fendi. He focused on leather goods in the '90s but was soon tapped by Tom Ford to design bags for Gucci in 2002. Michele spent over ten years moving up in the company until he was named creative director in 2015.

When given the role in 2015, Michele was also given "free reign to bring his idiosyncratic sense of vintage style to the Italian fashion house," reported *Business of Fashion*. Also in 2015, Michele received the International Designer Award at the British Fashion Awards. In 2016, he received the International Award from the CFDA. In March 2017, *Business of Fashion* reported Gucci's "exceptional [financial] performance across the board ... with a record first quarter revenue increase of 51 percent—its strongest in 20 years."

As soon as Michele gained creative agency and freedom, an element of grace came to the brand that had not been seen before. It started with the fall 2015 menswear collection shown at Milan Fashion Week. In Gucci's YouTube video of the show, a soft strum of a guitar accompanies Kazu Makino of Blonde Redhead singing "The One I Love." The lyrics seemed to harken to an inner, suppressed voice, a being that could not "play" or be at ease.

The models walked a bare, if not utilitarian, gray runway—almost setting the stage as the back of a mind. Then a raspberry pussy bow blouse emerged on a male model paired with Birkenstock-like sandals. The model following showed a deeper raspberry beret, softly puffed, with a geometric pussy bow blouse and carrying an elbow length messenger bag just a slouch shy of a lady's purse. Lace peeped out from under a crew neck sweater. Robin's egg accompanied granite gray. A classic trench joined

Birkenstocks. Fur, middle-of-the-night slippers glanced up from under crisp, pleated office trousers. A ruffle danced at the wrist of a blouse. A lace camisole creeped out from under a shearling-lined peacoat. More bows at the neck, this time dainty enough to befit a French classmate of Ludwig Bemelmans's Madeline. "If there was a masculine heart to each of those items," wrote Tim Blanks in his review on *Vogue*'s website, "the defining details were eccentric old-ladyish."

Blanks also recognized a reorientation. "Is a granny's pussy-bow blouse still a pussy-bow if a willowy teenage boy is wearing it? Or is it, as today's show notes claimed, 'a renewal of possibility'?" wrote Tim Blanks in his June review. "Alessandro Michele has brought a radically different culture to Gucci."

Androgyny is the subtle—but pure—linen cloth that Michele lays over his creative kitchen before he cuts into design. The hair length and soft bone structures in the 2015 show were pleasant, but perhaps not as purposeful as in his fall 2017 ready-to-wear collection. Michele produced one show with both male and female models wearing the same fashion and walking the same runway. Both sexes, possibly all genders, shared style and were unified.

"I have known *strong* minds with imposing, undoubting, Cobbett-like manners, but I have never met a *great* mind of this sort," wrote Samuel Taylor Coleridge in 1832.

"And of the former, they are at least as often wrong as right. The truth is, a great mind must be androgynous." Shari Wattling added a note in the Broadview Press edition of *A Room of One's Own*, interpreting Woolf's reaction to that comment from Coleridge. "Coleridge conceives of poetic genius as an ability with which the imaginative mind may understand Nature's opposites from one enlightened perspective, or consciousness. He coined the term 'esemplastic,' meaning 'capable of shaping into one,' to describe this imaginative property." One hundred and eighty-five years after Coleridge and eighty-eight years after Woolf, *Vogue*'s Sarah Mower wrote this of Michele's Gucci collection: "Michele wasn't making any claims that his first amalgamated female/male collection show for Gucci was a bolt from the blue, a revolutionary turn against the last season. On the contrary, he finds it easier to focus when both sexes are considered together."

"This is always my world," Michele said to Mower. "I want to swim in my ocean."

I don't believe seamless gender in fashion is moral, just as I don't believe one show for women and one show for men is immoral. I listen. And after listening, I've learned that this generation, my generation, has asked questions on the topic of gender breathlessly; perhaps more than anyone in history. My first chapter, one overlaying questions of "segregated" media with the words of Woolf on the "androgynous mind" was not original to me. I am sure that, directly or indirectly, many others in beauty, fashion, and magazines have wondered if we'll ever get more freedom than we have now. (That is, the freedom to be ourselves and no one else.)

Freedom indeed is the gift that millennials are blamed for sugarcoating, and the gift that America sells each day. Those who restrict it in these three industries know now that their work is excellent, but is it also everlasting? Forgive the Washingtonian for dangling legacy, but I'll also assert that I am neither patriotic nor boastful when I guarantee that the limitations I urge broken here will be broken soon. I'm not saying it because I believe progressivism is the future, and that this book guides these three industries toward that future. It's the opposite.

This work exists so that it can be burned. I'm here with you so that I can be laughed at, undermined, and ignored. I encourage the others, all those inside Mag World, to believe that their opposition is as tangible as one book, one person, one small group of people, or one generation. If they rely on that safety, they will feel satisfied devoting themselves to extinguishing the messenger. Time will pass. Energy will expire. And it will still feel good, it will be such a relief, to see that the exact tangibility they attacked was merely a force of an intangibility that belongs to no one … least of all to me.

INDEX

@keikei_xo, 345
"flash bulb memory", 270
"I'm No Angel",314
"Mad Men", 254-255
"Project Runway", 341
"real women", 255, 260, 306,
"The One I Love", 351
"We're not selling reality";, 258
20-20-20 rule, 156
24/7 Wall St., 82
A Midsummer Night's Dream, 66
A Room of One's Own,7, 138, 353, 379
a weekly diet, 179
Aborigines, 55
Aboutaleb, Britt, 348
Absolute Beauty, 311, 325
Academy of Costume and Fashion, 350
Accutane, 214
acidophilus, 203-204
acne, 272, 277, 287, 289, 315, 363, 366, 368, 373, 391, 408, 412, 416, 423, 436
actresses, 11, 23, 66, 132, 187, 189, 219
Adams, Rebecca, 287, 288
Adele, 217
advertising, 2, 118, 136, 144, 153, 197, 255, 296, 495
Adweek, 254
Africa, 97, 99
aging hair, 56
Airola. Paavo, 175
Alba, Jessica, 235, 240, 241, 243
alcohol, 81, 154, 199, 201, 211- 215 .
Alexander McQueen, 340, 347-348
Allen, Woody, 219, 221, 223
allicin, 191
Allure, 196, 324
almonds, 6
alpha hydroxy acids, 183, 214
alpha-linolenic acid, 192, 196
Amed, Imran, 310, 315-316
American Apparel, 227
American Express, 254
American Girl, 151
American InterContinental University of London, 340
American Journal of Public Health, 283
American women, 30, 323, 341, 367
amino acids, 247, 345, 365
anchovies, 368
androgynous, 9, 10, 353, 379
androgyny, 352
Anglo-Saxon, 52-53
Aniston, Jennifer, 217
annamaya kosha 173
Annie Hall, 117, 336, 362
anorexia, 111, 124, 145, 250, 268
Anshel, Jeffrey, 155,
antimony, 33, 36, 46, 55
antioxidant, 145, 180, 182-197, 202, , 219-224
Anxiety UK, 157
Ap0E4 gene, 169
Apfel, Iris, 295
Aqua Tofana, 70

Aquetta di Napoli, 70
Arabia, 38, 45, 46, 56
Archer, Theresa Miller, 318
Aris, Sarajane, 163
arsenic, 40, 70
artichokes, 191
artifice, 28, 41, 47, 117
artificial aids, 48, 68
Ashley, 232, 239, 245
Asia, 54, 56
Asian models: underrepresented, 319
asses milk, 45-46
Assyrians, 34, 37
Athens, 38-39, 45,
atours, 53
Augustus, 43
Aurora, 20-23
Austen, Jane, 9
Australia, 55, 150, 160, 183
avenanthramide, 341
Avocados, 353
Ayurveda, 310, 333, 337, 396, 436
Ayurvedic, 163-164, 169, 171-173, 175, 177- 178, 198, 205, 211-212, 217- 219, 228
Ayurvedic Beauty Care, 163, 169
B vitamins, 179-180, 182
Babylonians, 35-36
Bacall, Lauren, 599
Bailly, Jenny, 160
balanos, 34
Balsamo Innocenziano, 62
Baltimore School for the Arts, 340
Banana Republic, 254-256
Bangle, Chris, 276-277, 301
Bans, Lauren, 101-102,
Bantu, 55
Barbie, 82-83, 346, 372
barley, 44, 46, 181, 205
barley water, 44, 59, 181
Barthélemy, Jean-Jacques, 38
bathe, 45, 217-218
BBC Newsnight, 116
beards, 35
beauty industry, 32- 33, 37-38, 60-61, 66, 70-71, 73-74, 76, 79-80, 83-84, 90, 92,-93 , 95-99, 104, 107, 111-113, 116, 118, 124, 128 -130, 136-137, 139
beauty marks, 66
beauty spots, 60, 66
beets, 187
behavioral economics, 80, 91
benzoyl peroxide, 214
Berlin, 64
Berlin, Isaiah, 263
berries, 184, 190, 205
beta hydroxy, 214
beta-amyloid plaque, 169
betalains, 355
Big Think, 19
Bill Cunningham New York, 290
bioflavonoids, 204
biotin, 182, 192
Bispebjerg Hospital in Denmark, 166
Black Arts Enterprise, 1
black hair to blonde, 45
black tea, 197
blackberries, 184
blackheads, 43, 215
Blanks, Tim, 315, 352
bleeding, 76, 214
blewe haire, 52
blonde, 39, 45, 61, 118, 137, 233, 334

blood sugar, 179, 201
Blue Grotto, 141-142, 144
blueberries, 184, 190
BMW Group, 277
body mass index (BMI), 15, 104, 123
BoF, 345
Bonfire of The Vanities, 60
Bonivetta, 57
Born This Way, 113
borrowed face, 49
Bossladies, 310, 317
Bourne, Leah, 349
Bradshaw, Carrie, 335
Brady, Tom, 246
Brant, Harry, 248
Brant, Peter, Jr., 248
Braun Kronberg, 83, 274,,
Brazil, 135, 315
breakfast, 180, 190, 198
breasts, 34, 47, 57, 95, 255
Brexit, 317
Britain, 8, 52, 134, 168
British Advertising Standards Authority (ASA), 124, 344
British Vogue, 323
broccoli, 174, 189-190
Brodbeck, Melinda, 133-135,
Bryant, Janie, 255-256,
Bryant, Lane. 314
Brzezinski, Mika, 197
buckwheat, 181-182
Bugbee, Stella, 117-119, 311, 320-327,
bulgur, 181
Bündchen, Gisele, 246
Burberry, 340
Burton, Sarah, 347-348
Business of Fashion, 310, 315-316, 345, 351
business of modeling, 235
Caesar, 51
calcium, 190, 194-195, 203-204
callanetics, 166
Campbell (the company), 187
Canada, 135
canola, 186
Capri, 141
carmine, 42, 47
carotenoids, 179, 185, 188, 192
Carpe Jugulum, 53
cayenne, 191
Celtic, 52-53
cerise, 42
Cescau, Patrick, 133
chalk, 45, 48
Chanel, 237
Chapman, George, 68, 75
Chase, Edna Woolman, 318
chia, 195-196
Chicken of the Sea, 260
China, 16, 131, 257, 315-316
Chinese Center for Disease Control and Prevention, 195
Chinese medicine, 131
choline, 192
Chopra, Deepak, 212
Christ, 49, 50
Christian Science Monitor, 104
chronic stress, 148
Chung, Jen, 121
chyawanprash, 205-206
cilantro, 202
cinnamon, 35, 61, 199, 202-203, 213.
cleanse, 81
Clement of Alexandria, 49

Clooney, George, 108
clothing . . . communicates, 333
clustering, 91
CNN, 155
cocoa, 198
cod liver oil, 203
Coenzyme Q_{10} (CoQ_{10}), 204, 221
Colbert, Dr. David, 154
cold crème, 40
Coleridge, Samuel Taylor, 9-10, 352-353
collagen, 145, 152-153, 166, 182, 184, 186, 189, 192, 194, 201, 210-214, 221-222, 224
collagen complex,214
coloring hair, 34
Columbus, 55
Comme des Garçons, 343, 345, 347
Computer Vision Syndrome, 155
concubines, 69
Condé Nast, 310, 312-313, 315, 321
Copeland, Dr. Michelle, 170, 172, 175-176, 202, 210, 214, 216, 220, 224
Copeland, Misty, 254
CoQ_{10}, 204, 223
Corson, Richard, 27-34, 36, 38-39, 46, 50-51, 53-70
cortisol, 145, 148-150, 168-169
cosmetic, 209
Cosmeticians, 33, 38, 56, 79, 81
cosmetics, 28, 31-44, 49-51, 55-56, 58, 60-63, 70-71, 75-76, 80, 143, 209-210, 213
Costa-i-Font, Dr, Joan, 124
Costume Institute at the Metropolitan Museum of Art, 293
Costume Institute in New York, 336
Courage in Journalism Award, 311
Coveteur, 331, 323, 325-326
Cowles, Charlotte, 123-124
cranberry, 184
crocus, 35
cumin, 202-203,
Cunningham, Bill, 290-301
curvy, 101-103
Cutler, R. J., 327
Daily Mail, 147
Daily Telegraph, 323
Dargis, Manohla, 114
dark chocolate, 197-198
Darling, 310, 317-318
Darwin, Charles, 54
de Coincy, Gautier, 54, 71,,
de Filippis, Ashley, 131
de la Renta, Annette, 294, 299
de Medici, Catherine, 56, 62
de Montaigne, Michel, 63
de Poitiers, Diane, 63
Delevingne, Cara, 247, 249
Dell'Orefice, Carmen, 292
della Porta, Giambattista, 61, 65, 71
depilatory, 40
Dermatology Times, 144, 152,
dermis, 166, 186, 210-211,
De-Stress Mi, 131
Deutsch, Donny, 106
Diet Pepsi, 86
dietary principals, 175
dinner, 114, 185, 190, 199, 203,
Dioscorides, 59
Discworld, 53
Divergent (motion picture), 109
diversity, 16, 38, 42, 90-91, 122, 135, 137, 262-264, 310, 315, 342
docosahexaenoic acid (DHA), 193
Dogwoof, 231

Do-In, 166
dolls, 72, 83, 121
domestic face, 46, 75
Dominicans, 60, 62
Don Quixote, 299
Dove, 124, 132-136
Draelos, Dr. Zoe, 145,
dragon's blood, 46
dreams, 72, 94-95
Drexler, 350
drugs, 45,152, 162, 241
317
Duke University, 161
Dunham, Lena, 116
Dunne, Anthony, 277, 301
Dyer, Jade, 160
Earhart, Amelia, 77
early Christian period, 49
Eat, Pray, Love, 19
eating disorders, 74, 79, 112
eating well, 178
Eberhard Karls University, 167
Edelman, 133, 135
editorial malpractice, 307
editors, 13, 17, 23, 80, 248, 262, 283, 302, 307, 309-311, 313, 325, 327.
eggs, 35, 44, 191-192
Egypt, 32-35 68,72
Egyptian eyeliner, 33
Egyptians, 32-35
eicosapentaenoic acid (EPA), 193
elastin, 166, 182, 184, 192, 194, 210-211, 222, 224
electrolyte levels, 167
Elizabethan women, 29, 63, 66
ellagic acid, 182, 184, 205
Elle magazine, 114, 348
Ellen, 257, 313
Elliott, Stuart, 260-261
England, 30, 51, 54, 63
Enheduanna, 52
environment, 6, 17, 80, 113-114, 124, 127, 143-145, 149, 159, 160, 206, 210, 256, 275, 277, 280, 284- 285, 287-288, 292-294, 297, 304-305
epidermis, 166, 182, 210-211, 217,
erucic acid, 190
esemplastic, 353
Etcoff, Dr. Nancy, 134
Europe, 51, 56, 62-64, 239,
European women, 50
Evans, Erin, 133-135
exercise, 7, 14, 60, 70, 105, 132, 150, 163-172 216, 227, 326
exfoliate, 37, 217,
exhaustion, 249
extract of crocodile dung, 42
eye bags, 107, 228, 286
eye care, 218
Fabula, 48
faith, 96, 161-162, 320
Fallon, Jimmy, 128
false hair, 53
Fanning, Dakota, 122, , 258, 344
fashion . . . is about vocation, 330
Fashion Institute of Technology, 340
Fashion Law Institute at Fordham Law School, 265
fashion week, 18, 243, 246-248, 263,
Fashionista, 257, 349
Fast Company, 350
Fendi, Silvia Venturini, 350
fennel, 44, 203, 218
Ferrera, America, 116
Fey, Tina, 254
fiber, 175-196

fibroblast cells, 166, 182, 210-211
Firenzuola, Agnolo, 57-59, 72
first black cover girls, 261
fish oil, 204
Fitness magazine, 184
FitzGerald, Niall, 133
flavonoids, 183, 204
flaxseed, 196
Florence, 60, 62
folate, 180-191, 196
folic acid, 192
Food . . . what and how to eat., 173
Food and Drug Administration, 119
Forbes, 349
Founding Fathers, 263
France, 56, 134, 267
France-- passes law banning excessively thin models, 267
François Nars, 128
frankincense, 31, 34, 44
French Federation of Couture, 300
French Ministry of Culture, 300
friendship, 149, 151
fruits, 182
fucus, 48
Fukasawa, Naoto, 286, 288, 301
Gabanna, Stefano, 33
Gaelic, 53
Gagliana, Mona Bettola, 58
Galen, 40
garlic,191, 203
gazelle's dung, 34
Genetics, 89, 105, 159
Germanotta, Stefani, 113
Geronimo Balloons, 317
Gilbert, Elizabeth, 19, , 324
ginger tea, 203
Girl Model, 231
GLA (gamma-linolenic acid), 205
Gladwell, Malcolm, 85-92,, 135
Glamour UK, 185, 190, 193,
Glamour magazine, 102, 261-262, 312-315, 344,
Globe and Mail, 83, 315
glycemic index, 177, 179, 185, 201,
glycolic acid, 214, 218
God, 30, 49, 63, 66, 74, 107, 162, 331,
Golden Globes, 111
Gomez, Selena, 249
Good Morning America, 312
Google, 1-3, 317, 330
Gotch, Jen, 317
Gothamist, 121
Goulding, Ellie, 249
grains, 179
grapeseed, 186, 224, 227
Great Britain, 135, 168
Greece, 38-42, 264
Greek, Greeks, 38-42, 49,72, 250
Grey Poupon, 88
Griffin, David, 270 -273, 301
Griffith, Ivor, 53
Guardian, 315, 350
Gucci, 350-353
Haiken, Melanie, 111-112
hair coloring, 34
Hamlet, 66
Han, Christina, 128,
Hannah and Her Sisters, 118
Harding, Kate, 313
Harlow, Jean, 209
harmonizing your lifestyle, 213
Harousseau, Philippe, 135
Harper's Bazaar, 319
Harris, Sarah, 350

Hartmann, Margaret, 313
hartshorn, 44
Harvard, 46, 134, 150, 162, 162, 315
Harvard Business School, 323
Hastreiter, Kim, 291, 298
Health Impact Assessment, 149
Health magazine, 102
healthy choices for models?, 258
Heatherton, Erin, 358
Helen, 72
Hendricks, Christina, 102, 255-256, 487
henna, 32-33, 55,
Henry VII, 54
hepatotoxin, 154
heptapeptides, 214
Herrick, Robert, 67
Hessian soap, 46
Hindu, 29, 163
hippopotamus fat, 35
Holiday, Ryan, 121-122
Hollywood, 72, 97, 98, 101, 108, 110, 114, 117, 125, 128, 335
Holmes, Sally, 97-99, 119
Homer, 38, 250, 273
Homerian Greeks, 38
Honest Beauty, 125-126
honey, 43- 44, 57, 61, 65, 205198,
Hong Kong, 316
Horace, 42
horizontal segmentation, 88-91, 135
horse manure, 51
Horyn, Cathy, 325. 327, 348
Hou, Kathleen, 104
How To Choose a Wife, 67
how to eat, 206
Huang, Qin Shi, 257
Hurley. Elizabeth, 81
Hydrate Mi, 130
hydration, 131. 148, 154, 176, 211
hydroxycitric, 205
hyperbole, 13
Ignatian Examen, 146
Illyrian iris, 43
immune function, 147, 161
incense, 34, 43-44, 324
India, 37, 205, 315
Indiana University, 157,
indigo, 55
Indus Valley, 37-38,
Instagram, 17, 251, 278, 309, 314, 317, 337
Institutional Venture Partners, 125
insulin, 154, 184, 201
Integrity Toys, 346
International Day of Persons with Disabilities, 103
International Designer Award, 351
International Herald Tribune, 311
International Women's Media Foundation (IWMF), 583
Interview, 109
Iran, 31
iron, 33
Ischomacus, 41, 46,
Israel – bans "underweight" models, 123, 267
It's All Good, 173-174
Italian Renaissance, 56
Italy, 56, 60, 62, 63, 70, 110, 134, 141,
Italy -- passes laws banning underweight models, 268

J.Crew, 347, 349
James, Kat, 176-178, 200-, 206, 214, 218, 223, 226-227,
Jane Eyre, 7
Japan, 69, 134, 190, 232- 246,
Jason Wu doll, 346
JCrew.com, 349
Jed Root, 110
Jenner, Kendall, 249
Jezebel, 36,
Jezeble (magazine), 112, 246, 263, 313,
Johansson, Erik, 278-282, 301
Johnson, Beverly, 262
Jongerius, Hella, 283, 301
Jonson, Ben, 64
Jordan University of Science and Technology, 168-169
Journal of Agricultural and Food Chemistry, 188
Journal of Clinical Oncology, 150
Journal of Nutrition, 198
Journal of Nutritional Biochemistry, 197
Journal of the American Dental Association, 168
journalism, 8, 12, 16, 80, 272-273, 306, 310, 321, 324, 326
juicing, 97
Juvenal, 46
kale, 187-188
Kaling, Mindy, 117
kapha, 165, 211
Karan, Donna, 349
Katniss, 114-115
Kawakubo, Rei, 345
Kelley, David M., 288-289, 301
Keys, Alicia, 116
Kironde, Katiti, 262
kiss of death, 70
Kitchens, Simone, 314
Kiwi, 183-184, 189
Klein, Jeff, 266
Kloss, Karlie, 247
Koda, Harold, 293, 294
Koffler, Larry, 135
Kohl, 31, 33
Kors, Michael, 102
kosmetikos, 209
Krant, Dr. Jessica, 154,
Kwan, Amanda, 341
Kyoshi, Takahama, 287, 301
L'Oréal Paris, 123
La Grotta Azzura, 141
Lady Gaga, 111-113
Lagerfeld, Karl, 350
Laguna, 58-59
Lancôme, 416
Lane Bryant, 314
Language123, 1
Late Night, 128
Lawrence, Jennifer, 113-115, 117
Le Roman de la Rose, 53
lead, 33, 36, 40,42-43, 46, 48, 58-59, 65,
Leive, Cindi, 310-315
Leno, Jay, 81
Les Copains, 350
leukocytes, 147
Lever Brothers, 132
LGBTQIA, 10, 341
Liberty And The News, 80, 92, 307
Lifestyle choices, 131, 160, 163
Lightspeed Venture Partners, 125
linolenic acid (CLA), 200
liposuction, 97-98, 104-105

Lippmann, Walter, 12, 18, 80, 92-95, 108-109 307, .
Livestrong Foundation, 164, 166-168, 170, 192, 194
Lohan, Lindsay, 101
London School of Economics, 124, 134
long life elixir, 62
Loren, Sophia, 107
lotus, 35-36, 191
Louis Vuitton, 342
Luc, Jean, 300
Lucas' Pawpaw Ointment, 183
Lucian, 44
lunch, 190, 198,
lust for fantasy, 72
lutein, 187-188, 191, 205, 204
lycopene, 188, 205, 224
Lycoris, 48
Lycurgus, 41, 43
Lyons, Jenna, 347, 349-350
Machirori, Edna, 311
mackerel, 192-193
Madison Avenue, 260
Madison, James, 264,
Madlen, 236-237, 243-244
magazines "for women", 8
magnesium, 179-183, 196, 203
MAKE, 124
Makino, Kazu, 351
MANA Products,128
manganese, 33, 180-182, 187, 189-191, 196
Manna of St. Nicholas di Bari, 70
mannequins, 15, 98, 103-104, 121-122
Marc by Marc Jacobs, 342
Marc Jacobs, 122, 258, 341-345, 347
Marchesa, 111
Marie Claire, 101
marijuana, 153
Mariwalla, Dr. Kavita, 167-168
marjoram, 34-35
Martial, 42, 48, 73
Martone, Lorenzo, 343
Mason, Nicolette, 341
Mattel, 82-83
Mayans, 55
Maybelline, 316
Mayer, Marissa, 115
Mayo Clinic,120
McDermott. Maeve, 342
McKinsey & Company, 315
McQueen, Alexander, 347-348
Medes, 35
Medicis, 62
meditation, 146-147, 160, 162, 208
melanin, 192
melatonin, 146, 156, 187, 197
melissa water, 62
men's colognes, 35
Menander, 39
Mennis, Sir John, 69
mental health, 157
Mercurie sublimate, 40
mercury, 40, 58-59, 193
Merriam-Webster, 2, 330
Mesopotamia, 31-32
Mexican study, 152
Michele, Alessandro, 350-353
Middle Ages, 50, 54, 63, 74
Midnight in Paris, 116
millennials, 261, 310, 317, 354
Miyu, 134
Mobile Mindset, 156
Model Alliance, 265

models need to be *adults*, 258
models, labor laws for, 264
Mohenjo-Daro, 36
moisturizers, 219-220
Monash University, 160
Monroe, Marilyn, 237, 254
Montreal Gazette, 102
moralists, 30
Morocco, 69
Moscherosch, Johann Michael, 62
Moschino, 316
Moskowitz, Howard, 85-92, 95, 135
Moss, Adam, 321
Moss, Hillary, 247
Moss, Kate, 116, 264, 342
Mouyiaris, Nikos, 128-130
Mower, 354
MSNBC's Morning Joe, 106
mulberry, 40, 48
multitasking, 157, 159, 239
multivitamin, 203
Murgatroyd, Stephen, 163
muse, 71-73, 76, 117, 125, 139, 245, 331
Muslim women, 69
myrrh, 34, 44
Nadya, 231-246
Naiman, Dr. Rubin, 146
nanoparticles,144-146, 152
Naples, 61, 141
narcissus bulbs, 44
National Center for Biotechnology Information (NCBI), 1
National Geographic, 17, 270, 273, 288
natural beauty, 49, 54, 111, 121, 136, 210
NBC News, 135
neck-to-waist ratio, 104, 105
Needleman, Deborah, 311, 324
Netherlands, 134
neurocognitive function, 169
New World, 55
New York Fashion Week, 247, 263, 41
New York magazine, 101, 247-248, 255, 265, 320-321, 343
New York Times, 5, 11, 100, 114, 132, 149, 251 260, 299, 344, 348
New York Times Magazine, 5, 100, 320
news magazines, 17-18, 283
niacin, 193-194, 221
Nike, 260-261
Nordstrom, 316
Noto, Gloria, 110, 207
nourish the skin, 219
O Magazine, 149-151, 166
Obama, Michelle, 346-347
Objectified, 5, 16, 84,100, 251, 256, 259, 274, 276-277 283, 286 288
oesypum, 47
Officier de l'Ordre des Arts et des Lettres, 300
OKCupid, 101
OKREAL, 322, 325-326
Old Bay Seasoning, 203
oleic acid, 186
olive oil, 34, 39, 185-186, 217-218, 221
Olson, Elizabeth, 132
omega fatty acids, omega-3, omega-6, 180-194, 200, 203
Omniture, 321
Oprah, 19, 81,
Ora, Rita, 247

Orbach, Dr. Susie, 134
organic, 126, 136, 181, 185, 200, 284
Oriental, 56
origanum, 34
orpiment, 36
orris powder, 62
Oscars, 97, 99, 109, 113
Ostad, Dr. Ariel, 153
Out magazine, 343
Ovid, 42-44, 47-48, 71, 73
oysters, 194
Oz, Dr. Mehmet, 146-147, 166, 169, 175-176, 182, 188, 190, 192, 195, 197, 199, 201, 203, 204, 210-211, 216, 220-221, 223,
P.O.V, 231
paederos, 40
painted stuffe, 49
Pakistan, 36
Paltrow, Gwyneth, 174-175, 180, 186, 189, 192, 195, 202
panic attacks, 249
pantothenic acid, 183, 186, 221
Papain, 183
paparazzi, 251-252, 293
Papaya, 176
Paper, 291, 298
Paris fashion week, 244
Parker, Sarah Jessica, 335
Parker-Pope, 149-150
patching, 64, 66
Penn State University, 133
Peptides, 191
perfume, 31, 33-34, 35-38, 42, 45, 56, 62,63, 69, 128,
Perry, Katy, 81-82
Persia, 28, 35
petroleum, 126, 214-215
Petronius, 41
Petrou, Dr. Ilya, 144-145, 147, 148, 152
pH balance, 211
phosphorous, 192
phosphorus, 180-181, 193-194, 196
photograph shares a moment, 271
photographer: selling "perfection" in women's and fashion magazines, 275
photography, 17, 270, 272-273,
photography: digital editing, 285
photojournalism, 272-273, 278-280. 282-285, 287-288, 292, 302-304, ,
photojournalism: "being in the right place at the right time." 279
Photoshop, 12, 17, 74, 91, 94, 121, 123, 257-258, 278-281 283-285, 303
physicians, 59
Pictsies, 53
Picture Me, 265
Pike, Helena, 316
pink grapefruit, 188
pitta, 165, 211
plastic surgery, 74, 106, 137
Plat, Hugh, 64-65
Plato's *Republic*, 12
Plautus, 41
Plutarch, 41
pollution, 127, 130, 144-145, 195, 210
Polycyclic aromatic hydrocarbons (PAH), 145
polyphenols, 179, , 197
Pomegranate, 182
Pompeia, 45, 46
Pope Clement I, 42
Pope Innocent XI, 62

Portugal, 134
potassium, 181, 183-184, 187, 189-190
powdered ash, 47
Powell, L. H., 160
Prada, Miuccia, 336, 344, 349
prana, 165, 200
Pratchett,Terry, 52
prayer, 146, 160,-162, 206, 208, 308
presleep hygiene, 146
Pret-a-Reporter, 110
Price is Right, 233
Price, Candy Pratts, 327,
pride, 35, 67-68, 103, 273, 346
Priestly, Miranda, 336-337
Pro Infirmis, 103
probiotics, 204
Propertius, 42
prostitute, 240-241
prostitution, 241
protein (eggs, fish, nuts), 191
Provine, Dr. Robert R,, 164
Psychological Science, 151
psychophysicist, 86, 90
publishers, 23, 80, 283, 308, 321
pumice stone, 35, 46
pumpernickel, 181
pumpkin seeds, 147, 196, 199
Punch, 52
punicalagin, 182
Purchas, Samuel, 69
Pythagoras, 209
Queen Elizabeth I, 63
Queen of Naples, 54
Queen Puabi, 35
quick-silver, 40
quina elixir, 62
quinoa, 180
quinones, 145
Quips Upon Questions, 67
Racked, 344
Raichur, Pratima, 165, 172-173, 174-178, 203, 205, 207
Rams, Dieter, 83-85, 274, 301
raspberry, 185, 351
Rawsthorn, Alice, 16, 256
Recommended Dietary Allowances (RDAs), 204
red bell peppers, 189
red grapes, 185
red niter, 43
red wine, 146, 154, 182, 185, 199
red-carpet, 98
Reed, Nikki, 102
refined sugar, 181, 201
Regina water, 62
religious activity, 160
Renaissance, 56, 58, 60-63, 74
renewable sources, 127
Renn, Crystal, 102
resveratrol, 185, 199, 224
Retin-A or Renova, 214, 221
riboflavin, 191
rice, 180, 189
Rihanna, 247
Rocha, Coco, 255
Roizen, Dr., 166, 169
role model, 124, 253-254, 259
Roman lady's bathroom, 45
Roman women, 48
Rome, 42-43, 48, 72, 309
Romeo and Juliet, 273
rose-leaves, 44
rosemary, 61, 202, 224, 226-227
rouge, 33, 35, 39-41, 43 46, 51, 56, 262

rutin, 182
rye, 175, 181
Sabella, 48
Sachs, Andy, 336
Sachs, Melanie, 163-166, 168-171, 175, 178-179, 198-202, 206-208, 210, 212-219, 221, 223-227
Sacks, Danielle, 350
Sadeghi, Dr. Habib, 173-175
safflower oil, 186, 216, 219
saffron, 35, 37, 47, 61
sal-ammoniac, 44
salmon, 190, 192-196, 198
Santa Maria Novella, 62
sardines, 192-194,
Saris, John, 69
Sauers, Jenna, 246-247, 313
Savino, Senator Diane, 266
Savonarola, Girolamo, 60
scalp massages, 226
Scarborough. Joe, 106
Schell, Ole, 265
Schumer, Amy, 116, 314
Scotland, 53
Seattle Times, 341
seaweed, 40, 191
sebaceous glands, 148, 210,
sebum, 152, 190, 210, 226
Seckel, Al, 281-282, 301,
selenium, 179, 181, 191-193, 196-197, 224,
Self-Esteem Project, 136
Seneca, 45
seraglios, 69
Sex and the City, 346
Seydoux, Lea, 118
Shakespeare, 66, 273
shampoo, 125, 183, 190, 225-226
sheep fat, 46
sibbersauces, 30
Sidibe, Gabourey, 101
significant moment, , 270, 301, 303
silicone, lanolin, and dimethicone, 214
Singer, John, 67
Siriano, Christian, 340-342
six tastes, 178
skin care, 97, 123, 130, 143, 209, 211-212.
Slate, 321
slaves, 45, 48
Sleeping Beauty, 20
slubbersauces, 59
Smithsonian Museum of American History, 347
smoking, 152-153, 340
snacks, 199
social media, 111-112, 151, 157-158, 251-252, 309, 312, 315, 314, 343
social support, 160-162
Soliman, 40
Somaliland, 38
Sonksen, Chelsea, 310, 317
Sotai, 166
Sowell, Victoria, 317
spaghetti sauce, 85, 87-88
Spain, 56, 59
Spar, Debora, 159, 323-324
Sparta, 41-42,
spices, 35, 56, 201-203, 205, 207, 213
spikenard, 34-35
spinach, 287-288
Spirituality, 161-163
St. Ambrose, 49
Stampler, Laura, 121
standardization, 104-105, 121, 138,

256,-257, 308
Stanford University, 157
stibium, 36
stilbenes, 185
Stober, Dan, 157
Stoeffel, Kat, 248-249
Stone, Emma, 109
StrategyOne, 134
strawberries, 184
Streep, Meryl, 116
Stubbes, Philip, 30
Style.com, 321
Styles, Harry, 247
Suckling, Sir John, 67
Sudan, 55
sulfide of mercury, 40
sunblock vs sunscreen, 225
sunscreen, 119, 125, 223
Super Bowl commercials, 106
superfoods, 205
superseeds, 194-195
Surface magazine, 321-322, 324, 327
Surflet, Richard, 66
Swarthmore College, 311
sweat glands, 210
sweet potatoes, 190
Swift, Taylor, 249
Switch Modeling Agency, 233
Switch Models, 236
tai chi chih, 166
Tai, Connie, 129-131
Talbott, Shawn, 169
Talley, Andre Leon, 319, 346
tanning, 74, 79, 120, 318
tannins, 131
Taoist, 166
tattoos, 53-56, 308
Tchaikovsky, Peter Ilych, 21-22
TED, 85, 90, 270, 278, 281
Teen Vogue, 102, 310,
Teigen, Chrissy, 315
telomeres, 147
Temperley, 340
tentipellum, 44
tetracycline, 214
Texas Heart Institute, 167
The Art of Love, 47
The Beautiful Skin Workout, 172
The Business of Fashion, 315
The Canterbury Tales, 51
The Countrey Farme, 66
The Cut, 97, 101, 104, 117, 123-124, 128, 130, 255, 300, 311, 320-322, 324, 326
The Descendants, 108
The Devil Wears Prada, 346
the first problem of the model, 245
The Gap, 336
The Hollywood Reporter, 110
The Honest Company, 124-126
The Huffington Post, 154, 156, 158,
The Hunger Games, 114
The Journal of the American Medical Association, 149
The Lady's Toilet, 44
The Metabolic Method, 169
The National Sleep Foundation, 170
The Odyssey, 273
The Picture of Dorian Gray, 345
The Real Truth About Beauty, 134
The Science of Good Husbandry, 41
The September Issue, 327
The Spectacular Now, 109
The Truth About Beauty, 176
thiamin, 181
Thomée, Sara, 155

three B's rule, 155
thyme, 34,-35, 202, 227
Tibullius, 42
Time magazine, 121, 254, 342
tocopherols, 204
Tofana, Giulia, 70
Tom Ford, 350
tomatoes, 188-
Tonight Show, 81
toothpaste, 61
Touraine, Marisol, 267
toxic, 127, 152, 177, 202
toxins, 167, 176-177, 179, 199-200, 210
Traister, Rebecca, 324
Trump, Melania, 342
Trump, President Donald J., 316
Tuke, Thomas, 67
tuna, 192-193
Turkish women, 69
turmeric, 191, 202, 205
Turshen, Julia, 173-175, 180, 186, 189, 192, 195, 202
Tuscan wheat, 44
Tutankhamun, 32
tweenage, 157
Twitter, 112, 321, 344
Unilever, 132-133
University College London, 150
University of Gothenburg, Sweden, 156
University of Maryland, 158, 164
University of Maryland Medical Center, 161
University of Utah, 159
University of Virginia, 150
Ur, 35
US Army, 104
USA Today, 341
UV radiation, 197, 211
vallentine, 52
Vandals, 309
Vanity Fair, 128-129, 316
vata, 165, 211
vegetables, 187
Venus, 56
vermilion, 36,40, 42
Verner, Amy, 315
Victoria's Secret, 15, 257, 265
virgins milk, 65
Vivienne Westwood, 340, 345-346
Vlasic, 87
Vogue, 81, 262, 292, 310, 320-323, 327, 346, 350-353
Volpi, Dr, David, 154, 156
Vreeland, Diana, 310, 319-320
Vreeland, Reed, 320
W&T Seafood, 194
Wachler, Dr. Biran Boxer, 155
Walker, Rob, 5-6, 100
Wall Street Journal, 82, 119,
walnuts, 188, 196-197
Walters, Barbara, 115, 347
wantonness, 50
Washingtonian, 254
Watson, Emma, 116
Watson, Julie, 104-105
Watson, William Hough, 132
Wattling, Shari, 353
wax, 34, 47, 63, 75,
We See Beauty Foundation, 128
Weiss. Bea, 81
Weisz, Rachel, 123, 338
Wells, Linda, 324
Welteroth, Elaine, 311
Wheat Germ, 181

white lead, 37, 40, 43, 46, 48, 58
Whitney, Ruth, 312
Wilde, Oscar, 345
William Morris Agency, 343
Williams, Serena, 116
Wilson, Rob, 251, 259
Winslet, Kate, 116
Wintour, Anna, 297, 299, 319, 321, 323-324,327, 336
Wischhover, Cheryl, 130-131
Wit Restored, 69
Women's Health, 195
women's magazines, 17-18 93, 283
Women's Wear Daily, 123
Wonder Women: Sex, Power, and the Quest for Perfect, 160, 324
Woodley, Shailene, 108-111, 113, 117
Woolf, Virginia, 1, 7-10, 24, 75, 137-139, 318-319, 323, 353
Woolrich, 318
WORK Magazine, 111
World Health Organization, 123, 149, 267
World Heritage Encyclopedia, 250
Wright, Geoff, 147
wrinkle-fighting secret, 34
Wu, Jason, 346-347
Xenophon, 41
yellow ochre, 33
yoga, 147, 165, 168-169
yogurt, 198-199, 203
You: Being Beautiful, 166
zeaxanthin, 187-188, 191
Zencirli, Jihan, 317
Ziff, Sarah, 264-266
zinc,180-181, 191, 194, 196, 205, 224-225

Made in the USA
Middletown, DE
29 June 2017